THE AGARIA

THE AGARIA

VERRIER ELWIN

GYAN

Published by

GYAN

Gyan Publishing House
5, Ansari Road
Daryaganj, New Delhi-110002
Phone: 011-47034999, 9811692060
E-mail: books@gyanbooks.com

Distribution Network
gyanbooks.com
India, USA, Canada, UK, Australia

ISBN: 978-93-7447-121-0 (HB)

First Published, 1942

2nd Impression 2026

Printed at: Gyan Press, Delhi.

THE AGARIA
Author: VERRIER ELWIN

Patharia Agaria bringing ore out of the pit.

THE AGARIA

By

VERRIER ELWIN

With a Foreword by

SARAT CHANDRA ROY

INDIAN BRANCH

HUMPHREY MILFORD
OXFORD UNIVERSITY PRESS

To

Mr and Mrs J. R. D. Tata

FOREWORD
To Special Vanya Prakashan Reprint

As we take a glimpse at the rich and diverse heritage of this vast country, we discover that the tribal societies have taken an active part in the process of fusion of races and cultures. Their contribution to the creation of the amorphous mass of myths and legends, religious traditions and customs of India has, truly speaking, been phenomenal.

Nevertheless, it is also true that our tribal societies have been undergoing recurrent culture shocks and their absorption in what is considered to be the 'mainstream' is not only a debating point with anthropologists and sociologists but a live issue in determining development strategies.

No society should be disturbed and for tribals even development can assume an intrusive character if undertaken without a thorough understanding of their social and cultural roots. About tribals, even now, so little is known and that too is coloured by our own perceptions. The data available through the Census reports or the studies sponsored by the Anthropological Survey of India, serve a very useful purpose but the studies of field anthropologists alone provide intimate and sympathetic understanding of the tribal way of life.

Verrier Elwin was an outstanding scholar, who explored the tribal areas of Mandla and Bastar districts in his own inimitable style. He lived here for twenty-five years and was able to achieve complete identification with tribals in these parts of the erstwhile Central Provinces.

Vanya feels privileged in bringing out reprints of the rare works of such great scholars as Verrier Elwin, Grigson and others. These works are an enduring testimony to their spirit of adventure, sacrifice and wisdom, and our venture is a humble homage to them. We convey our deep gratitude to all those who helped us in this.

V.G. NIGAM
Chairman, Vanya Prakashan

FOREWORD

Mr Verrier Elwin is too well known to students of social anthropology to need any introduction. His latest book, *The Baiga*, is a classic of Indian ethnology. His earlier books, *Leaves from the Jungle*, *Phulmat of the Hills*, and *A Cloud that's Dragonish*, reveal an intimate familiarity with primitive life and mentality among the forest tribes of India which is rare not only in a European but even in educated Indians.

So far, little of any ethnological interest or validity has been published about the Agaria, except short notes on the Asur and the Birjhia by W. H. P. Driver in Pr.A.S.B., 1887, and meagre and faulty references in such works as Risley's *Tribes and Castes of Bengal* and Crooke's *Tribes and Castes of the North-Western Provinces.* It is none too early then that Mr Verrier Elwin has published this monograph written in the light of intimate personal knowledge, deep sympathy and first-hand investigation conducted scientifically.

The Agaria share with the Baiga and other neighbouring tribes many of the social customs and habits which go to fashion much of the pattern of their lives; and as these have been described in detail in Mr Elwin's previous monograph on the Baiga, the present volume, the author tells us in the Preface, may be regarded 'as in some sense supplementary to *The Baiga*'. In that work the author discussed very fully 'an attitude to sex, a system of magic, a scheme of primitive jurisprudence, a policy for the future that would apply equally to any of the tribes inhabiting the Maikal Range'. So too with other and smaller matters. Thus, 'the chapter on dancing in *The Baiga* may be taken as applying equally to the Agaria of Mandla'. 'Kinship rules, avoidances, the law of inheritance, pregnancy and menstruation rules, birth customs are the same as among the Gond.' Agaria marriages are of the ordinary *sāt-bhānwar* type, with a few special features which have been noted in the Preface.

These cultural resemblances with their neighbours do not, however, imply that the Agaria lack a distinctive and vigorous life of their own. Far from it. Besides possessing a highly developed totemistic organization, the Agaria have a striking and distinctive mythology which controls and vitalizes to an unusual degree the material culture of the tribe. In this volume we have an illuminating study of the Agaria's special contribution to magic, and 'the tribal neurosis of fear and magic' which, the author tells us, has made at many times a painful impression on his mind.

We are here introduced to a tribe that has lived every moment of their lives for an ancient craft and by a living myth.

The 'marriage of myth and craft', as the author tells us, 'is the central theme of the book and gives the Agaria great significance'. 'If this book,' the author further says, 'lacks the intimate human touches of *The Baiga*, that is due to the character of the people. The Agaria are a people absorbed in their craft and their material; they seem to have little life apart from the roar of the bellows and the clang of hammer upon iron. Few of them live to a great age, they have poor memories, there are few outstanding personalities among them.'

This study of Agaria myths is one of absorbing interest. Mr Elwin shows how the myths lie at the root of the social relations and the religious and economic structure of Agaria society. These myths reveal the fundamental ideas regarding life and nature, and sentiments attaching to these ideas in the Agaria's mind. Although the age-old rituals of a tribe are generally found to be more or less dramatizations of their ancient myths, myth and ritual not unoften influence each other to a considerable extent. Again, as in the myths of other pre-literate tribes, there occur in Agaria myths some obvious inconsistencies and even contradictions between different versions of the same legend, not to speak of local variations. As Mr Elwin says: 'The Agaria myths are confused and contradictory. Their heroes blend into one another and change their character and even their sex—Lohasur, for example, is sometimes male and sometimes female. But they are alive. And as long as they live, the primitive smelting industry cannot altogether die. Lohasur must have his temple, and Agyasur be honoured in the Virgin Fire.' But the primitive recounter of myths is obviously unconscious of these inconsistencies and contradictions.

Speaking of the different theories propounded by different Western ethnologists regarding the origin of totemism and their application to Indian facts, our author makes the pertinent observation that in all these discussions insufficient attention has been paid to the Indian evidence and to the light which folk-tales can throw upon the subject. In support of this contention, Mr Elwin goes on to say: 'In India everywhere, and certainly among the Agaria, we can see the strength of the fears which may so easily gather round inanimate objects. In the folk-tales we see these objects endowed with life and speech and acting in a sometimes hostile, sometimes friendly, way on human affairs. It is very common for a house which has been the scene of ill-luck or death to be deserted; a bed on which someone has died must not be used again . . . The Agaria stories suggest some such quite obvious and simple origin for totemism. Someone is bitten by a horse and his children first avoid and then honour the horse so that they will not be bitten again. Probably the many sections of the Bagh or Baghel sept are composed of descendants of people who, long ago, were killed by tigers.' The author certainly does not mean, however, to suggest that the origin of totemism even in India admits of a one-key solution. It is not intended to ignore that, like most other social phenomena, a multiple origin of totemism is not only possible but probable in India as elsewhere.

Thus some of the folk traditions regarding the origin of a few clan-affiliations among the Agaria, as also other aboriginal tribes of India, refer to material help or succour received by some ancestor of the clan from some member of an animal or a vegetable species in dire extremity, resulting in a magical pact of alliance or allegiance with it entered into by the human ancestor of the clan, which is to remain valid for himself and his posterity. Again, among the Birjhia Asur of the Ranchi District in Chota Nagpur some families practise what is called individual totemism, and some change the totem-name of a family in every fourth generation.[1] One and the same origin cannot certainly be attributed to the more usual hereditary form of totemism and such divergent or aberrant forms of totemism.

Mr Elwin is inclined to think that on the whole the Agaria (though known by different names in different places) are 'all ultimately one tribe', and 'something more than a branch, or a collection of branches of another tribe or tribes', inasmuch as 'they have the same mythology, they worship the same gods, they have the same magic'. He further suggests that 'the Agaria and Asur are descendants of a tribe which is represented by the Asura of Sanskrit literature' and 'it is possible that this ancient Asur tribe invaded the Munda country in Chota Nagpur, were driven back by the Mundas, rallying under the standard of their deity Sing Bonga, to the very border of Bihar, and thence spread west and north through Surguja and Udaipur, Korea and the north of Bilaspur, a weaker branch fittering down to Raipur, until in the Maikal Hills they found a congenial home and a plentiful supply of iron'. Dr Reuben, Professor of Sanskrit in the Ankara University, is also inclined to the view that the traditions of the present-day Asur on the hills of the borderland of Ranchi, Jashpur, and Palamau appear to connect them with the Asura of Hindu mythology. But he finds that although they represent a cultural stratum different from that of the Munda and other agricultural 'Kolarian' or Proto-Australoid tribes and also from that of such hunting Proto-Australoid tribes as the Birhor, Baiga, etc., there is some difficulty in connecting the Asura of Sanskrit literature with iron and iron-smelting. On the other hand, among considerations that might be suggested for connecting the Agaria and Asur with the Proto-

[1] *J.B.O.R.S.*, XII (1926), pp. 147ff.

Australoid Munda tribes might be mentioned the ancestral name 'Sabar' ('Sai' in 'Sabar Sai' being an honorific title of kings derived from the Persian word 'Sahi' for king introduced into India after the Muhammadan conquest)—a name which more than one section of the Munda-speaking tribe of Kharias mention as that of their traditional ancestor.[1] Again, the Santal are called *Savar* by their neighbours, the Nal Paharia; and another Munda-speaking Proto-Australoid tribe living in Orissa and the adjoining tracts of the Madras Presidency is known as the *Savar.* General Cunningham[2] has advanced reasons for concluding that in early times where the name of *Savara* is used, it probably covers all the different divisions of the 'Kol' (Munda) tribes 'who in early Aryan times, spread far and wide over the Central Hill Belt of India'. The traditions of the Agaria and Asur themselves speak of the slaughter of all the Asur-Agaria males by the God of the Munda through a trick, though one of the legends speaks of a brother and a sister alone surviving and their union resulting in the propagation of the present tribe of Asur or Agaria, and another legend speaks of an escaped Agaria woman who was then with child finding shelter in the house of a Gond, where she gave birth to the male ancestor of the present tribe of Asur-Agaria. Mr Elwin quotes earlier writers like Ball, Drake-Brockman, etc., who regard the Asur-Agaria as a branch of the Munda tribe, but suggests that there is a distinct physical and cultural resemblance between all sections of the Asur-Agaria, they have the same professional technique and the same mythology, they worship the same gods and have the same magic, and thus must be all ultimately one tribe, although 'not one homogeneous tribe, as there are many different sections, diversified by small customs and even by name, owning no relation to each other'. This, however, does not militate against the supposition that the different sections of the Asur-Agaria people came originally from the Proto-

[1] S. C. Roy, *The Kharias* (Ranchi, 1937), p. 30.

[2] *Report of the Archaeological Survey of India*, XXVII, pp. 125, 139.

Australoid Munda stock, even though perhaps from different branches of it. And it is not improbable that the nucleus of the present-day tribe of Asur-Agaria might have been formed by the few stray survivors of the ancient Asura in Chota Nagpur and swelled and consolidated by accretions from different branches of the Munda stock who took to iron-smelting as their occupation. Mr Elwin says that among the Agaria-Asur there are few outstanding personalities, but ancient Sanskrit literature refers to numerous Asura celebrities and their achievements.[1] But as regards this it might be said that the present-day Asur are degenerate descendants of their distinguished ancestors. As Mr Elwin notes, 'Their spirit has been broken by long decades of slow material decline'.

As regards the suggestion that the possession of the same professional technique, same mythology, same magic and same worship indicates that they must all ultimately be one tribe, it might be pointed out that there are instances to show that when economic necessity or convenience brings together members of different tribes of the same or similar cultural level, and particularly of the same original racial stock, they often build up by fusion a new cultural and physical type and in course of time acquire a consciousness of kind akin to 'caste-feeling', and constitute one homogeneous people. This is particularly the case when geographical or other conditions favour their comparative segregation from other cultural groups. On the other hand, when the economic motive that led to the original aggregation and fusion of different families into one homogeneous people weakens and fails, disintegration may set in and different sections may adapt themselves to their respective changed economic and social environments and adopt new occupations, after their social customs and worship. This is what we now find among the Asur-Agaria tribes of the south-western parts of the Ranchi plateau. It is significant

[1] In Sorensen's *Index to the Mahabharata*, we come across pages of lists of mighty Asura heroes, great architects and so forth. For similar lists of Asur celebrities, see Keith's *Index to the Rigveda*.

that some sections of them do not now know either Lohasur or Agyasur or Koelasur or Logundi Raja. The only trace of ritual connected with their ancient occupation now survives in the annual sacrifice to the god of the anvil and hammer (*sanrsi kutāsi puja*). In several of their settlements even iron-smelting has been given up owing to increasing rigours of forest regulations.

Leaving aside speculations about tribal origins and ancient history, about which one can never be certain, when we look into the material parts of the book, we are filled with admiration at the clear and comprehensive, accurate and scientific and yet deeply sympathetic delineation of the life and manners and mentality of one of the poorest and lowliest but withal most interesting forest tribes of India. Indian ethnology is fortunate in securing the whole-hearted (and let us hope lifelong) services of a consummate scholar and a sturdy champion of the poor and the oppressed in Mr Verrier Elwin, whose name is now a household word among the aborigines of the Central Provinces.

S. C. Roy

Ranchi,
November 10, 1940

CONTENTS

LIST OF ILLUSTRATIONS

MAPS

PREFACE

Through the enterprise of the Oxford University Press and the generous assistance of the great House of Tata, this book goes to the printers in the middle of a war. A book about iron is not wholly out of place in wartime (this war, as no other, must 'move by her two main nerves, Iron and Gold in all her equipage') even though it must seem absurd, even fantastic, to turn from the millions of tons of death-dealing steel employed in modern battle to the few thousand tons smelted annually in the little clay furnaces of central India and used for the simplest human implements—ploughshares, axe-heads, sickles. Yet in the end the Agaria may have the advantage; their iron is magic iron, vestal iron that is powerful to protect from earthquake and lightning and every assault of ghostly enemies; for centuries their simple ploughs and harrows have raised rich crops in the wild uplands of the Maikal Hills. This aboriginal iron has brought the law of plenty to the jungle: that civilized iron is bringing the law of the jungle to the lands of plenty. In the old days, says the Agaria legend, 'iron was used as food, not for weapons'.

The Agaria are the iron-smelters and blacksmiths of the Central Provinces of India. They are most numerous and characteristic in the Maikal Hills and in the lonely *zamindaris* of Bilaspur, but an 'Agaria belt' may be traced all the way from Dindori to Neterhat. It is not possible to say how many there are: the Census of 1911 put the number at 9,500; but the Agaria tribes go by several different names and are often confused with the Hindu blacksmiths, the Lohar, and the Agharia cultivators. Their origin must remain in obscurity, but it is a fascinating speculation to connect them with the Asura, the ancient enemies of the gods, the metal-workers who brought to an end the age of stone.

It is not possible to say exactly when iron was first produced and worked in India, but it must have been at a very early date. Neogi has suggested that an iron engine of war was in use between 2000 and 1000 B.C., basing his opinion on the *Black Yajurveda.*[1] Herodotus says that the Indian soldiers in Xerxes' army had arrows of cane tipped with iron.[2] The famous iron column at the Kutb Minar near Delhi is probably three thousand years old, and its seven or eight tons of metal were manipulated with an amazing and mysterious skill.

Later, the *wootz* steel of Hyderabad was widely admired as the material from which Damascus blades were furnished, and other ancient arms of India. 'Many of the weapons', says Lovat Frazer, 'are of very great antiquity, and show remarkable qualities of workmanship. The art of damascening upon soft steel was widely practised in India, chiefly in connexion with arms. It was only after the downfall of Sikh independence in the last century that it almost ceased to be associated with the manufacture of swords and armour and was thereafter employed only in the adornment of more peaceful products.'

An excellent account of the ancient iron industry of India has been given by W. H. Schoff in an article 'The Eastern Iron Trade of the Roman Empire'.[3] Mr Schoff, who was Secretary to the Commercial Museum in Philadelphia, points out that there is ample evidence for the importation into the Roman world of antiquity from some eastern source of the finest grade of steel then known, and that it all points towards India rather than China. *Ferrum Indicum* appears in the list of articles subject to duty at Alexandria. Indian iron and steel appears in the Periplus among the imports into Abyssinia. We get some indication of this ancient trade from the account of Phoenician commerce in Ezekiel (XXVII, 19): 'Dan also and Javan going to and fro occupied in thy fairs; bright iron, cassia and calamus were in thy market.'

Early metallurgists knew little of artificial alloys, and the quality of their metals depended on the character of the ores

[1] Neogi, *Journal of the Royal Society of Arts*, 1914, Vol. LXIII, p. 43.
[2] Book, VII, Chap. LXV.
[3] J.A.O.S. Vol. XXXV (1915), pp. 224ff.

they used and the effectiveness of their primitive methods of smelting. In Egypt, for instance, we find that some iron was produced from the native ore by smelting with papyrus, but the industry disappeared at an early date when it met the competition of better metals from Asia Minor derived from magnetic sand and forest timber, and from Elba, Spain and the Alps, where rich ores were also found together with ample timber. The Roman Empire had an abundant supply of ordinary iron from within its own borders, and its imports of that metal were limited to qualities beyond its own ability to produce. This iron which it imported from the East, as has been ascertained from examination of existing specimens, was really a good grade of charcoal steel yielded by native processes jealously held secret and unknown to the Romans.

Herodotus, in his catalogue of the troops of Xerxes, says that 'the Indians were clad with garments made of cotton, had bows of cane and arrows of cane tipped with iron'. Ctesias mentions two wonderful swords of Indian steel had from the King of Persia, and it is recorded also that the Malli and Oxydracae made a gift to the victorious invader Alexander of 100 talents of Indian steel. Salmasius in his notes on Pliny, refers to an early Greek chemical treatise on 'The Tempering of Indian Steel', and Colonel Yule, in his notes on Marco Polo, has traced this trade from source to destination. It was this same Indian steel which was used in the manufacture of the famous Damascus blades of the Arabs in the height of their prosperity, and which was regarded as essentially a different metal from ordinary iron, being called by the Arabs *Hundwany*, 'Indian', whence the curious word 'Andanic' or 'Ondanique' of the mediaeval writers, the fine steel used for swords and mirrors. Cordier notes that this 'Hindi' metal used for mirrors has passed into Spanish in the form of *allinde* and *alinde* first with the meaning of steel, then that of steel mirror, and finally with that of any metallic foil for making mirror-glass. The Arab, Edrisi, says: 'The Hindus excel in the manufacture of iron. They have also workshops wherein are forged the most famous sabres in the world. It is impossible to find anything to surpass the edge that you get from Indian steel.' So Chardin says of the steel of Persia, 'They combine it with Indian steel, which is more tractable, and is much more esteemed.' Dupre says, 'I used to believe that the steel for the famous Persian sabres came from certain mines in

Khorasan, but according to all the information I have obtained, I can assert that no mine of steel exists in that province. What is used for these blades comes in the shape of discs from Lahore.'

In more recent times, the French gem merchant, Tavernier, who travelled India in the seventeenth century, mentions this steel industry in the 'Kingdom of Golconda', and remarks: 'They carry a broad sword like the Swiss, with which they both cut and thrust, and they suspend it from a belt. The barrels of their muskets are stronger than ours, and the iron is better and purer. This makes them not liable to burst. As for the cavalry, they have bow and arrow, shield and mace, with helmet and a coat of mail.' We are thus carried back by recent travellers both to the iron-tipped Indian arrows of Herodotus, and to the 'bright iron' of Ezekiel brought by merchants 'going to and fro'.

In the present century the iron industry of India has been transformed by the vast enterprises of the House of Tata. Had it not been for certain difficulties of coal and water, this book would never have been written, for Jamshedpur would have been established in the Central Provinces and the primitive industry would certainly have been absorbed. For in 1903 it was to Chanda District that Sir Dorabji Tata first went with Mr Weld on a romantic and thrilling voyage of discovery. Later, the chance discovery of an old map in the Nagpur Museum led Sir Dorabji to Drug and the wonderful reserves of ore at Dalli and Rajhara, even more remarkable than the entire hill of pure specular iron at Lohara in Chanda. But the supplies of coal and water were not equal to the ore, and in the end it was in Bihar that the greatest blast-furnace in the world came to be erected.

The ancient smelting industry has, of course, greatly declined. Yet neither famine nor foreign competition, heavy taxation nor a poor technique, social degradation nor the most pitiful earnings have succeeded in altogether destroying the little clay furnaces which may still be found in many parts of India, in Bengal and Bihar; in the Santal Parganas, Monghyr,

Sambalpur and Orissa; in the Kumaon Hills; in Mysore; in the districts of Malabar; in Salem and Trichinopoly; in Hyderabad; in several States in Central India and Rajputana; and above all in the Central Provinces.

One reason for this heroic persistence is the peasant's preference for tools made from the soft and malleable ores used by the village smelters. For example, in the iron head of the small axe, the hole which takes the wooden handle is made by hammering it out with a large nail while the iron is hot—which would be impossible with English iron. Again, the *karrahi*, a sort of large plate with handles, made in Jubbulpore, is made by continual hammering of the cold iron—a process which gives the metal a fine polish, but could not be applied to more brittle iron. The peasants also believe that tools made with the village iron are easier to mend when broken. A striking proof of its utility is seen in the suspension bridge which was built over the Bias River (in Saugor) in 1830, the iron for which had all been smelted in village furnaces at Tendukhera.

It has also been observed that village iron does not rust quickly, possibly because the use of a stone anvil siliconides the skin of the iron. 'I have seen native-made iron,' writes Wallace, 'forged on a stone anvil, and have observed that it does not rust like English iron when exposed to the weather. The iron-work of the car on which the gods of the Kulu Valley take the air has a fine brown patina and no rust flakes. It is all charcoal iron.'[1]

The scope of this book is strictly limited. The Agaria are a small and scattered people; their smithies are widely distributed across the countryside. Here you will find an Agaria home in a Baiga village, the women dressed in Baiga style, the children playing Baiga games. There you will find the smithy in a Gond, or a Dhoba, or a Kawar centre—and the Agaria taking something of the pattern of their lives from their surroundings. There did not seem to be any point in describing with the

[1] J. Wallace, *Journal of the Iron and Steel Institute*, 1908, No. I, p. 84.

fulness, for example, that I allowed myself in *The Baiga*, the customs and habits which the Agaria share with their neighbours and which have already been described elsewhere. This volume, then, may be regarded as in some sense supplementary to *The Baiga*. There I discussed very fully an attitude to sex, a system of magic, a scheme of primitive jurisprudence, a policy for the future that would apply equally to any of the tribes inhabiting the Maikal Range.

It was the same with other, smaller, matters. Take dancing, for example. There are no specifically Agaria dances, but this does not mean that the Agaria are not good dancers. The life and soul of the Gond Saila dances in Karanjia was Sujawal —an Agaria. In Sanhrwachhapar once I had arranged a display of Baiga dancing for some friends. 'What perfect rhythm your Baiga achieve,' exclaimed one of them pointing to the girl who was leading the line of women—she was Chinnibinni, an Agaria. The chapter on dancing in *The Baiga*, then, may be taken as applying equally to the Agaria of Mandla. The dancing of Bilaspur differs in many ways—there are, for example, twenty different kinds of Dhandha for men, and different types of Karma. But these again are not specially Agaria dances, and at Nunera—where there is an unusually large Agaria settlement—they danced very badly.

The life of Agaria children does not seem to differ greatly from that of their neighbours, except that they begin work in the smithy at a very early age. At first they simply work the bellows; later, the girls are taught how to prepare the furnaces, and the boys are initiated into the work of the forge. On the first day the boy offers incense to Lohasur and Koelasur, saying 'Be a shadow over me!' and he makes a reverence before the anvil and the heavy hammer. The friendships of children resemble those of the Baiga, though among the Chokh I found the Ganga-baru, or 'Sand of the Ganges' which I had not noticed elsewhere. Agaria children join in the ordinary village games; I only found one game which could be called their own—the Pasra-khel, which is simply an imitation of all the activities of the smithy.

Kinship rules, avoidances, the law of inheritance, pregnancy and menstruation rules, birth customs are the same as among the Gond. Agaria marriages are of the ordinary *sāt-bhānwar* type: a few special features may be noted. The Agaria, like the Baiga, and unlike the Gond, make a marriage elephant. As among the Gond, bride and bridegroom are adorned with crowns made of *chhindi*-palm leaves. When the marriage is over they go down to the nearest stream, and the girl hides the *kalsa*-pot and her husband has to find it. He has to draw an arrow through her bent arm and shoot a small image of a deer. When the new wife first enters her home, she steps across an iron nail which is placed on the threshold.

There is no Agaria language, and since these tribesmen live outside the Gondi area they usually speak a corrupt Hindi. The Asur of Neterhat, however, have their own Munda tongue, a so-called Aghori language noted by Sir G. A. Grierson.

But the fact that the Agaria in many ways resemble their neighbours must not be taken to mean that they do not have a highly distinctive and vigorous life of their own. The totemistic customs of the tribe are highly developed and of great significance. The mythology is striking and distinctive, and offers interesting parallels to the Baiga stories. It controls and vitalizes to an unusual degree the material culture of the tribe. The Agaria have their own special contribution to magic and I have studied this fully (though the chapter should be read in connexion with the chapters in *The Baiga* on the same subject) as well as what I have called the tribal neurosis of fear and conflict which has made at many times a painful impression on my mind.

If this book lacks the intimate human touches of *The Baiga*, that is due, I think, to the character of the people. Malinowski noted the very striking differences in temperament between the people of the Trobriand Islands and those of the neighbouring Amphletts. The Agaria are a people absorbed in their craft and their material; they seem to have little life apart from the roar of the bellows and the clang of hammer upon iron. Few of them live to a great age, they have poor memories, there are few outstanding personalities among them. I made many attempts to collect autobiographies as I did easily and successfully from the Baiga, but I failed to get anything worthy of a permanent record.

Yet the folk-lore and mythology of the Agaria is fascinating, and the tribe seemed to me to demand at least a short monograph because here was a people that lived every moment of their lives for an ancient craft and by a living myth. This marriage of myth and craft, which is the central theme of the book, gives the Agaria great significance.

Very little has ever been written about the Agaria and most of that little has been wrong. In the earlier provincial literature, which gives excellent accounts of the Gond and Baiga, there are only the scantiest references. In 1867 Colonel Ward considered, most unjustly, that the Agaria were drunken and lazy. When in 1909 Sir C. E. Low selected for Government assistance those village industries 'which had some vitality left and were thus capable of improvement' he did not include primitive iron-smelting. The Bourne Committee of 1930, which examined many of the indigenous industries of the Province, does not mention the craft of the Agaria. The Census of 1931 did not even enumerate them, though it briefly refers to them in the schedule as 'a caste'—although as one of the most primitive peoples in the Province they, if any, should have been described as a 'tribe'. The Census also makes the extraordinary statement that, in regard to the production of raw materials, only nine men and seven women were returned as engaged in the extraction of iron. 'Figures are not available for 1921 but those for the recent Census definitely indicate the death of an industry which was once important in certain districts.'[1] Actually, even with the numbers reduced owing to heavy taxation, there were over a hundred furnaces working in 1931. The industry was not dead yet.

[1] *Census of India, 1931*, Vol. XII, p. 237. For a criticism of Census facts and figures, see J. M. Datta, 'Inaccuracies in the Bengal Census Report, 1931' in *Sankhya*, III, Pt. II, pp. 163ff.

In *The Tribes and Castes of the Central Provinces*, Russell and Hiralal have a section on the Agaria. 'This article', they admit with engaging frankness, 'is compiled from papers by Mr Mir Padshah, Tahsildar of Bilaspur, and Kanhya Lal, clerk in the Gazetteer office.'[1] I cannot believe that this is how scientific work should be produced. I myself have had many years' experience of Tahsildars and other minor officials. They make excellent magistrates, and do exact and faithful work in the Treasury and Revenue Department, but they are not trained to observe ethnographic details. A Boiler Inspector can get an admirable focus on a boiler, but he does not know what to look at in a Gond marriage. Casual observation is nearly always inaccurate. Low-paid officials, with little interest in the subject, are apt to produce very dubious work. For example, the Tahsildars of certain Districts in the Province were asked to compile lists of villages in which there were Agaria smithies. This, you would say, was a simple enough business and, since Government taxes the smithies, almost a speciality of Revenue officials. Yet every list was hopelessly inaccurate and useless, not only for the purposes of science, but even as a guide to research.

Yet this blind reliance on the statements of subordinate officials—who, moreover, on account of the conflict between country and Government, are the last people to be able to get real information—seems to be taken for granted. Methods of research which would not be tolerated for a moment in Africa, Melanesia or Australia are accepted and established in India. Enthoven based his *Folklore of Bombay* and even his *Tribes and Castes of Bombay* on 'raw material' furnished by primary school masters! Risley's *Tribes and Castes of Bengal*, like all the volumes in the Ethnographic Survey of India, contains much misleading information. 'Inaccurate and even erroneous statements', says Mr S. C. Roy, 'are unfortunately not rare in Risley's accounts of different tribes, and indeed are inevitable

[1] R. V. Russell and R. B. Hiralal, *The Tribes and Castes of the Central Provinces of India*, Vol. II, p. 1.

in a writer whose information was in most cases not collected first-hand but was made up of varying information supplied by subordinate officers of Government and other correspondents, most of whom had little interest in the inquiries, had no clear idea of what was wanted and lacked the equipment and discernment needed to discriminate between things bearing the same names but differing in essentials.'[1]

Russell and Hiralal's volumes suffer from the same defect. Whatever the authors themselves have written is valuable and authoritative. But the bulk of the book is vitiated by the way it was compiled. Mr Grigson, for example, in his admirable *Maria Gonds of Bastar*, has again and again to correct Russell's statements. See his page 114—'Whoever gave the authors this information must have been drawing on his imagination'; his page 142—'There is no need to believe this picturesque story'; page 193—'Their account of Bastar generally is in many respects misinformed'; page 224—'Russell and Hiralal have again to be criticized for the generalization', etc.[2] Grigson also shows them to be largely incorrect in their account of the social organization of the Marias and rather emphatically contradicts them on the question of names. In fact, he is hardly ever able to quote the book except to correct it.

In their account of the Agaria, Russell and Hiralal are equally inaccurate, and for the same cause. They begin with the highly controversial statement that the Agaria are 'an offshoot of the Gond tribe'. They put the Maikal Range in the Raipur District. They allow the 'caste' only two, instead of half a dozen, endogamous divisions. Their list of septs is so incomplete as to be dangerously misleading, and they make the astonishing statement that 'the Agaria do not know the meanings of their section names and therefore have no totemistic observances'. The dead are not 'usually burnt', but even now are still buried. They do not 'worship Bara Deo',

[1] S. C. Roy, *Oraon Religion and Customs* (Ranchi, 1928), p. 322.
[2] W. V. Grigson, *The Maria Gonds of Bastar*.

Russell and Hiralal say that the Agaria 'do not eat beef' and imply that they have given up worshipping 'Lohar Sur' (*sic*) with a black cow. It is almost certain, it is true, that the Agaria told this to the Tahsildar and the Hindu clerk in the office, but it is incorrect. Their account of the iron-smelting industry is so meagre and incomplete that it gives a false picture of the life and interest of the tribe.

It must sound, I am afraid, ungracious and ungenerous to decry the methods and results of these older and pioneer scholars, but it is necessary because there is a dangerous tendency among the younger Indian anthropologists to follow their example. There is a tendency to scamp personal investigation on the spot, to make brief visits of a fortnight or less to a District and then write about it, to conduct inquiries from the veranda of a dak bungalow.

I was once present when a certain investigator was conducting some research into a very difficult question relating to the conduct of the sexes. We sat in the dak bungalow round a large table. The Sub-Divisional Officer was there, and a Tahsildar. There were two clerks with their pencils poised above writing-pads. The informant, literally trembling with fear, was led in by a *policeman* and made to *stand* before the table and there asked intimate questions about the morals of his people. Naturally he denied everything that he thought would offend the 'sahib' and said anything that he thought would please him.

You cannot observe mankind from the howdah of an elephant. There is no substitute for field-work. There is no substitute for life in the village, among the people, staying in village houses, and enduring the physical distress as well as the possible misunderstandings that may arise. Happily, the father of Indian ethnography, Mr Sarat Chandra Roy, has set the most shining example in this regard. His knowledge of the people about whom he writes extends over forty years. He has lived with them, shared their food and their homes. He speaks their languages with idiomatic intimacy. He has won their love and trust by fighting for them in the District

Councils and the Legislatures, and has defended scores of them in the Courts. Such a man will not be given misleading information. Specially among the aboriginals, the truth is told to those who are loved. It cannot be bought by presents of liquor and tobacco.

Mr Grigson also won the affection of the Bastar aboriginals by many measures designed for their protection, and he toured widely among the Maria villages in the State. Time is of great importance. Reuben's monumental *Eisenschmiede und Dämonen in Indien* was written after a sojourn of only a month among the Asur of Chota Nagpur. No scholar, however brilliant, can expect the results of such hastily gathered inquiries to be accepted. The value of Reuben's book, however, is great. He puts the modern iron-smelter into an almost cosmic setting, and allows us to see him against the vast background of Sanskrit mythology.

But long residence, intimate personal contact, knowledge of the local idiom and, in the case of foreign observers, trained Indian assistants, are necessary qualifications for the ethnographer in India. My objection to accepting the casual statements of uninterested officials naturally does not apply to the work of trained helpers.

In the preparation of this volume I have been fortunate in having the assistance of Sunderlal and Gulabdas, colleagues of nearly ten years' standing, who have been trained to a standard of very high accuracy in the simpler aspects of observation and investigation. They have the advantage of being non-aboriginals who have lived all their lives in tribal territory. They do not therefore suffer from the temptation to 'improve' their information in order to save the face of their tribe. On the other hand, since they are not 'converts' to a foreign religion they do not suffer from the equally dangerous tendency to exaggerate the evils of the social order they have deserted. They have dictaphone minds and can repeat accurately and without personal bias whatever they are told. I owe them both more than I can say for companionship on long and arduous journeys, for care in sickness and, above all, for accuracy.

My own qualifications for writing this book are simply those of long residence and intimate contact. For five years in Karanjia (Dindori Tahsil of the Mandla District) my nearest neighbours were Agaria, and I woke every morning to the roar of the bellows. Later, in Sanhrwachhapar and Patan, I was in constant touch with the Agaria in the neighbourhood and in Mawai, and assisted at all their ceremonies and watched every aspect of their industry. I have also made long tours in the Bilaspur Zamindaris, Pendra, Kenda, Lapha, Chhuri, Matin, Uprora, Pandaria, as well as in the Phuljhar Zamindari and the Raipur District. I have seen something of the work of the Lohar in Sarangarh State and the borders of the Sambalpur District. My acquaintance with the Asur of Chota Nagpur is necessarily slighter, but I spent some fruitful and interesting days on the Neterhat plateau with Mr W. G. Archer, I.C.S., himself an authority on primitive art and dancing and author of a brilliant collection of Uraon folk-songs. Later Mr Archer supplied me with exact and detailed information about the iron-smelters living within his charge as Census Superintendent of Bihar. To him and to his assistants, Babu Bishram Trofimus Toppo and the late Babu John Katkahi, I must express my gratitude.

I am indebted also to Khan Saheb F. K. Khan, to Mr H. S. Kamath, I.C.S., Mr R. K. Patil, I.C.S., and Mr Paramanand, I.C.S., for that assistance for which an anthropologist must always depend on officers of Government. Mr G. C. F. Ramsden, I.C.S., and Rao Bahadur K. N. Dikshit sent me photographs. Dr C. S. Fox, D.Sc., F.G.S., gave me valuable information; I owe a great deal to him and to the indispensable Records and Memoirs of the Geological Survey of which he is Director. Miss Durga Bhagvat gave me useful details of the Agaria she saw while touring in Drug and Raipur and still further increased my debt to her by reading the proofs. Mr M. B. Bhaduri, of Udaipur State, took great pains to collect, in a precise and methodical manner, material on points about which I needed information. Mr J. B. Le Patourel, Diwan of Jashpur, and Rai Sahib H. L. Varma, M.B.E., Minister of Surguja, made valuable surveys of the iron-smelters working in their States.

I am grateful too to Mr J. J. Ghandy, General Manager of the Tata Iron and Steel Company, as also to the Company's Chief Chemist at Jamshedpur, for arranging a chemical analysis and report on various specimens of iron-ore that I sent them; to Mr R. V. Leyden and Dr and Mrs Kronenberger for translating parts of Reuben's monograph on the Asur; to Mr R. D. Motafram for several drawings; and to Mr S. M. Ishaque for arranging for the maps to be drawn in his office at Jagdalpur.

The expenses of research were covered by a grant from Merton College; to the Warden and Fellows I must express my deep gratitude for their generosity and interest. I was also helped by the Sir Dorabji Tata Trust in my capacity as a research associate of its School of Social Studies, and the generous support of the Tata Iron and Steel Company made this publication possible.

I am also indebted to the Government of the Central Provinces and Berar for their assistance; to Mr. P. de Peterson for many tokens of sympathy and friendship; and to the Oxford University Press in Bombay which so valiantly accepted an unprofitable manuscript in a lean year.

Governments in India have not always treated their primitive iron-workers with sympathy and imagination; this makes it the greater pleasure to acknowledge the lively interest taken in the Agaria during the preparation of this book by several officials of the Central Provinces administration. To Mr V. K. Maitland, M.C., I.F.S., the Agaria community of Mandla and Balaghat owe a special debt, for it was he who without hesitation or delay took up the question of the heavy taxation of the furnaces directly I brought it to his notice and authorized a substantial reduction—which may actually save this ancient industry from decay. By the efforts of Mr W. V. Grigson, I.C.S., and Mr E. S. Hyde, I.C.S., than whom no greater friends and allies of the aboriginals exist, this reduction was applied to a still wider field.

Other friends too have given me support in fullest measure. Mr Shamrao Hivale was not greatly attracted by the Agaria—his people are the Pardhan—but as always his cheerful company, his universal friendliness, his quick and ready observation, and not least his ability to get our old Ford V8 out of any difficulty lightened my task and made it more effective.

When I sent him my manuscript, Mr S. C. Roy was confined to bed with an exhausting and painful illness. His Foreword to this book must have been one of the last things he wrote. Soon after sending it to me he died, depriving science of a patient, humble, exact, far-seeing scholar; the aboriginals, of an ardent and sincere champion; and those who loved him of a generous friend.

Mr W. V. Grigson read the proofs with meticulous care and made many important suggestions, saving me from a score of errors. To him I must join my friends, Maeve and Evelyn Wood. The isolation and disappointments of village life have made me perhaps abnormally sensitive to friendship and encouragement. Those precious things have always been given me by the Woods. In a dozen ways Evelyn has furthered the production of this book, and Maeve's admirable drawings lighten its duller pages.

VERRIER ELWIN

11 May, 1942
Patan Village,
Mandla District, India

NOTE ON TRANSLITERATION

As this is not a linguistic treatise, the system of transliteration has been kept as simple as possible for the convenience of the general reader. The safest general rule for the pronunciation of the italicized words is to give the consonants their values as in English and the vowels as in Italian. Words printed in roman type do not show long or short vowels, and I have written Sanskrit proper names in the conventional English manner; that is, I have put Rigveda instead of Ṛgveda and so on.

Currency and Weights

There are 16 annas in a rupee and there are, at the time of writing, 13 rupees and 3-4 annas in a pound sterling. A pice is a quarter of an anna. Rs.2-8-6 means two rupees, eight-and-a-half annas. A lakh is a hundred thousand and a crore is ten million.

Weights and measures differ from place to place, but in this book the following table is used:

16 *chattak* make 1 *seer*,
5 *seer* make 1 *kuro*,
20 *kuro* make 1 *khandi*

A *seer* is about 2 pounds avoirdupois.

CHAPTER I
THE AGARIA

I. *The Agaria Belt*

The word Agaria probably means a worker in *āg* or fire; *āg* is the root of Agni, the Hindu god of fire, or of Agyasur, the tribal demon who was born in flame. The Agaria are indeed the servants of the fire which they so constantly tend, and the name will not seem inappropriate to anyone who has watched by night their ghostly figures clothed in showers of sparks as they move to and fro in the weird light of the flames flickering above the furnace.

Another derivation is from *agar*, the name which in Rewa State is applied to the local iron-mines.[1] In Udaipur State, the name is traced to Agar Sai, Raja of the iron city Lohitpur. But in any case the blacksmith Agaria must not be confused with the Agharia, the great cultivating caste of Chhattisgarh who are said to take their name from Agra, or with the Agari, the salt-makers of Rajputana and the Panjab, who derive their title from the *āgar* or shallow pan in which they evaporate the saline water of lakes or wells.

The name Agaria proper is applied rather loosely to many of the primitive iron-smelters in the Central Provinces, in Rewa State, in Mirzapur, in the Surguja, Udaipur, and Jashpur States, to a branch of the Asur in Ranchi and Palamau, to sections of Korwa and Binjhia in Bihar and of Lohar in Bengal.

The Agaria do not form one homogeneous tribe; there are many different sections, diversified by small customs and even by name, owning no relation to each other, yet marked by a common appearance, mythology and technique. It is thus possible to trace an Agaria belt across the centre of India

[1] C. E. Luard, *Rewa State Gazetteer*, Vol. IV, p. 41.

within which the primitive iron-smelters are quite distinct from the Hindu iron-workers on every side of them.

In the Central Provinces, the blacksmith neighbours of the Agaria are mainly Lohar, from whom they may be readily distinguished even when, as in Raipur, they have adopted the Hindu name. There are certain features characteristic of the Agaria tribes everywhere.

The Agaria burn charcoal and extract iron from ore in small clay furnaces. It is rare for the Lohar to practise iron-smelting.

The Agaria use bellows of a particular kettledrum pattern and work them with their feet. A glance at Plate 25 will show the remarkable contrast between these primitive bellows and those used by the Lohar which are worked by hand. Many Agaria cover the bellows with cow-hide which the Lohar refuse to touch.

The Agaria worship tribal gods or demons, who are clearly associated with the ancient Asura, such as Lohasur (whose name does not occur in Sanskrit literature[1]), Koelasur and Agyasur. The very form of their names marks them as Asura and enemies of the Hindu gods. The Lohar, on the other hand, worship the ordinary Hindu gods and do not seem to have a special god of the forge.

The Agaria have an elaborate mythology of which the heroes are Logundi Raja, Jwala Mukhi and Kariya Kuar, but they are ignorant of the Hindu Vulcan, Twashtri or Vishwakarma, the artisan of the gods, who made the fiery weapon Agneyastra and revealed the Sthapatya-veda, the science of mechanics and architecture. The Lohar, on the other hand, who are ignorant of the tribal heroes, derive their caste and its profession from Twashtri or Vishwakarma.

Another interesting point in the mythology is that whereas the Lohar claim, as for example in Garhwal, that their ancestors furnished the Pandava with their weapons, in Agaria legend it was the Pandava who attacked and destroyed their iron city

[1] W. Reuben, *Eisenschmiede und Dämonen in Indien*, p. 300.

2. (*a*) Patharia Agaria of Pungaon, Mandla District.

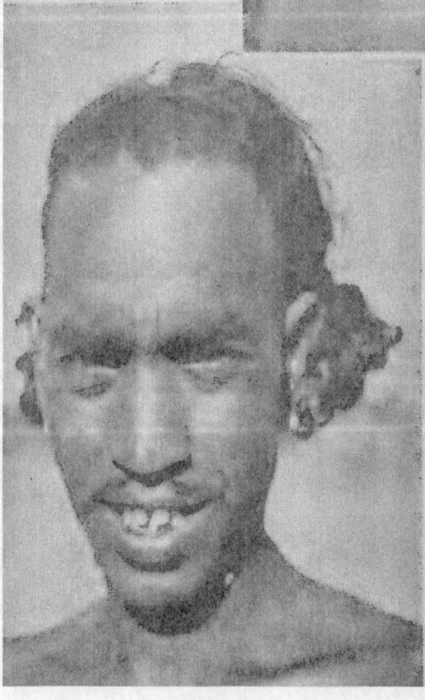

(*b*) Patharia Agaria of Pungaon, Mandla District.

3. (*a*) God-dhuka Lohar of Patandadar, Raipur District.

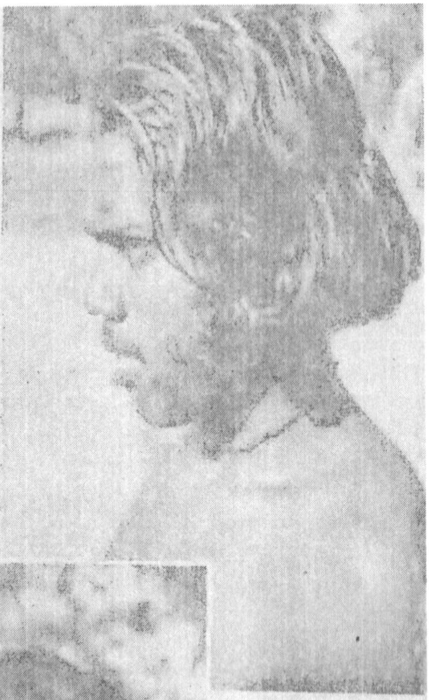

(*b*) God-dhuka Lohar of Patandadar, Raipur District.

and the old kingdom of Logundi Raja. Other stories attribute the city's destruction to the Hindu god Bhagavan or to the Hindu solar deity Narayan Deo or Suraj Deo. Here the Agaria hero Jwala Mukhi plays the part of Rahu the Asura and swallows the sun. There is a very strict taboo in Mandla among the Agaria on working in the sun. I will return to this later, but I mention these facts now because they are highly characteristic of Agaria legend and would never be found among the Hindu Lohar.

Finally, it is generally possible to distinguish an Agaria from a Lohar by looking at him. The Agaria are short, sturdy, square-headed, with broad heavy noses, thick-lipped, very dark in colour, with straight hair; the features are coarse and unattractive. They are rather stupid, dull and heavy. It is rare to see a beautiful Agaria woman. The Lohar are more finely built and of a generally lighter colour, taller, longer-headed, with mesorrhine to leptorrhine nose, and thin lips. The distinction will be seen most readily by comparing the Lohar of Sarangarh (Plate 5) with the typical Agaria (Plate 2).

Where we have the above conditions fulfilled, along with some tradition of the name Agaria, we shall be justified in regarding a group of iron-smelters, even if they now call themselves by some other title, as belonging to the true Agaria.

Let us now make a rapid survey of the 'Agaria belt', moving eastward from Mandla. In the Dindori Tahsil at the east of that District we find the Patharia Agaria; these may be regarded as the 'standard' Agaria—their culture is highly characteristic and fairly well preserved.

Moving further east to Bilaspur, there are Kalha Agaria in the foothills of the Maikal Range and in the remote zamindaris of the east. To the south are the God-dhuka Lohar of Raipur and the Gondi-speaking Agaria of Drug. All these are obviously related to the Mandla Agaria, by their physical characters, their professional technique, their mythology and their religion.

North from Mandla, there are Patharia in Rewa State, some of whom have migrated to Mirzapur. The Mirzapur

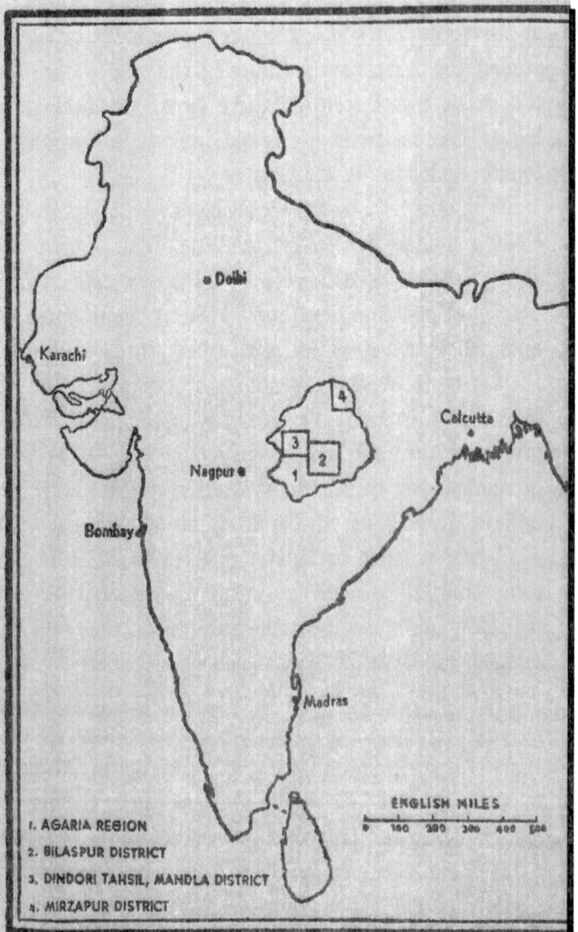

For further details of 1. Agaria Region, *see* map facing p. 6; for 2. Bilaspur Distr *see* p. 34; for 3. Dindori Tahsil, Mandla District, *see* p. 45; for 4. Mirzapur District, *see* p. 49.

Agaria worship Lohasur Devi and their smelting methods recall those of Mandla.

Turning east again, we pass through Surguja, Udaipur and Jashpur States into Chota Nagpur where we finally reach the Asur group of tribes, traditionally primitive iron-workers of whom one branch still bears the name Agaria. In Udaipur the blacksmiths are called Chokh (which they themselves say is synonymous with Agaria), Mahali and Mahali Lohar. In Jashpur the majority are Mahali Lohar.

How far are we justified in regarding the Agaria of the west, the Chokh of the centre, the God-dhuka Lohar of the south, and the Asur of the east as one tribe?

We must admit at once that there are many and obvious differences, for everywhere the blacksmith takes for his ordinary life much of the colouring of his neighbours. The Agaria of Mandla resemble the Gond and Baiga among whom they live; the Chokh resemble the Korwa and Gond of Chhattisgarh; the Asur of Chota Nagpur have the same dress, festivals, dances and even village dormitories as their Munda-speaking neighbours.

But all these tribes have a tradition of the name Agaria and sometimes use it. They erect the same general type of smithy, build the same kind of kiln, use bellows of the same pattern and work them with their feet. They all make Virgin Iron, and believe in its power. Many have a taboo on working in the sun. Anthropometric measurements are not available and in any case would prove little, for there has obviously been a great deal of inter-marriage between the smiths and their neighbours.

Although the mythology at the two ends of the belt is different, we can trace the gradual transformation of one type of legend into the other. Thus an Agaria story of north Udaipur gives us a link between the Agaria and the Mahali Chokh. 'Sabar Sai had twelve sons'—such is the story given by Kanpi Agaria of Dehidanr—'they were called the twelve Asur brothers. They were great smelters of iron. One of them took Mahali girls as wives and their sons became Mahali

Chokh. Logundi Raja was an Asur. He and his wife the Asurin are offered a pig before the iron-kiln.' Sabar Sai and Logundi Raja are the chief heroes of the Agaria legends of Mandla. In another village it was related how Sabar Sai reigned in Lohripur (a further parallel with Mandla) which is seven days' journey north-east from Assam. The twelve Asur brothers fled from Lohripur to Saraidi in Jashpur, where there are mountains of slag to be seen even today.

Other Chokh Agaria blacksmiths of Udaipur identify Logundi Raja and Sabar Sai, and even Logundi Raja and Lohasur. Yet another synonym is Agar Sai, from which the name Agaria is said to be derived. In Semipali village the Chokh Agaria said they were descended from the twelve Asur brothers and Sabar Sai; in Raimer village, they said that the founder of the tribe was Lohri Raja who was also called Loha Asur. Some Chokh of the north of the State (near the Surguja border) worship at the iron-pit Lohgund-Tinga (that is, Logundi Raja and his consort Tingamati), Asur-Asurin and Lohasur; others worship the twelve Asur brothers in the iron-kiln.

Although the Agaria of Mandla do not know the Asur-Asurin and the Asur of Chota Nagpur do not worship Lohasur or Logundi, we can see in the transition area how these tribal heroes and deities are identified with one another. The Agaria, Chokh and Asur regard themselves as separated by minor differences of food and custom—one, for example, fixes the bellows with a stone, another with a peg—but they recognize their ultimate similarity and relationship.

It was obviously impossible, however, for the Census authorities to classify these different tribes under one heading. The iron-smelters further complicate matters by changing their names from time to time, with the result that the 1891 Census Report declares that 'the tribes who follow the profession of smelting iron-ore have been returned in such various ways at the Census that it is difficult to ascertain what their real numbers may be'.[1]

[1] *Census of India*, 1891, Vol. XI, p. 205.

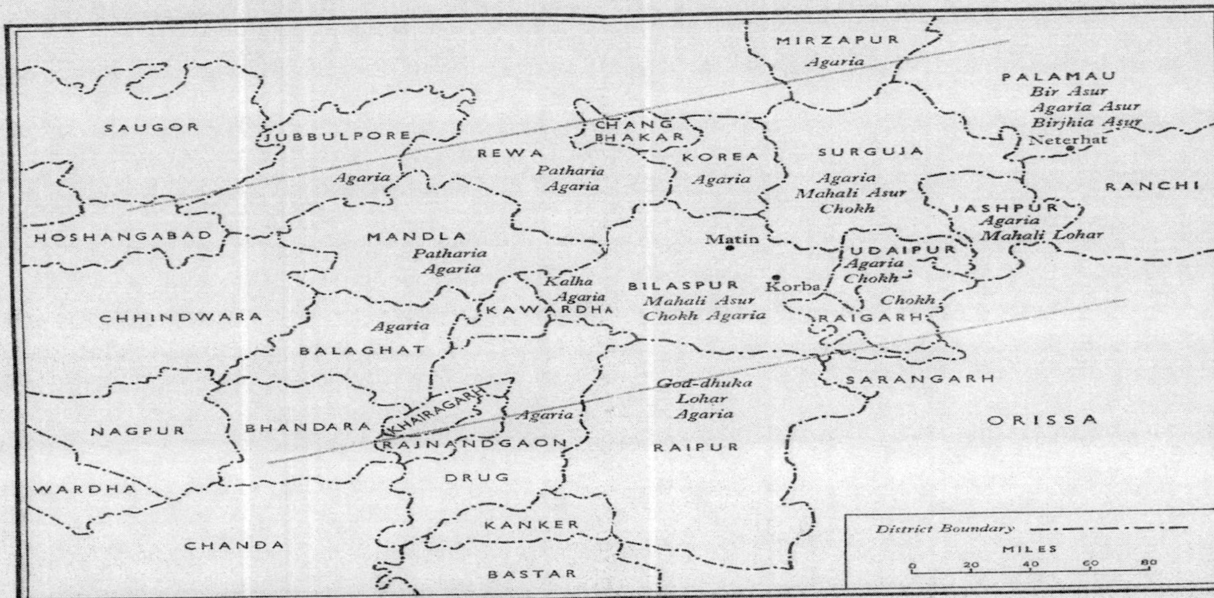

SKETCH MAP TO ILLUSTRATE THE AGARIA BELT

Sometimes the Agaria have returned themselves as Gond, often they have been confused with the Agharia. In Raipur in recent years they have taken to calling themselves Lohar. In 1921 they were tabulated only in Bilaspur and Surguja State. The population figures are thus almost wholly unreliable. We will, however, run quickly through the Census reports and tables to see whether at least some approximations to the facts can be discovered.

In 1881, there was a return for the whole of India of 210,918 Agaria, of which 22,957 were in the Central Provinces. Here they were obviously confused with the Agharia cultivators.[1]

In 1891, when Sir Benjamin Robertson was Census Commissioner for the Central Provinces, the Agaria were tabulated under three heads[2]:—

Agaria, under Gond tribes	326
Lohar Agaria	2,380
Agaria iron-smelters	2,470

To this must be added 414 Gondi Agaria and 242 iron-smelters in the States.

In 1891, while there were 84,112 blacksmiths in the Province, there were 3,070 people returned as occupied in iron-smelting. The castes employed were Kondar Gond (1274) in Saugor, Damoh and Jubbulpore, and Agaria and sometimes Gond elsewhere. There was a subdivision of Lohar called Agaria, chiefly from Jubbulpore, and 4,679 Gondi Lohar from the Satpura Districts. 'Both are in all probability mostly employed in collecting and smelting iron-ore.'[3] The Lohar Agaria are very probably Agaria who were trying to raise their status, an idea which would occur naturally to them in the Jubbulpore District, by calling themselves Lohar.

In 1901, when R. V. Russell was in charge of the Census, incorrect classification caused the number of Agaria to drop from 5,832 to 1,604,[4] and we are told nothing at all about them.

[1] E. V. Kitts, *Compendium of the Castes and Tribes found in India*, p. 2.
[2] *Census of India*, 1891, Vol. XII, Pt. II, p. 144.
[3] *Census of India*, 1891, Vol. XI, p. 199.
[4] *Census of India*, 1901, Vol. XIII, Pt. I, p. 179.

In 1911, on the other hand, there was a 90 per cent increase. The Agaria now numbered 9,500 and to this figure we should probably be right in adding 276 Mahali and 129 Asur, the only time, I think, that the Asur have been tabulated in the Central Provinces.

There were also 8,712 Panchal—the Lohar of the Maratha Districts, 451 Sikligar—a branch of the Lohar who specialize in cleaning swords, and no fewer than 181,590 Lohar, a very considerable increase on the figures of 1891.[1]

In 1921 the figures go down again and there are only 3,661 Agaria, a decrease of 61 per cent.[2] But this is explained. 'The apparent decrease of 61 per cent in their numbers is due to the fact that at the present Census they have only been tabulated in the Bilaspur District and Surguja State, where they are mostly found. They may also have been confused with the Agharias.'[3]

The Agaria were not tabulated at all in 1931.

Probably the 1911 figures, which were adopted by Russell in his article on the Agaria, come nearest to the correct figure for the Central Provinces. To get a complete total we should have to add figures for Rewa State, Mirzapur—where there were 1,186 Agaria in 1909—and Bihar. Possibly today there may be altogether some 15,000 Agaria.

II. *The Origin of the Tribe*

We now approach the important and difficult problem of who the Agaria really are. Are they a separate tribe, a tribe —as it were—on their own, which came into being long ago, perhaps at the time of the discovery of iron or its introduction into the Province? Or are they simply a conglomerate of those members of many different tribes who have taken to iron-smelting? Are the Patharia Agaria of Dindori a separate tribe or are they a branch of the Gond who have taken to the despised iron work and thus been gradually isolated as a special

[1] *Census of India*, 1911 (J. T. Marten), Vol. X, Pt. I, p. 229.
[2] *Census of India*, 1921 (N. J. Roughton), Vol. XI, Pt. I.
[3] *Census of India*, 1921, Vol. XI, Pt. I, p. 155.

community? The Chokh Agaria of Bilaspur have many affinities with the Korwa; are they a group of Korwa who have taken to iron-smelting?

We may illustrate the problem from other parts of India. Risley, for example, describes how the Lohar of Bihar and Western Bengal 'are a large and heterogeneous aggregate, comprising members of several different tribes and castes, who in different parts of the country took up the profession of working in iron'.[1] Thus, the Kokas Lohar seem to be Barhi who had to separate from the parent stock. The Kamarkalla Lohar may be 'a degraded offshoot from the Sonar caste'. The Manjhal-Tuiya of Lohardaga may similarly be a branch of the Turi.

In Bastar, this process may be seen actually at work at the present day. Grigson, describing the Maria blacksmiths, remarks that 'these blacksmiths appear to be of Maria stock, speaking the Maria language, indistinguishable physically, having the same phratries and clans, and following the same customs. Enquiry showed in every case that some of the blacksmiths either had themselves once been cultivators or had fathers who were originally cultivators. In some cases they had obtained cultivators' daughters as wives; but these appeared all to be runaway matches without the consent of the girls' parents; in other cases cultivators had become blacksmiths in order to marry blacksmiths' daughters. Halba and Telanga neighbours refer to them often as Kammar by caste; but so far as the word can be used of them, it is clearly rather an occupational term. Yet for some reason the aboriginal everywhere looks down on the smith, and as soon as a Maria takes to this occupation he must live with his fellow-smiths either in a separate village or hamlet, or segregated in a separate part of the village.'[2]

[1] Sir H. H. Risley, *Tribes and Castes of Bengal*, Vol. II, p. 22.

[2] W. V. Grigson, op. cit., pp. 175f. The ban on the blacksmith in Bastar, however, is not absolute. Muria-Lohar boys and girls are sometimes admitted to membership of the village dormitory. In some Maria villages of Dantewara I was told that it was only the Naiko Lohara (the first ancestor of whom had intercourse with a corpse) who were avoided.

It is obvious that where there is a social ban on any occupation, the evolution of a new tribe from those who take to it is greatly accelerated. A sub-tribe of Korwa in Surguja, Jashpur and Palamau was already known in Risley's day as the Agaria-Korwa, for they made axes from iron of their own smelting, and a similar group of Binjhia was known as the Agaria-Binjhia. [1] Both these groups are now probably merged in the main Agaria tribe. The Savara have a division called Luara or Muli who work in iron and are separating from the original tribe. [2] Some of the Kharia also smelt and work iron, but have not yet become a separate group. Mr S. C. Roy believes that the present-day Asur of Bihar are simply a tribe of Munda or Kol stock which has adopted the characteristic occupation of the ancient Asur and with it the tribal name. [3]

What then of the Agaria? Are they 'an offshoot of the Gond tribe', as Russell thought, [4] formed in some such way as Grigson noticed among the Maria? In 1891 the Agaria were classified by Sir B. Robertson among the 'Tribes allied to Gonds' [5] along with, for example, Bhattra, Muria and Maria, and he observes that the Agaria in the C.P. 'are looked upon as Gonds, and have frequently described themselves as such at the enumeration'.[6] Similarly, in 1921, Roughton described the Agaria as 'a small Dravidian tribe which is an offshoot of the Gonds'.[7] P. N. Bose, then Deputy Superintendent of the Geological Survey of India, wrote in 1887 an account of the iron industry of the Raipur District. His remarks on the Raipur iron-smelters are doubly interesting on account of the fact that the name Agaria is now scarcely heard in the District. 'The furnaces', he says, 'are worked by a class of Gonds who style themselves Agarias or Pardhans. They almost invariably speak the Gondi language, which their

[1] Risley, op. cit., Vol. I, p. 512.

[2] E. Thurston, *Tribes and Castes of Southern India*, Vol. VI, p. 308.

[3] S. C. Roy, *The Asurs; Ancient and Modern*, p. 2.

[4] R. V. Russell and R. B. Hiralal, op. cit., Vol. II, p. 3.

[5] *Census of India*, 1891, Vol. XI, p. 182.

[6] ibid., p. 205.

[7] *Census of India*, 1921, Vol. XI, Pt. I, p. 155.

brethren of the plains have quite forgotten, and would not scruple to eat cow, buffalo, etc., which the latter who aspire to the title of Hindus would never touch. Iron-smelting must be a very old industry with the Gonds. Their traditions ascribe their first settlement in Kachikopa Lahugarh, or the Iron Valley in the Red Hills, and the only metal for which they appear to have a name in their language is iron.'[1]

If this is correct, we can see the entire social process at work in Raipur. A group of Gond takes to iron-smelting. Despised by their brethren they become a separate group under the name of Agaria. Later they see in Hinduism a chance to recover something of their social position and they begin to call themselves Lohar, forgetting either that they were Gond or Agaria.

It may be added that the Agaria have the same customs and beliefs as the Gond, often the same septs. But this would be equally true of the Korwa among whom many of the Bilaspur Agaria have their homes, while in Chota Nagpur the Agaria Asur share custom, religion and totems with other Munda tribes.

The older writers generally refer to the iron-smelters of Ranchi and Palamau as Agaria,[2] though today these are more often called Asur. Ball's authority may be given as supporting S. C. Roy. In Palamau, he says, 'the Agarias, it is considered by the best authorities, belong to the Munda family of aboriginals; but another tribe, the Kol Lohar, are, it is supposed, Uraons'.[3] And elsewhere he says that in the Ramgurh Hills—he was speaking of a date before 1880—there

[1] *R.G.S.I.*, Vol. XX, Pt. IV, p. 170. According to Hislop (*Papers relating to the Aboriginal Tribes of the C.P.* (1866), Part II, p. 20) the words for iron in India are—

Kachchi in Gondi and Gayeti, *Kachi* in Rutluk and Maria, *Yinamu* in Naikunde Gondi, *Loha* in Kuri and Muasi, *Iemu* in Keikadi, *Inumu* in Telugu, *Irumbu* in Tamil and Malay. In Sanskrit, iron is *ayas* and *lauha*.

[2] L. S. S. O'Malley, *Palamau District Gazetteer*. Revised edition by P. C. Tallents, pp. 137f.

[3] V. Ball, *Jungle Life in India*, p. 479.

were Kol, using small furnaces, whom he thought identical with the 'Aguriahs' of Hazaribagh and Palamau.[1]

The Mirzapur Agaria are, according to the *Gazetteer*,[2] of non-Aryan origin and connected with other Dravidians such as the subdivision of the Korwa described by Dalton[3] and Risley,[4] the Parahiya and the Mandla Agaria.

On the whole, however, I am inclined to think that the Agaria are something more than a branch, or a collection of branches, of another tribe or tribes. There is a distinct physical and cultural resemblance between all sections of the Agaria: they have the same professional technique, they have the same mythology, they worship the same gods, they have the same magic. Unless they are all ultimately one tribe I cannot understand how the cult of Lohasur should be so widespread and so vigorous among them. Otherwise I would have thought that this cult and the memory of such tribal heroes as Logundi would have disappeared before the all-prevailing influence of Hinduism and the more powerful cult-heroes like Twashtri or Vishwakarma.

This belief is strengthened if, as I hope to show in the next chapter, the Agaria and Asur are descendants of a tribe which is represented by the Asura of Sanskrit legend.

I suggest it is possible that this ancient Asur tribe invaded the Munda country in Bihar. They were driven back by the Munda, under the rallying standard of their deity Sing-bonga,[5] to the very borders of Bihar, and thence spread west and north, through Surguja and Udaipur, Korea and the north of Bilaspur, a weaker branch filtering down to Raipur, until in the Maikal

[1] Ball, op. cit., p. 225.

[2] D. L. Drake-Brockman, *Mirzapur. A Gazetteer*, p. 3.

[3] E. T. Dalton, *Descriptive Ethnology of Bengal*, p. 221.

[4] Risley, op. cit., Vol. I, p. 4.

[5] cf. W. H. Driver, *Notes on Some Kolarian Tribes*, *J.A.S.B.*, 1889, Vol. LVII, Pt. I, p. 7. Mr B. C. Mazumdar suggests that the names of two villages, Mundagarh and Asurgarh 'lying in proximity to each other in the zemindary of Kashipur in the State of Kalahandi' witness to the ancient struggle between the two tribes (*The Aborigines of the Highlands of Central India*, Calcutta, 1927, p. 22). See also E. F. O. Murray, *The Ancient Workers of Western Dhalbhum*, J.R.A.S. Beng. Letters, Vol. VI, No. 2, p. 80.

Hills they found a congenial home and a plentiful supply of iron. The migration to Mirzapur through Rewa seems to have occurred in recent times, at least since the British occupation.

These movements were controlled by two chief factors—a supply of ore and a forest of *sarai* trees, from which charcoal suitable for use in the furnaces can best be made.

III. *Character of the Agaria*

The Agaria are a pleasant and mediocre race. Their chief faults are those of timidity and dullness. Writing in 1867, Colonel Ward described them as 'the laziest and most drunken of all the Gonds'. He says again how the forges are generally set up near the mines 'as the people are much too lazy to carry the ore any distance'[1]—an unusually stupid remark, for every industry in the world tries to get its factory as near as possible to the source of supply.

As a matter of fact, the Agaria are a very hard-working people. The conditions of their life are strenuous and exacting; I myself have seldom spent more exhausting days than in their company. The long tramp through the forest, the cutting of the trees and the tedious and smoky business of making charcoal, the journey home with laden baskets—this alone is no light labour. The pits where iron may be dug are often in the most inaccessible places and require long climbs in the hills, followed by digging with small picks in a confined space. The work of the smithy is heavy enough: often I have watched the household rise at three or four in the morning and work on till ten or eleven without food or refreshment. When the long labour of the smithy is over, there is sometimes work in the fields, or on the tobacco-patch, or they have to carry their wares to a distant bazaar. The Chokh have a rule that the day following a big bazaar should be observed as a holiday.

[1] H. C. E. Ward, *Report on the Land Revenue Settlement of the Mundlah District*, p. 131.

Nor are the Agaria, at least at present, specially drunken. I think they drink much less than the Baiga. In Bilaspur, the excise policy was at one time driving them to drugs such as *gānja* and *bhang*, the inevitable result of forcing the political fad of prohibition on primitive people.

The Agaria are not nearly so jolly and amusing as the Baiga. They are not good company, and there are very few whose personalities stand out memorably. They are thin, timid, anxious little men, depressed and hungry. Some of the younger men, however, are not unlike young Baiga, good-looking, friendly and affectionate. Deo Singh of Umaria, Buddhu of Bahapur, Kuar Singh of Gaura, Anath of Dumarkachhar are interesting and attractive youths—but as compared with the Baiga, how few come to the mind! Anath is particularly affectionate: 'I will go anywhere with you', he used to say. 'I don't like being away from you for a moment.' Murwa and Nanas of Karanjia were two very attractive boys; we employed Murwa for some years as a teacher and he did well at it—the children liked him. Nanas might have grown up into a leader of his tribe; he was a good craftsman and sensitive and intelligent. But he developed tuberculosis and died while still young. His elder brother Sujawal is a famous singer and dancer, very popular, a great social success.

The Agaria, in view of their occupation, are fairly clean, and they keep their houses and smithies in good order. They are generally believed to be honest, and except for a group of railway thieves near Pendra Road, do not often come into the courts.

But work among them was difficult and sometimes depressing. They were not deliberately uninformative, but most of them had very little to say. Yet they are good craftsmen and could easily be trained, and it would be a thousand pities if they were to die out.

Owing to their craft the Agaria have more to do with the outside world than some other aboriginals. 'If you think iron is nothing,' so runs one of their proverbs, 'look out of your house and see it wandering all over the three worlds.'

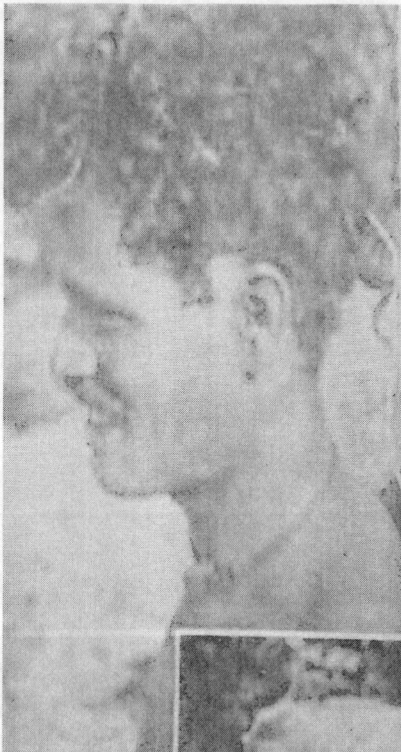

4. (a) Mahali Asur of Singhia, Bilaspur District.

Khuntia Chokh of Dumarkachhar, Bilaspur District.

5. (*a*) Hindu Lohar of Sarangarh.

(*b*) Hindu Lohar of Baldidih, Raipur District, wearing leaf hat.

There is iron everywhere, and it is all 'their' iron. It all comes from Lohripur. It is born there and the world goes to steal it. When the rat sent by the Hindu Bhimsen burrowed under the city, the iron flowed out and away across the world.[1]

The Agaria are specially fascinated by trains and no wonder, for here are iron and fire and coal combined in a gigantic moving furnace. An Agaria who had actually travelled in a train—I only know one who has—composed the following Karma song which was sung in the wilds of the Motinala forest.

> *Hai Re!* The train whistles, it is leaving Bilaspur.
> In front is the train, behind is the signal.
> The villagers leave their work and run to see it.
> At every station the engine takes coal and water.
> In front runs the wire to give the news.
> Behind, we sit clutching our tickets in our hands.
> In front goes the motor,
> Behind goes the cycle.
> Leaving their food, the children run to see.

In the Pendra Zamindari a number of Agaria live very near the railway line (the B.N.R. line that connects Katni with Bilaspur). In 1937, villagers from Karangra, Bijawar and Korja raided the line, and removed a number of fish-plates, trolley-refuge indicators, iron sleepers and rail-keys. They hid the spoil in the jungle and gradually turned them into spears, arrow-heads and axes. When they were caught, six Agaria were sentenced to six months' imprisonment apiece. But the punishment did not have any great effect, for in 1940, men from Bijawar, Tikakalla, Korja and Sarbera—two of them were ex-convicts from 1937—carried off a number of fish-plates from the storeyard at Pendra Road and buried them in the fields.

The Agaria have no politics. 'We were born and ripened under the English Raj', said an Agaria in Motinala, 'and all our money goes to stuff that scarecrow.' But in the same

[1] See pp. 96f.

breath he was calling the British Government 'Bhagavan'. 'The British are Bhagavan, for they create the *jiv*.' The *jiv*, which is often used for the soul, can also mean anything that works, or goes by itself, like a gramophone, or a train. 'Some *jiv* have blood, some not, but they are all the same.'

Four months after the war had started, I found many Agaria in the Motinala Range who had not heard of it. But shortly afterwards in Lapha Zamindari I was mistaken for a recruiting officer, and I started a panic in a bazaar in Udaipur State among the people who thought I had come to carry them away for the war. I have met many Asur, Chokh and Patharia who had never heard of Mahatma Gandhi or the Congress. In the Karanjia Range there was an old Agaria who believed Gandhi to be a god, and every year offered him coconut, supari and incense. But in parts of Bilaspur near the road, I found some bitterness against the Congress on account of the high price of liquor. Here it was seven-and-a-half annas a bottle, compared with two annas in Mandla. 'What is the use of stopping our liquor,' said an Agaria bitterly. 'This has become *gānja-ilāka*, the Province of Ganja, and that is worse for us.' This is very true, for the effect of *gānja* on a man is far more devastating, and many of the Chokh Agaria have taken to the habit with disastrous results.

I do not know of any C.P. Agaria who have become Christians, but in Bihar some of the Bir Asur have been converted to Catholicism. There is little outward change; they continue to practise their craft in the old way, go almost naked save for a crucifix round their necks, and maintain most of the old tribal dances and even the tribal dormitories.

Some insight into the character of the Agaria is gained from a study of their proverbs, though they are not rich in these. They are undoubtedly proud of their craft and the physical strength that enables them to perform it. 'If the Agaria swings his hammer, how will the iron not be shaped?' 'Even iron can be destroyed by these—by hammer and tongs, chisel and punch.' 'O neighbour, what are you staring at? Come and lift up my hammer yourself.'

The Agaria like to feel that, even if their social standing is low, everyone has to come to them. 'Everyone comes to say, *Rām rām.* He answers *Johār.*' The Agaria are the mainstay of the village economy and they know it. 'The black iron is born in the Agaria's house, and the world enjoys the sweets of it.'

The Agaria sometimes compare themselves to the Sonar goldsmiths, so much more well-to-do, yet in the Agaria's view, no happier. 'The poor Sonar must tap tap tap a hundred times: the Agaria does it with a single blow.' 'He who has gold in his house—death is near him. He who has iron in his house can live secure.' 'Gold is the brother of the Sonar; iron is the brother of the Agaria,' but in the long run iron brings safety and happiness.

For the Agaria is absorbed in his business. 'The Agaria cares not for going here and there; all his intoxication is for his hammer.' He is lord in his little smithy. 'The tongs are yours, the hammer is yours. Hammer away just as you like!' Love affairs may be ruinous to his trade. 'If the heart is abroad, who will care for the smithy?'

One or two proverbs reveal the Agaria in unexpectedly reflective moods. Just as God seems to care little for the fate of his creatures, so 'what cares the bellows-blower for the fate of the cinders?' God too makes no distinctions between man and man. 'O Brother Agaria, O bellows-blower, you make no distinctions', for you put into the same fire the finest sword and the roughest axe-head or sickle. [1]

[1] Risley gives some proverbs about Indian blacksmiths in an Appendix to his *People of India* (London, 1915), App., p. xii, but I have only heard the first among the Agaria.

'One stroke of a blacksmith is worth a goldsmith's hundred.'

'The Lohar is a bad friend: he will either burn you with fire or stifle you with smoke.'

'Sparks are the lot of a blacksmith's legs.'

'If you live with a blacksmith, your clothes will be burned.'

'A blacksmith's shop—like the place where the donkeys roll.'

'To keep house like a Kammalan (blacksmith)' —said of a slovenly man.

'The Kammalan's cloth—so thin that the hair on his legs shows through and so dirty that it will not burn.'

About death there are a few thoughtful lines, not proverbs, but in a Karma song from Mawai in Mandla District:

O they will carry you away, and your soul will weep.
The hammer says, 'Listen, O Agaria, do not make me!
Tomorrow or the day after you will die,
And then who will use me to strike the iron?'
O they will carry you away, and your soul will weep.
The pick says, 'Listen, O Agaria, do not make me!
Tomorrow or the day after you will die,
And I shall be used to dig your grave.'
O they will carry you away, and your soul will weep.

CHAPTER II

THE ASURA

The age-long and bitter war between the Gods and the Asura is represented by the *Mahabharata* as beginning at the Churning of the Ocean. In a strange and wonderful passage, the great poem describes how Gods and Asura stand on either side to pull the serpentine churning-cord to and fro until from the ocean appear many objects of delight which the greedy Gods desire to appropriate for themselves. A struggle follows for possession of the moon and the nectar of immortality. Vishnu, in the shape of Maya, bewitches the Asura and in despair they see all the treasure passing from them. Rahu the Asura takes a draught of the elixir of life, yet before he can swallow it Narayan the Sun strikes off his head. It rises to the sky with loud and dreadful cries and his body crashing to earth makes hills and forests tremble. But Rahu's head is now immortal and ever fights against sun and moon, and the Asura, embittered by the trick which robbed them of so many precious things, begin their endless and ever-futile war against the Gods.

In the *Rigveda*, the word 'Asura' is generally a term of honour: [1] Varuna and Indra are so called: [2] Agni is an Asura; [3] and the greatest of all the Asura is Rudra or Shiva,[4] the only malevolent Aryan deity. But already in the *Rigveda*, especially in the later books, there are hints of the coming enmity. The Asura gradually separate from the Aryans; they are called demons, 'hostile in speech',[5] and enemies.[6] By the close of the Rigvedic period, the Arya hosts have defeated the Asura and reduced them to the level of demons.

1 *Rigveda*, I, 35, 7.
2 ibid., I, 24, 14.
3 ibid., IV, 2, 5, and VII, 2, 3.
4 ibid., V, 12, 11.
5 ibid., VII, 18, 13 and VII, 6, 3.
6 ibid., X, 23, 5.

There are other 'hostile beings' in the *Rigveda* often classed with the Asura. These are the Daitya, Danava and Dasa. They are 'noseless',[1] 'black',[2] 'without rites',[3] 'indifferent to the gods',[4] 'without devotion'[5] and 'lawless'.[6] They are worshippers of the phallus.

Although many passages seem to refer to superhuman foes, others may well apply to human enemies, and it has often been suggested that these black and hostile beings are the aboriginal tribes who opposed and for a time checked the Aryan advance. Keith thinks that the Asura are the enemies of the gods, and the Dasa and Rakshasa are the enemies of men. But probably too rigid a distinction should not be drawn between the Asura and their allies.

At this period certain famous Asura are already emerging—Pipru (whose name may mean ''The Resister') and Varcin ('The Shining')—the first has fifty thousand black warriors, the second a hundred thousand. Another leader is Namuci, 'He who will not let go'.[7] They are defeated by Indra, an event which may reflect an actual defeat of the aboriginals under their patron gods.

From now onwards the word 'Asura' definitely means an enemy of the gods. Keith notes the change from the *Rigveda* where the word normally applies to the gods themselves and the conflict is only between individual Asura and Gods, to the *Brahmana* where the struggle is between hosts of Asura and the Gods, and the Asura are established as enemies.[8] This degradation, he suggests, is due possibly to the influence of Iranic dualism, more likely to 'the apparent form of the word as a negative to *sura*, from the base *svar*, denoting light, for by the time of the *Upanishads* we meet the word "*sura*" denoting "a god" derived by this popular etymology from *asura*, which is really connected with *asu*, "breath"'.

[1] *Rigveda*, V, 29, 10. [2] ibid., I, 104, 2. [3] ibid., X, 22, 8.
[4] ibid., VIII, 70, 11. [5] ibid., IV, 16, 9.
[6] ibid., VI, 14, 3 and IX, 41, 2.
[7] A. Berriedale Keith, *Indian Mythology*, pp. 67ff. [8] ibid., p. 84.

By now we find the Asura described as being created by Prajapati, who, finding that darkness came from them, pierced them with the darkness and overcame them. Vratra is the chief Asura and the tale of Namuci is elaborated. Large numbers of new names are given to the demons in the *Grihya Sutra* and again later in the *Mahabharata*, but there is no connexion between these and the names in the Agaria mythology. Svarbhanu, the Asura, eclipses the Sun and is resisted by Atri.

The Asura are now described in the severest terms—they are insolent, sacrificing to themselves, lying, deceitful. There are many accounts of battles between the Gods and the Asura; in one of these Indra and Vishnu defeat the Asura who then held the world, and demanded as much as Vishnu could step over in three strides. These covered the three worlds, the Vedas and speech.[1]

In Epic and Puranic times this titanic struggle still held the imagination of poets and philosophers. In the Epics, the host of the Asura flings itself time and again at the great power of the Gods in never-ending conflict. The Gods always are victorious, but there is no limit to the number of the demons. There are many kinds of Asura—Daitya, Danava, Rakshasa. The Picaca, often identified with the Rakshasa, are spoken of together with the Magadha and Kalinga 'which seems to prove them to be the original people of the country (the aboriginals)'.[2] Fausböll thinks that the Naga also are aborigines. They are very powerful; they use mountains and trees as weapons; they are skilled in sorcery.[3] Mahisha fights with a mountain as missile; Keshin uses a mountain-peak; Ravana uses magic. They have their homes in caves of mountains, in the depths of Patala or at the bottom of the sea. They build three great forts, of gold, iron and silver, and thence attack the three worlds. But they fail, as always,

[1] *Aitareya Brahmana*, VI, 15.

[2] V. Fausböll, *Indian Mythology according to the Mahabharata*.

[3] *Mahabharata*, III, 12131.

and are cast out of heaven. Arjuna's war with the Asura [1] is told in detail and his destruction of their cities described.

The appearance and customs of the demons are terrible. The *Mahabharata* describes them as cannibals,[2] living on flesh and blood,[3] of great strength and courage, dark as a thunder-cloud, with red eyes, frightful appearance, great teeth, red hair and beard, spear-shaped ears, neck and shoulders as thick as tree-trunks. They wander by night, transform themselves into alluring shapes to draw men to destruction, they stop penance and offerings.[4] Nothing is too bad for them.

Such, briefly, are some of the terms in which this great rivalry and battle are described. It is hard to resist the conclusion that it must reflect some long and bitter struggle in ancient India. Among those who accept—perhaps more fully than he should—the historical interpretation of these passages is Mr Banerji-Sastri who has studied the conflict in great detail.[5] 'The Vedic struggle', he concludes, 'drove the Asura from the Indus Valley; the epic conflict routed them in the Madhyadesa and the subsequent readjustment lost them the Gangetic Valley and pushed them southwards. The Nagas were the spearhead and backbone of the Asura people in India. Daityas, Danavas, Rakshasas, Kalakanyas, Kaleyyas, Nivata-kavachas, Paulomas, etc., are offshoots and families. With the downfall of the Nagas ended organized Asura supremacy in India. And the remnants of Nagas who once ruled Gosringa in Khotan, had to seek shelter in places still bearing their name, *e.g.* Nagpur, Chota Nagpur, and are today completely absorbed in the Dasa aborigines haunting woods, mountain fastnesses, and desolate regions, of the jungles of Assam, of Chota Nagpur and the Vindhya range.' [6]

As I have already suggested, the conventional view of the Asura and allied demons is that they were the ancestors of the

[1] *Mahabharata*, III, 11903ff.
[2] ibid., I, 6102.
[3] ibid., II, 715.
[4] *Passim.*
[5] A. Banerji-Sastri, 'The Asuras in Indo-Iranian Literature', *J.B.O.R.S.*, Vol. XII, pp. 110ff.
[6] 'Asura Expansion by Sea', *J.B.O.R.S.*, Vol. XII, p. 356.

Indian aboriginals. The first, I think, to challenge this was Mr Sarat Chandra Roy [1] who has suggested that we have here a reflection of the worldwide contest between the denizens of the Stone Age and the new metal-working people who invaded and disturbed it. He has drawn attention to the fact that there is a 'widespread tradition among the Mundas and several other aboriginal tribes of Chota Nagpur of the previous occupation of the country by a metal-using people called the Asuras who are said to have been routed by the Mundas with the help of their deity Sing-bonga. The iron-smelting activities of the Asura, tradition says, greatly disturbed the even tenor of existence of the Munda and other deities who were as yet innocent of the use and manufacture of metals.' One such legend, given us by the Asur of the Neterhat Plateau, will be found recorded on page 101 of this book.

Mr Roy also refers to the existence of numerous ancient ruins of brick buildings in which are found various objects, particularly of terra-cotta, while near by are traces of working in copper or iron. These buildings are attributed to the ancient Asur as are also many graveyards of great antiquity, in which both Neolithic and copper implements have been found. With these facts Mr Roy relates the existence of the iron-smelting Asur and Agaria of modern times.

Mr Roy is not altogether happy about this theory; indeed he points out that, although according to Munda tradition the Asur introduced the use of iron into Chota Nagpur, 'very few iron objects have been found in the Asur graves—except a few iron rings, arrow-heads and bangles. In the building-sites, a number of iron spear-heads and arrow-heads, besides some knives, *kukris* and sickles have been found.' [2] Elsewhere he says that far from there being any special emphasis on iron in the Asur remains, three ages appear to meet in the Asur of Munda tradition—the Stone Age, the Copper Age and the Early Iron Age. [3] Dr Reuben recognizes a similar difficulty in connecting the Asura of the Sanskrit literature with iron.

[1] S. C. Roy, 'The Asurs: Ancient and Modern', *J.B.O.R.S.*, Vol. XII, pp. 147ff. [2] *J.B.O.R.S.*, Vol. VI, p. 404. [3] *J.B.O.R.S.*, Vol. I, p. 253.

On the other hand, the Agaria traditions add no little support to the suggestion that the Agaria-Asur of today is descended from and in the same line of business as the Asura of old legend. In the first place there is the similarity of name. This persists not only in the name given to the tribe in Chota Nagpur and to a sub-tribe of the Agaria in Surguja and Bilaspur, but also in the names of the Agaria demons—Lohasur (*i.e.* Loha Asur), the demon of the iron-kiln; Koelasur, the demon of charcoal; Agyasur, the demon of fire.

Again, the Asura of Sanskrit mythology hold the very place which tradition assigns to the blacksmith all over the world. The Deva, like the fairies and spirits of Europe, belong to the Age of Stone. The Asura, like the blacksmith, is the new, disturbing, hostile bringer of the Age of Iron. This is the real reason for the implacable enmity between the Gods and the Asura.

This conflict finds many echoes in the Agaria legends: just as Vishnu cheats the Asura out of their share in the rich products of the churning of the ocean, so Bhagavan tricks the first Agaria Raja, Logundi, and destroys his city. As Arjuna and the Pandava fight against the Asura and capture their forts, so do the Pandava, led by Bhimsen, attack and destroy Lohripur, the Agaria citadel. As the Àsura Rahu for ever seeks to devour the Sun, so does the Agaria Jwala Mukhi, and in Mandla at least there is a strong tradition of enmity between the Sun and the tribe and a strict taboo on working iron in the Sun's rays.

Geography can give us little help, but it is just worthy of mention that, according to Reuben, near Jubbulpore there were three metal castles of the Asura;[1] and the upper part of the Narbada, the home of the most characteristic Agaria, is the main region of the mythical Asura.[2] An iron fortress of the Asura is mentioned in the *Rigveda*.[3]

It is true that the connexion of the Asura with iron is not very close, but there is some connexion. Roy tells how the

[1] Reuben, op. cit., p. 300. [2] ibid., p. 302. [3] ibid., p. 301.

Munda describe the old Asur giants as 'a *pūndi* or white people of enormous stature, strength and agility, who could in the course of one night walk a hundred miles with giant strides to attend dances at distant villages and walk back to their own homes before dawn. They are said to have lived in huge brick palaces, to have been engaged most of their time in smelting copper and iron, and the tradition goes that they even ate iron and blew fire from their mouths.'[1] The power to eat iron was characteristic of the first Agaria, and many such fiery meals and excrements are described in the mythology. On the other hand Reuben says that fire-eating is not ascribed to the Asura of Sanskrit literature.

In the later period, however, in the Epics and Purana, we hear of iron demons. Thus in the *Mahabharata* we read of four demons made of iron who punish a bad king at the behest of a saint.[2] They are demons with iron faces and one has an iron head (Ayahsiras). Another demon with an iron arrow is Ayahsanku.[3] One of the demons killed by Krishna is Lohajandha.

In the *Vishnu Purana*, we read how the saint Gargya eats iron as an asceticism offered to Siva in order to get a son who could not be overcome by the inhabitants of Mathura who had laughed at his childlessness. The son was the dark-faced Kalayavana, the most dangerous of all Krishna's enemies.[4]

In the *Linga Purana*,[5] which gives an account of different lingams, some are golden, some copper—for the Aditya, but the Daitya and Rakshasa produce and worship an iron one. The Asura are not specifically mentioned here, but they are described as lingam-worshippers,[6] a characteristic also of the early Asur. In this Purana, the Asura are also called 'dark as the blue petals of a lotus'.[7]

Many Purana contain the story of the milking of the earth and tell how the gods use a golden bucket, ancestors a

[1] *J.B.O.R.S.*, Vol. XVIII, p. 372.
[2] *Mahabharata*, III, 192.
[3] ibid., I, 59, 23; 61, 10.
[4] *Vishnu Purana*, V, 23, 3.
[5] *Linga Purana*, I, 74, 1.
[6] ibid., LXXXI, 24-37.
[7] Roy, *J.B.O.R.S.*, Vol. I, p. 248.

silver, the mountains a crystal, the Yaksha a pot of unburnt clay, the Gandharva lotus leaves, the Naga pumpkins, and the Asura an iron bucket.[1]

No one has studied this problem more elaborately than Dr Reuben, and we cannot end this chapter more fittingly than by quoting the conclusion to his *Eisenschmiede und Dämonen in Indien*.[2]

> I conclude that *one* source of demon-mythology in India comes from the old iron-smelters. As blacksmiths they appeared sinister and suspicious to their neighbours, being regarded as sorcerers and masters of a secret art . . . Thus one can understand the admiration for Maya and the condemnation of the Asura. Apart from that, the buffalo, vulture and snake totemists of the Central Indian hills existed as one source of the Asuras, and the conception of evil spirits which confront the good ones in a dualistic way exists throughout Eurasia in a primitive and high form.
>
> The main difficulty is: has the tribal name Asur anything to do with the Rigvedic deity-term Asura? It is, in my opinion, insufficient to say that the Arya called the Asur demons because of their occupation as blacksmiths and that the Asur adopted the name without knowing its meaning. That would solve the problem in a simple manner, but world-history is not simple—and what people would accept such a demon name? Do any parallels exist?
>
> It is too simple, too, to say: Asur and Asura have nothing to do with each other and are words of different languages, as Assur in Babylonia is a similar-sounding but not related name. To these ideas one could add the fact that old buildings of the Asur, because of the similarity of names, were taken as Asura by the Arya, or not first by the Arya, but by the Munda people of the old Gangetic civilization. One has to note, however, how the Munda people of today identify the Asur with demons in their Asur myths. Further they say that they found the Asur in the country before they themselves came; but that is difficult to combine with the idea that they had learnt the term Asura as 'demon' from the Arya and used it for the Asur who received the name Asur only by this way.

[1] *Vishnu Purana*, I, 188.

[2] Reuben, op. cit., pp. 302ff. Translated for me by Mr R. V. Leyden. I have simplified the spelling of Sanskrit names.

The temptation is great to combine with this problem that of the change of meaning in the old word Asura from 'God' to 'Demon' which for many decades has been one of the chief problems of the more ancient history of Indian religion. Could not one difficulty ease the other? It is said today that this change of meaning only occurred relatively late in India, during the youngest period of Rigvedic poetry. Only then did the group of Deva worshippers become victorious over the Asura worshippers—these had previously co-existed in peace. The Deva-god-term is certainly Indo-Aryan because of its etymology; it is joined by the 'Asura' term in common Aryan times, perhaps in connexion with Varuna who is the real Asura in the *Rigveda.* Some interpreters of the *Rigveda*, however, have felt Varuna to be something foreign with 'southern' influence, meaning that he springs (at least partially) from the Near-Eastern city civilization of the Bronze-Stone Age. If, however, the etymology 'Asura-erus' (Lat. master) proves to be correct this would appear as already one component of the Indo-Aryan, which would agree with Koppers' view. This would save the popular etymology 'Varuna-Ouranos' . . .

One could, therefore, argue: the god-term Asura changed to Demon, *i.e.* enemy of the gods, because of the conflict between the Arya and the Asur; or one could put the old Gangetic civilization yet between both; it met the Asur, developed the Vishnu-idea of the fight between gods and demons (which, however, has already inner Asiatic sources) in the combat between its herdsmen and the Asur. The Aryan civilization, arriving in the Gangetic plains, took over this idea from them.

One could object: how does such a minute tribe attain to such significance? Anyone who has travelled in India and seen Lake Pushkara, Mount Mandara, the temple of Vindhyavasini, is astonished to see how small these most sacred places of Indian mythology are.

More difficult is the question to which cultural type the ancient Asuras are to be related. The mythological Asuras are often Shivaite. Asura Varuna has 'southern' characteristics. But today the 'male' note is more outspoken in the Asur (even as Varuna is said to be a component of the central Asiatic Heaven God). One should expect that somehow they already had this note, otherwise they could not have fitted in without a break into the hunter totemism

> of Chota Nagpur. Are they Shivaite only because they were fought by Vishnu?
>
> I cannot go beyond these quite uncertain answers to these hypothetical questions. The questions, however, and the material collected deserve further investigation.

I would certainly not venture to give a more certain answer than Dr Reuben's in solution of a problem about which we have the most scanty evidence. But there are at least hints and indications that the modern Asur and their neighbours and kinsfolk the Agaria are linked with whatever metal-working tribes were represented of old by the Asura and by their later descendants, the earliest Asur.

CHAPTER III

GAZETTEER

The Central Provinces are rich in minerals, the most important geological formations being the Dharwars with their rich deposits of manganese ore, iron-ore, steatite, red ochre and dolomite; the Gondwanas with coal and clay; the laterite with its bauxite and building stone; and the alluvium with its store of brick-clays. The various mineral industries established in the Province recorded the following figures for the year 1938 [1]:—

	Tons
Coal	1,658,626
Manganese ore	646,465
Limestone and Kankar	551,978
Clay	60,252
Bauxite	4,634
Ochre	2,924
Steatite	2,189
Iron-ore	611

But although the production of iron-ore ranks lowest among the industries,[2] the region has great reserves of iron: in Bastar State alone the reserves of ore are estimated as from 114 to 610 million tons.[3]

The iron-ores are found in four geological formations, viz. laterite, the Chikiala and Barakar divisions of the Gondwana, the Bijawar, and the Dharwar, of which the last is the most important to the modern smelter.

[1] *R.G.S.I.*, Vol. LXXIV, Part III.

[2] In the whole Province, during the period 1909–13, an average of 428 primitive furnaces produced an average annual total of 557 tons. Today, production is probably less than a third of this.

[3] For a discussion of the iron resources of Bastar State and the possibility of exploiting them commercially, see H. Crookshank, 'The Iron-Ores of the Bailadila Range, Bastar State' in *Transactions of the Mining, Geological and Metallurgical Institute of India*, Vol. XXXIV, Pt. 3, pp. 254f.

> Lateritic ores are most abundant near Katni in the Jubbulpore District, but are also found in Drug, Saugor, Yeotmal and other districts. In the Jubbulpore District the lateritic ores are well seen at Bijori and in the Kanhwara hills; in the latter locality three bands of ore, ranging from two to two and a half feet thick, are estimated to contain forty-nine million tons of ore. Further south in this district the upturned edges of the Dharwar hematites are capped by lateritoid limonitic ores formed by replacement.
>
> Brown and red hematite occur abundantly in the sandstones of the Chikiala stage in the valley of the Pranhita, and are smelted in native furnaces at Yemlapali in Hyderabad territory and at neighbouring localities in the Chanda District. The ores of Barakar age occur as ironstone zones at two horizons in the Raigarh-Hingir coalfield in Raigarh State, being most abundant near Kodoloi.
>
> Iron-ores are also found in the Bijawar rocks in Nimar, Hoshangabad and Narsinghpur. In the two former districts the ores are almost invariably hematite, obtained from breccias occurring in the Bijawar series near the junction with the Vindhyans, or from debris derived from the same rocks. There is no evidence that these ores exist in sufficient quantity to interest a modern smelter, although they have been largely used in the past by the native smelter. [1]

At first sight, it might be expected that the distribution of the Agaria would follow that of the iron-ore, but this is not so. In Chanda, for example, where there are 'enormous and splendid accumulations of ore',[2] Agaria are not found: the smelting is done by Gond and Teli. The reason for this is probably the willingness of the Agaria to use ores that are comparatively valueless. To quote the *Geological Survey* again,

> Iron-smelting was at one time a widespread industry in India and there is hardly a district away from the great alluvial tracts of the Indus, Ganges and Brahmaputra, in which slag-heaps are not found. For the primitive iron-smelter finds no difficulty in obtaining sufficient supplies of ore from deposits that no European iron-master would regard as worth his serious consideration. Sometimes he

[1] Sir L. L. Fermor, 'Mineral Resources of the Central Provinces', *R.G.S.I.*, Vol. L, p. 283.

[2] Sir G. Watts, *Dictionary of the Economic Products of India*, Vol. IV, p. 507.

will break up small friable bits of quartz-iron-ore schist, concentrating the ore by winnowing the crushed materials in the wind or by washing in a stream. Sometimes he is content with ferruginous laterites, or even with the small granules formed by the concentration of the rusty cement in ancient sandstones. In ancient times the people of India seem to have acquired a fame for metallurgical skill, and the reputation of the famous *wootz* steel, which was certainly made in India long before the Christian era, has probably contributed to the general impression that the country is rich in iron-ore of a high-class type. It is true that throughout the Peninsula, which is so largely occupied by ancient crystalline rocks, quartz-hematite and quartz-magnetite schists are very common in the Dharwarian system, the system of rocks that lithologically, as well as in stratigraphical relationship, corresponds approximately to the Lower Huronian of America. But most of these occurrences consist of quartz and iron-ore so intimately blended that only a highly siliceous ore of a low grade can be obtained without artificial concentration.[1]

The value of the mineral deposits is thus no guide to the distribution of the aboriginals who exploit them. We must, therefore, now proceed to a somewhat tedious exploration of the area District by District and State by State, in order to discover the past and present distribution of the Agaria. For convenience of reference we will make our survey in alphabetical rather than administrative or geographical order.

We begin then with *Balaghat District*, where the lovely Maikal Hills find their end and the consummation of their beauty. Iron-ore is found in the zamindaris of Bhanpur, Kinhi and Bahela:[2] that used by the Agaria was mostly lateritic, though possibly ferruginous Chilpi shales were also used as a source of iron: specimens of hematite have been obtained from this formation at Ragholi in Saletekri. There were once large numbers of Agaria in this District. 'Iron-smelting was widely practised all over the Dhansua and Bhanpur forests, till the practice was prohibited in those belonging to Government. There are now only one or two

[1] *R.G.S.I.*, Vol. XLVI, p. 99.

[2] *Balaghat District Gazetteer*, p. 232.

furnaces working in Bhanpur.'[1] There was iron-smelting also in the Kinhi Zamindari, 'but to an insignificant extent only'.[2] *The Agricultural Ledger* says (in 1898) that 'formerly there were about fifty families in this District engaged in smelting iron, but at present the industry has almost ceased to exist'.[3] At this date only five furnaces were working. There were four in 1912. Although the Deputy Commissioner had informed me that the industry was extinct, Mr Grigson saw a furnace and forge in action at Arwar in the Supkhar Range and heard of others in Baihar.

Bhandara District. In the earliest Settlement Report of this District, written in 1867, A. J. Lawrence reports that 'the best iron-ores are found near Chandpore, Lanjee and Pertabghur. That of Chandpore is generally considered to be the best. The ore is smelted with wood fuel in clay furnaces of a very primitive kind. It is exported to Nagpore in the shape of small, imperfectly smelted pigs of iron. At the Jubbulpore Exhibition of 1866 the Local Committee of the Bhundara District was awarded a special prize for the capital collection of iron-ore, smelted and wrought iron. This assortment was selected to be forwarded to the Agra Exhibition of 1867.'[4] Watts adds that the ore was lateritic and that excellent iron was obtained from the mines of Agri and Ambajhari. In the middle of the last century there were 162 furnaces.[5] In 1897, there were 14 furnaces operating in the Tirora Tahsil which gave employment to 56 men and 28 women, producing altogether 45,696 seers of iron during the year.[6] There is no evidence to show who the smelters were, but it is probable—on geographical grounds—that they were Agaria. The industry now appears to have become extinct.

[1] *Balaghat District Gazetteer*, p. 19. [2] ibid., p. 232.

[3] *The Agricultural Ledger*, 1898, Mineral and Metallic Series, No. 12, 'The Iron Industry in the C.P. A memorandum containing extracts from the reports furnished on the subject by Deputy Commissioners and Forest Officers.' Compiled by R. S. Hole, Assistant Conservator of Forests, C.P.

[4] A. J. Lawrence, *Report of the Land Revenue Settlement of the Bhundara District*, p. 6.

[5] Watts, op. cit., p. 508. [6] *The Agricultural Ledger*, p. 5.

Bilaspur District. We come now to Bilaspur and the beginning of the great plain of Chhattisgarh. As early as 1820, Major P. Vans Agnew was noting that 'iron was to be found in the zamindaris of Matin, Ooprodah, Koorbe and Chooree'. He describes the 'iron vessels' which were imported from Mandla (and presumably made by the Agaria there) into Chhattisgarh.[1] While limestone is perhaps the commonest rock at the surface all over the plains of Chhattisgarh, iron-ore is found in the hills to the north of Bilaspur and in the beautiful Pandaria Zamindari. Excellent magnetite has been found on the borders of the Kenda and Lapha Zamindaris.[2] In the Korba Zamindari ore is often picked up on the surface, as for example round Godma, Rajgamar, Thakurkheta, Kachandi, Kaldamar and other villages. There is a legend that the best ore of all used to be found on the Tapra Hill (near Katghora) and many Agaria used to go there for it. But one day a stream of blood issued from the iron-pit, the earth roared and quaked, and those who went there died. So they no longer venture near. 'For the Mother of all the iron in the world is there.' It is curious, however, that neither in Bilaspur nor in Mandla has there been a survey of the iron deposits on a scale comparable to that undertaken in other parts of the Province.

Yet Bilaspur and Mandla form the real home of the Agaria and it is hard to understand why Watts should say that though in Bilaspur there are 'ores in many places, they are not worked in any considerable scale'.[3] The population of Agaria in Bilaspur was over two thousand in 1891 and rose by six hundred in the next two decades. It dropped to 1921 at the next Census, but is said to be again increasing, probably as a result of immigration from the east. In the Mungeli Tahsil, there are

[1] P. Vans Agnew, *A Report on the Subah or Province of Chhattisgarh, written in 1820*, pp. 9 and 10.

[2] Sir A. E. Nelson, *Bilaspur District Gazetteer* (Allahabad, 1910), p. 192. For the geology of Bilaspur District, see Ball 'The Geology of the Mahanadi Basin' in *R.G.S.I.*, Vol. X, pp. 167ff. and King 'The Chhattisgarh Division' in *R.G.S.I.*, Vol. XVIII, pp. 169ff.

[3] Watts, op. cit., p. 507.

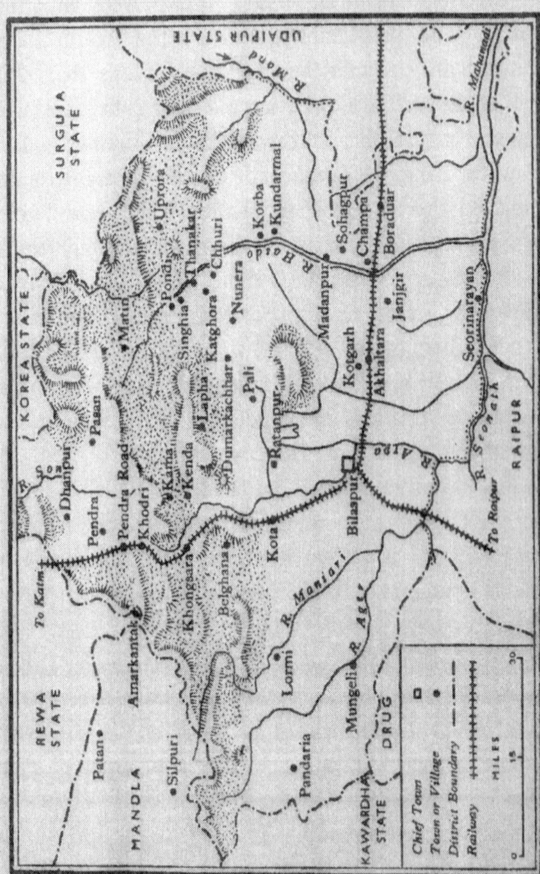

SKETCH MAP OF BILASPUR DISTRICT

indeed only a few households of Agaria (they were working 10 furnaces in 1939 and 8 in 1940): these are Kalha Agaria and are distinguished by the fact that they have adopted the dress and the customs of the lowlands. The main body of the tribe has its home in the zamindaris of the north. Here is to be found some of the wildest and most inaccessible country in the Province. In the Matin and Uprora Zamindaris, in Lapha, in Korba, in Chhuri, in Pendra and Kenda live two great sections of the tribe, the Khuntia Chokh and the Mahali Asur. Both say that they have come from Surguja in the east.

Chang Bhakar State. This small State which 'projects like a spur'[1] into Rewa from the east, where it is bounded by Korea, returned a population of nearly five hundred Agaria in 1911. If this is correct, they probably belong to the same group as the Mandla and Rewa Agaria. It is said that the ploughshare used in the State, which is exceptionally light, is made of iron obtained locally.[2]

Chanda District. In 1891 the Census recorded 27 Agaria for this district, but it seems as though in the main the iron-smelting industry has passed into other hands. The *Gazetteer* says that it is carried on by various castes—in Bramhapuri by Gond, Gowari, Dhimar, Teli and Khaire Kunbi; in Garhchiroli by Teli; and in Sironcha by Mannewar.[3] I do not know whether these smelters have formed themselves into a separate tribe or not. But whoever is available to work it, the District has a wonderful supply of ore. With the exception of the Chikiala ores in the valley of the Pranhita, the iron-ore deposits of Chanda are all situated in the Archaean tracts, where they form well-marked bands (possibly beds) usually associated

> with Dharwarian rocks.[4] The ore is usually hematite associated with banded hematite-quartzites, but magnetite is sometimes present. At least ten separate deposits have been located, and although they have not yet been exhaustively prospected, there is little doubt that some of them are of large size. The two best known are Lohara, where the iron-

[1] E. A. de Brett, *Chhattisgarh Feudatory States Gazetteer* (Bombay, 1909), p. 306.

[2] ibid., p. 312.

[3] *Chanda District Gazetteer*, p. 230.

[4] *R.G.S.I.*, Vol. L, p. 286.

ore forms a hill three-eighths of a mile long, 200 yards wide, and 120 feet high, and has been traced for a further distance of 2½ miles; and Pipalgaon, where a very fine mass of red hematite has been located.

In 1875 unsuccessful experiments were made at Warora in smelting iron-ore from Lohara and Ratnapur with Warora coal and a few years later a scheme was proposed for the establishment of modern iron works at Durgapur on the Erai river to smelt the ores of Lohara and Pipalgaon with charcoal fuel, the suggested scale of production being 25,000 tons of pig iron annually. Nothing, however, resulted from this proposal, and the Lohara deposit is now leased to the Tata Iron and Steel Co. Ltd, and held in reserve, except when small quantities of this very low-phosphorus ore are required for special purposes at Jamshedpur. The quality of the Chanda ores can be judged from the following analyses:

	Fe	SiO_2	S	P
Asola	65·99	3·89	..	..
Dewalgaon ..	61·2	11·04	..	..
do. ..	67·76	1·50	..	..
Lohara ..	69·21	0·82	0·012	0·005
Pipalgaon ..	71·05	4·5	trace.	trace.
Poser ..	69·8	..	..	..
Ratanpur (limonite)	49·7	26·0 (insol.)		..

There were 23 furnaces at work in 1897. By 1909 the number had sunk to 9, but it rose again to 20 in 1913, only to decrease again gradually until today not more than 4 are numbered.

Damoh District. This district, which has now been amalgamated with Saugor, returned a population of 148 Agaria in 1891 and 18 in 1911. I know nothing about the iron work here except for a note in *The Agricultural Ledger* (1898) which, in view of the Census figures, may be taken as probably referring to Agaria.

There are certain blacksmiths, two in number, in Mauza Koopi in the Hatta Tahsil, who purchase iron-ore at the rate of 24 maunds per rupee from Mauza Deora in the Chhattarpur State; they smelt it and extract refined iron and make therefrom utensils, such as pans, *tawas,* etc. Retail purchasers take these to the North West Provinces for purposes of trade and sell the pans at 3 or 4 seers per rupee and *tawas* at 4 to 6 seers per rupee. The blacksmiths prepare a kiln in the earth, put the iron-ore into it and obtain the metal in a superior form. They purchase coal for smelting purposes from villages. They do not pay any Government dues, but the Malguzar (landlord) levies a duty of Rs.16 per kiln per annum in lieu of the fuel obtained by them from the Malguzari forest.[1]

Drug District. This District was separated from Raipur in 1906, and its Agaria population is allied to that of the parent District. The 1911 Census gives a population of only 3 Agaria, but at the same date there were 39 furnaces at work, a typical example of the untrustworthiness of Census figures. The Gazetteer says that in 1907 there were 19 Agaria furnaces in the Sanjari Tahsil and probably there were other furnaces in the Dondi-Lohara Zamindari, at Killekonda, Ungara and Hirkapur.[2] The number of furnaces rose to 92 in 1920 as a result of 'the cheap and ample labour available owing to the failure of crops', but it declined again the following year to 26 and has since slowly decreased till today there are only a few furnaces left. This is the more remarkable since Drug, like Chanda, holds some of the best iron deposits in India. These were first recognized by P. N. Bose in 1887.[3] The area was later explored on behalf of Messrs Tata and Co. by Mr C. M. Weld and a large area in the Dondi-Lohara Zamindari in the western part of the District was taken up under prospecting licence for detailed examination.[4] Sir L. L. Fermor gives an interesting description of these iron-ores which, on account

> of their resistance to weathering agents, stand up as conspicuous hillocks in the general peneplain. The most

[1] *The Agricultural Ledger*, 1898, p. 1.

[2] Sir A. E. Nelson, *Drug District Gazetteer*, p. 114.

[3] *R.G.S.I.*, Vol. LIII, Part III, p. 181.

[4] *R.G.S.I.*, Vol. L, p. 287. The zamindari was at that time included in Raipur District.

striking of these is the ridge which includes the Dhalli and Rajhara hills, extending for some 20 miles in a zigzag, almost continuous line, and rising to heights of sometimes 400 feet above the general level of the flat country around. The iron-ores are associated with phyllites and are often of the usual type of banded quartz-iron-ore schists characteristic of the Dharwar system. But in places, thick masses, apparently lenticular in shape, are formed of comparatively pure hematite, and one of these in the Rajhara hills has been subjected to very careful examination by diamond drilling. The Rajhara mass was carefully sampled across the surface at each point selected for a drill hole, and the ores obtained were also analyzed in lengths representing successive depths of 10 feet each from the surface, giving altogether 64 samples, which were assayed for iron, phosphorus, sulphur, silica and manganese. The average results obtained for the surface samples were as follows: Fe, 66·35; P, 0·058; S, 0·108; SiO_2, 1·44; Mn, 0·151 per cent; while for the cores the averages were Fe, 68·56; P, 0·064; S, 0·071; SiO_2, 0·71; Mn, 0·175 per cent.

In this mass the prospecting operations thus proved the existence of 2½ million tons of ore carrying about 67·5 per cent of iron and a phosphorus content slightly below the Bessemer limit. The quantity estimated is that which may be regarded as ore in sight, while almost certainly much larger quantities may be obtained by continuation of the ore-bodies beyond their proved depth.[1]

It will be of interest to add another, much earlier account of the Dondi-Lohara Zamindari by P. N. Bose.

The richest and most extensive ores of the district are to be found in this Zamindari. Furnaces exist at *Killakora*, *Ungara*, *Hirkapur*, etc. The hill of Dhalli, for about 7 miles of its length, is full of good hematite, which is developed in hard, red, rather thin bedded ferruginous Chilpi sandstone. The villages of Dhalli and Kondekassa once possessed a very large number of furnaces, but they have been given up, owing, I heard, to the Zamindar of Lohara having raised the duty levied on iron furnaces.

[1] *R.G.S.I.*, Vol. XX, Part IV, p. 169.

6. Muria Lohar of Phulpad, Bastar State.

7. Patharia Agaria girls of Umaria, Mandla District

Analyses.—Four specimens of the ores brought by me were analyzed by Mr E. J. Jones, of the Geological Survey, with the following result:—

		Percentage of iron
1.	Dhalli	72·92
2.	do.	67·41
3.	Chutrala	63·82
4.	Wararbandh	53·24

The first variety of the Dhalli ore appears to be the best that has as yet been found in this country, as will be seen from the following comparison:—

	Dhalli (Raipur)	Lohara hill[1] (Chanda)	Agaria[2] (Jabalpur)	Sanlow[3] (Rajputana)	Dechaun[4] (Kumaon)
Percentage of iron	72·92	69·208	68·28	66·00	55·13

Fuel and Water Supply.—All the places mentioned above, except Magarkund and Wararbandh, are situated in fairly wooded forests; and those near Dhalli, especially to the west and south-west of it, are exceptionally good, so much so that a charcoal furnace on a large scale could possibly be maintained here to advantage. The fuel used for reduction of ore in the furnace is obtained from *dhaora*, *sarai* and similar trees of comparatively little economic importance, teak and other timber-yielding trees being not allowed to be cut down for the purpose. For refining, bamboo charcoal is employed.

Of all the places tabulated above, Dhalli is most advantageously situated as regards supply of water, several springs in the neighbourhood yielding it in a very pure form. Mr E. J. Jones of the Geological Survey, who kindly analyzed a sample of the spring water, detected the merest traces only of lime and chloride in it.

Flux.—Flux is never used in the furnaces which I saw at work. The Raipur (Lower Vindhyan ?) limestone is usually not far off from the iron-ore localities.

As regards Dhalli, the nearest outcrop of it is at a distance of 20 miles. One specimen of the stone, analyzed by

[1] *Manual of the Geology of India*, Vol. III, p. 388.

[2] *R.G.S.I.*, Vol. XVI, p. 97.

[3] *Manual of the Geology of India*, Vol. III, p. 395.

[4] ibid., p. 409.

Mr Hiralal, of the Geological Survey, gave the following result:—

Carbonate of lime	83·50
,, ,, magnesia..	2·00
Oxide of iron and alumina	0·90
Insolubles	13·60
	100·00

Mr R. K. Patil, I.C.S., Deputy Commissioner of the District in 1940, informed me that in that year 'there were twenty-one Agaria families living in four villages—Bhadur, Br. Boriya, Bhatagaon and T. Boriya in the Pannabaras Zamindari of the Sanjari Tahsil. Thirteen of these families were carrying on their ancient craft and the others helped them. There was one more village—Paiwara—in the Sanjari Tahsil where a few Agaria were reported to be living. In the past, there were Agaria in the villages of Hitkasa, Nalkasa, Puswada, Bahmani, Katrel and Kopedesa but it is said that these have emigrated to Kanker State.'

Jashpur State. In this State, which lies south-east of Surguja and borders Udaipur on its eastern boundary, the Khuria plateau consists of trap-rock topped with volcanic laterite, and it is said that iron is obtained in a nodular form in the hilly tracts and smelted by the 'aboriginal tribes' for export. In the 1911 Census the State returned 53 Agaria.[1] I am indebted to Mr Le Patourel, the present Diwan of the State, for the latest figures.

These, excluding the Khuria Zamindari, are as follows:—

Agaria	21 households
Asur	25 ,,
Chokh Agaria	5 ,,
Deo-dhuka Lohar	18 ,,
Jait Lohar	8 ,,
Mahali Lohar	746 ,,
Maghaia Lohar	16 ,,
Kol Lohar	3 ,,
Lohar	77 ,,

[1] De Brett, *Chhattisgarh Feudatory States Gazetteer*, op. cit., pp. 277ff.

The number of furnaces and forges in operation is most encouraging.

Forges	.. .. ..	839
Furnaces	.. ..	486

The Asur have generally abandoned iron work for cultivation and the Agaria also seem to be no longer practising iron-smelting. But when necessary they make and repair their own implements for household use. The Mahali Lohar appear to smelt their iron in much the same fashion as in Mandla, using wooden bellows covered with deer-skin or cow-hide according to the strength of the local Hindu influence. These they work with their feet. In the Pandrapath area at least they worship Lohasur. Others are said to honour Vishwakarma. They make *kuāri lohā*, have a taboo on working in the sun, and many eat beef.

Jubbulpore District. In 1891 no fewer than 1,850 persons returned themselves as Agaria, but this number dropped in twenty years to 273. The number of furnaces also dropped from 28 in 1898[1]—a total which was maintained until 1913 or later—to only 1 in 1925; and the industry has probably expired before the competition of market iron which is particularly strong in a District with such good communications. When Mr Grigson was Deputy Commissioner of Jubbulpore in 1937, he saw several abandoned furnaces along the border of the Jubbulpore and Sihora Tahsils; and he noted that the blacksmiths attributed the abandonment of iron-smelting to the forest rates, the raising of which they said had made it cheaper to buy the raw material from the bazaar.

But the District, though long famous for its iron-ores, would not apparently be suitable for the establishment of a new Tatanagar.

[1] *The Agricultural Ledger*, 1898, pp. 1 and 8. But R. S. Hole remarks that the iron-smelters in Jubbulpore were 'invariably poor, low-caste individuals, such as Dhimars, Lodhis, Kachhis, Patharis, Chamars, Gonds, etc., and very rarely Lohars, i.e. workers in iron, or blacksmiths, by caste'. Possibly these came to regard themselves as Agaria after adopting their profession.

The hematite deposits, apparently interbedded with the Dharwar phyllites, had for years been supposed to be very rich, but prospecting operations conducted in this area by E. P. Martin and H. Louis have shown that while iron-ore is widely distributed, and the foundations in which it occurs are prominent in the district, there are no rich ore-bodies of large size that could be relied on for the output necessary to maintain an important industry, and most of the ore, being in the form of soft micaceous hematite, would be physically unfit in its natural condition for use in a blast furnace. Generally, also, the ores in this district contain a proportion of phosphorus too high for acid Bessemer steel.

The following analyses, extracted from Messrs Martin and Louis' report (*Agricultural Ledger*, Calcutta, 1904, No. 3), give an idea of the nature of the ore in the principal occurrences in the Jubbulpore district:—

	Iron	SiO_2	S	P	Moisture
I. Agaria hill. Lateritic cap covering most of the hill. 3 samples.	57·58	7·28	0·02	0·125	0·45
	56·85	8·17	0·02	0·125	0·67
	45·67	13·90	0·03	0·187	0·69
Soft micaceous hematite schists. Ore-layers only. 2 samples.	60·70	7·45	0·019	0·075	0·25
	58·40	8·40	0·022	0·081	0·33
II. Agaria ridge. Bed of hematite 4 to 5 feet thick, dipping 50°	50·07	11·37	0·036	0·074	0·44
III. Jauli. Soft banded hematite-quartz-schists. Picked samples.	64·67	3·70	0·027	0·023	0·30
	54·64	16·05	0·033	0·200	0·48
	65·50	3·37	0·032	0·110	0·33
	55·22	17·32	0·030	0·053	0·21

The hematite ores occur interbedded with Dharwar phyllites.

Near Sihora siliceous brown hematites were found, poorer in iron, but physically more suitable for the blast furnace, and in this area there occur patches of manganiferous iron-ore.[1]

[1] cf. *R.G.S.I.*, Vol. XVI (1883), pp. 101–3; *Trans. Min. Geol. Inst. Ind.*, Vol. I (1906), p. 99 and *M.G.S.I.*, Vol. XXXVII (1909), pp. 814, 815, 821–3.

8. Birjhia Asur girl of Jam Tola, near Neterhat.

9. (*a*) Patharia Agaria youth in dancing-dress, from Mandla District.

(*b*) Agaria bridegroom wearing leaf-crown for his marriage (Mandla District).

The following analyses were obtained from samples obtained at Mansakra (Silondi) near Sihora:—

	Fe	Mn	SiO_2	S	P	Moisture
Wider band ..	52·15	0·36	14·70	0·022	0·385	0·10
Narrower band ..	44·95	6·28	14·55	0·027	0·352	0·27
Manganiferous iron-ore	24·45	21·47	19·60	0·022	0·163	0·80

The above ores occur as lateritoid replacement products on the upturned edges of the Dharwar hematite ores.[1]

The chief centres of Agaria activity in Jubbulpore were certain villages eight to ten miles south-east of Sihora—Agaria, Jauli, Partabpur and Saroli, where there was a good deposit of schistose hematite. At Ghughra, east of Sihora, a good steel called *kheri* was produced from the manganiferous ore obtained there.[2] Sir L. L. Fermor mentions Majhgaon near Sihora as 'very accessible, so that the indigenous processes of iron-smelting can be readily studied'.

Khairagarh State. This is a small State lying on the western border of the great Chhattisgarh basin. No Agaria have been tabulated here at the Census, but there must at one time have been groups of them, probably allied to the Drug Agaria. In the western part of the State north of Dongargarh there lies a jungle-clad hilly country which is full of iron-ore. Ore is found in the forests of Barnara and Gatapani. A mining lease was once granted to the Indian Manganese Company of Calcutta.[3] P. N. Bose speaks of the furnaces at Borla, Katulkassa, and Banjar, 'probably aggregating twenty in number. The ores mostly occur in soil covering basaltic rocks which appear to be intrusions in the Chilpis; but rich hematite, among beds of red sandstone, is also met with.'[4]

Kanker State. This wild and beautiful State, which lies to the south of Raipur, has deposits of iron-ore in its hills and

[1] Fermor, op. cit., *R.G.S.I.*, Vol. L, p. 287.

[2] Sir A. E. Nelson, *Jubbulpore District Gazetteer*, p. 260. See also *Imperial Gazetteer*, p. 51.

[3] *Chhattisgarh Feudatory States Gazetteer*, p. 179.

[4] P. N. Bose in *R.G.S.I.*, Vol. XX (1887), p. 168.

these are 'worked up locally into ploughshares, etc.'.[1] Kanker returned an Agaria population of 64 in 1911.

Kawardha State. The Maikal Range runs through the north-east section of this State, and the aboriginals of these remote and almost inaccessible tracts are closely related to those of Mandla. There were 458 Agarias here in 1891 and 129 in 1911. The Gazetteer states that the iron in Rengakhar and Boria Zamindaris is 'worked locally'.[2]

Korea State. This little State, which is 'virtually nothing but one vast mass of hill ranges, crowding in on one another and covered with dense forests',[3] is neighboured by the Surguja and Rewa States and the Bilaspur District. It is thus in the middle of the Agaria belt. We read that 'iron is found, but not in large quantities. It is worked to some extent by a class of Gonds locally called Agarias'.[4] But Korea had the third largest population of Agaria in 1911, when 956 were returned.

Mandla District. The Agaria here seem to be confined to the Dindori Tahsil, which is bordered by Rewa State to the north and Kawardha to the south-east. In the rugged and lovely uplands of the Motinala, Dindori and Karanjia Ranges live the Patharia or Mukhi Agaria, who are distinguished by the fact that they fix their bellows in place with stones. They numbered 564 in 1891 and 793 in 1911, but the number of furnaces dropped from 65 in 1909 to 19 in 1939. *The Agricultural Ledger* reports that, in 1897, there were 51 furnaces producing during the year 9 tons of iron. 'The owners of 18 furnaces in the Dindori Tahsil obtain the ore from the Rewa State or other parts of the District.'[5] I do not know why this should have been so, for the lateritic ores of the Dindori Tahsil are generally considered good. Although Sir R. Temple did not mention Mandla in his survey (in 1862) of the iron resources of the Central Provinces, Colonel Ward five years later was discussing the excellent and plentiful iron in the hills of Mandla. 'Iron', he says, 'is plentiful all along the Mykul range to the

[1] *Chhattisgarh Feudatory States Gazetteer*, p. 77.
[2] ibid., p. 155. [3] ibid., p. 295. [4] ibid., p. 301.
[5] *The Agricultural Ledger*, op. cit., p. 3.

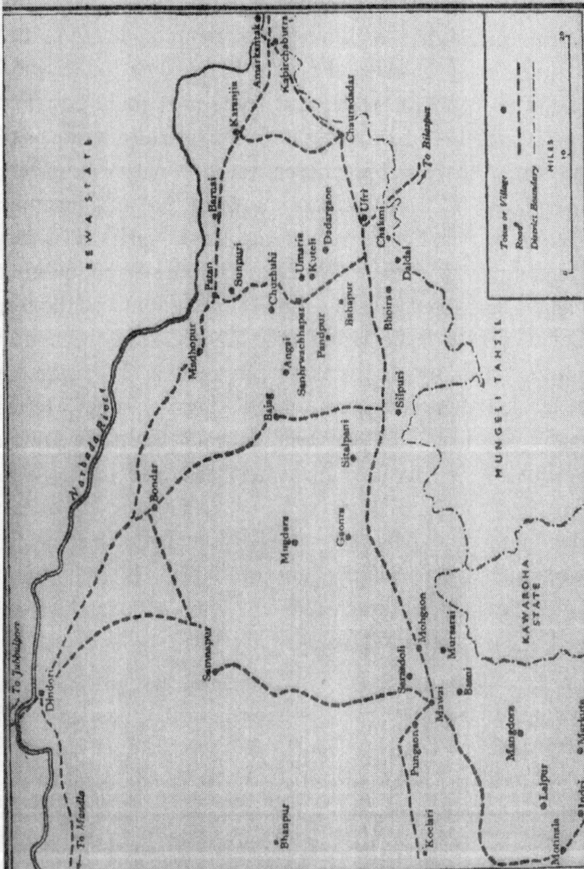

SKETCH MAP OF DINDORI TAHSIL, MANDLA DISTRICT

south-east, and in many other parts of the district the mines are only worked sufficiently for internal consumption with, perhaps, the exception of the Mowye mines, the iron from which has obtained a little more than mere local reputation.' The ore, he says again, is to be found near the surface, it is 'very plentiful' and is dug 'with but little labour'. The quality is sometimes 'very good' and 'ought some day to become a source of profit to the District, if trade in it could be a little more developed'.[1] In 1872 Captain Forsyth also wrote of the 'abundant' resources of Mandla in iron.[2]

The *Mandla District Gazetteer* speaks of the 'excellent iron' of the Agaria who live near the Baiga Chak; theirs is the only 'peculiar industry' of the Province. 'The ore is either quarried, or found lying about on the surface of the ground in the form of boulders of a reddish hue, the tinge having been communicated to it by the blood of the goddess Sita, who was shot by Laxman in mistake for a stag.'[3] The Gazetteer specially mentions 'a hill between Mohgaon, Sarasdoli Anuwar and Murserai in the Raigarh tract, and also in the Phen Valley'.[4]

The Agaria of Mandla themselves distinguish with some care between the various kinds of ore available. In the Dindori Tahsil at least half a dozen different kinds are classified and named. They are as follows:—

1 & 2. *Chawariya.* This is considered best of all, in the Karanjia and Motinala Ranges as well as in Bilaspur. It is dug from pits.

3. *Bhawariya.* This is also good. It is dug from pits in the Motinala Range.

4. *Pondo.* This is gathered from the surface of the ground in the Motinala Range. It is considered a good, pure, heavy iron.

[1] Ward, op. cit., p. 87.

[2] J. Forsyth, *The Highlands of Central India*, p. 370.

[3] F. R. R. Rudman, *Mandla District Gazetteer* (Bombay, 1912), p. 64.

[4] ibid., p. 147.

5. *Katarra* is collected from the banks of streams. It is not considered to be good.

6. *Charki* is dug from pits in the Motinala Range. It is not very good and tools made from this are said to break readily.

7. *Jak-makka* is dug from pits in Motinala.

Through my friend Mr Evelyn Wood I sent specimens of each of these to the Tata Iron and Steel Company at Jamshedpur. The General Manager, Mr J. J. Ghandy, was good enough to have them analyzed by his Chief Chemist and to send a report, the gist of which I quote.

> The iron content in the iron-ore samples runs from about 49% to 56%. Usually the Agaria do not mind a rather low-grade ore if it is soft and easily smelted. I presume these are all soft ores and it may be that their judgement as to what constitutes a good ore may depend partly on the physical condition of the ore, which I have not been able to judge. However, I note that the sample called *katarra* which is considered not good, is very high in phosphorus, and the sample called *charki*, the tools from which are said to break readily, is high in titanium, which may give them some difficulty in smelting. The three samples, *bhawariya* and *chawariya* from Mawai and Bajag, which they consider good, are all rather high in manganese and low in titanium and two of them low in phosphorus. The sample they consider best of all (the *chawariya* dug from pits in Mawai) has a high silica-to-alumina ratio, low titanium, low phosphorus, and fairly high manganese. These seem to be the factors that determine the value to the smelters rather than the iron content which is low in all the samples submitted.

The chemical analysis of these specimens, together with an analysis of metal after work in the furnace, and of slag, will be found in Appendix I.

The Khuntia Chokh of Bilaspur have a different classification. They classify the ores as follows:—

Bechra. This is the best of all. It is '*haldi*-coloured'.

Chawariya-pondo-jalposi. A heavy, whitish ore, considered good, but less heavy than the following:—

Pondo. A good heavy ore.

Pakna. Very good. The next best after *bechra.*
Dudhia.
Gondli-purut. It breaks open like the shells of an onion.
Kharahatta. A poor and brittle iron is extracted from this.

It is perhaps worth noting for purposes of comparison that in the Palamau District of Chota Nagpur, the Agaria (probably the Agaria Asur) recognized three varieties of ore—'*bali*, i.e. magnetite, *biji*, i.e. maematites from coal measures, and *dherhur*, i.e. hematites from laterite. *Bali* is first broken up into small fragments by pounding, and it is then reduced to a fine powder between a pair of mill-stones. The hematite it is not usual to submit to any other preliminary treatment besides pounding.'[1]

In Jeypore Zamindari, Miss Durga Bhagvat tells me, two kinds of ore are distinguished. 'About three miles from the Likhma station of the Raipur Forest Tramway there is a fairly big colony of the "Lohar"—they are mockingly called Agaria, but are ashamed to own the name. They said that there are two types of iron ore—male (*pharus*) and female (*māī*). It is considered lucky when both ores are found lying side by side. The female ore is reddish, light, sparkling and rich. The male ore is black, heavy and cheap.'[2]

Mirzapur District. The Mirzapur District of the United Provinces projects southwards to the borders of Surguja, having Rewa on its west and Palamau to the east. It is thus surrounded by Agaria territory, and we shall not be surprised to find 938 Agaria in 1891 living in that part of the district that lies south of the Son. In 1909 the number had increased to 1186.[3] The Agaria themselves said (in 1896) that five or six generations ago 'they emigrated from Rewa, hearing that

[1] V. Ball, *M.G.S.I.*, Vol. XV, Part I.

[2] The Baganda call hard ironstone male, and soft ore female, and mix them before smelting. J. Roscoe, *The Baganda* (London, 1911), p. 379. The Jur tribe of the Sudan also regard iron ore as having male and female elements which must be mixed before iron can be produced. T. C. Crawhall, 'Iron Working in the Sudan', *Man*, Vol. XXXIII, p. 41.

[3] D. L. Drake-Brockman, *Mirzapur. A Gazetteer* (Allahabad, 1911).

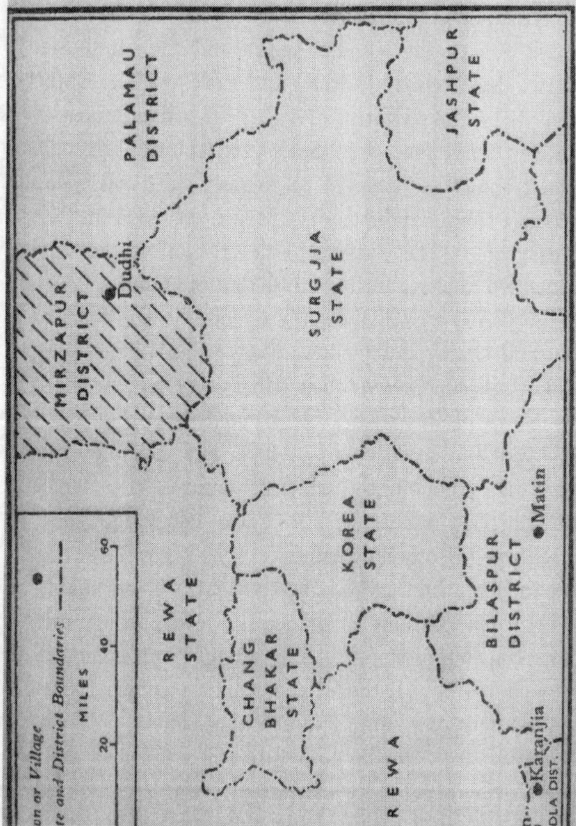

SKETCH MAP SHOWING RELATION OF MIRZAPUR DISTRICT TO THE REST OF THE AGARIA TERRITORY

they could carry on their business in peace in British territory. Their first settlement was in the village of Khairahi in Pargana Dudhi. Their headquarters in Rewa are at the village of Rijaura: they do not make any pilgrimages to their original settlements or draw their priests or tribal officials from there.' [1]

The Mirzapur Agaria, says Crooke, are 'almost certainly connected' [2] with the Mandla Agaria and the subdivision of the Korwa described by Dalton [3] and Risley.[4] The Gazetteer considers them linked with such other Dravidian tribes as the Korwa and Parahiya.[5] On both geographical and cultural grounds I should be inclined to connect them with Mandla. The passage from Mandla through Rewa to the Dudhi Pargana is an easy one. The Gazetteer's description of the smelting methods used in Mirzapur resembles that of Mandla. A glance at Plates 30 and 33 will show the likeness in the form of the furnace and the type of bellows used. The Mirzapur Agaria also take Lohasur Devi as their tribal deity, and worship her in the month of Pus with a black female goat that has never borne a kid and some cakes of flour and molasses fried in butter.[6] They honour the *sāl* tree,[7] planting it in the centre of the marriage booth, whence Crooke concludes 'that tree marriage was the original custom'.

Like their brethren in Mandla, they eat beef—probably now in secret. One curious difference, however, which must be due to social conditions—probably a large population of Lohar in the vicinity—is that the Mirzapur Agaria 'confine themselves almost entirely to mining and smelting iron'.[8] 'He does no blacksmith's work: all he does is to smelt the iron and work it up into rough ingots, which are afterwards converted into axe-heads and agricultural implements by the Lohar, who is admittedly a recent immigrant into the hill country and utterly repudiates any connexion with the iron-smelter of the jungles.' [9]

[1] W. Crooke, *Tribes and Castes of the N.-W. Provinces and Oudh*, p. 3.
[2] *ibid.*, p. 1.
[3] Dalton, op. cit., p. 221.
[4] Risley, op. cit., Vol. I, p. 4.
[5] *Gazetteer*, op. cit., p. 24.
[6] Crooke, op. cit., p. 8.
[7] ibid., p. 4.
[8] ibid, p. 1.
[9] ibid., Vol. III, p. 372, Article 'Lohar'.

The Gazetteer adds that some tools are, in fact, made by the Agaria, but most by the Lohar. 'The iron has a high reputation for tenacity and endurance, and over 1,400 axes, spades and other implements made of it are annually sold in Ahraura.'[1]

Nandgaon State. P. N. Bose noticed in 1886 that 'lateritic ore was abundant over an area of eight square miles' in this state 'at Bhawa, Jurlakhar and Chuḥuri (depopulated), now worked only at Jurlakhar, where he saw four active furnaces', though even this village was deserted the following year.[2] The Gazetteer (1909) says that prospecting licences were being taken out for the exploitation of the iron and manganese ores which were found at Nadai, Ghumka, Patwa, Chhuria and several other villages, and adds a rather mysterious note that 'about twenty years ago iron used to be manufactured locally by native methods, but this industry had to be given up owing to the expense'.[3]

Narsinghpur District (now amalgamated with the Hoshangabad District). Of this district Sir L. L. Fermor writes,

> At Omarpani near Tendukhera in the Narsinghpur district both hematite and limonite occur irregularly distributed in fissures and hollows among the Bijawar limestones and quartzites, and were formerly smelted extensively by indigenous methods. In 1855 to 1857 some 70 to 80 furnaces were at work with a production of about 140 tons of iron annually. This metal was of unusually good quality, and a portion of it was converted into steel by re-heating, hammering, rolling in burnt cow-dung, and plunging into water. No estimate of the quantity of ore available appears to have been made.[4]

In 1830, as we have already noticed, a suspension bridge over the Bias River in Saugor was made with ore that had been entirely smelted in the Agaria furnaces at Tendukhera. Watts points out that the ore here is somewhat calcareous—the gangue being partly limestone which produces the same effect as a purposely added flux.[5]

[1] *Gazetteer*, op. cit., p. 24. [2] *R.G.S.I.*, Vol. XX, p. 168.
[3] *Chhattisgarh Feudatory States Gazetteer*, p. 100.
[4] *R.G.S.I.*, Vol. L, p. 284. [5] Watts, op. cit., p. 508.

By 1898 the number of furnaces in Narsinghpur had dropped to 25 and in 1909 to 4.[1] The population of 78 Agaria in 1891 went down to only 9 in the next twenty years.[2] It is interesting to note that Mr Bourne thought that the determining factor in the failure of the District to regain its previous population of 1881 has been 'the construction of the railway with the resulting decay of local cottage industries which followed the increasing importation of manufactured articles'.[3]

Raigarh State. This State is linked with the Agaria belt through Jashpur, Udaipur and Bilaspur which border it to the north and west. In the south, however, Sarangarh State has no Agaria, the iron-work of the area being done by Hindu Lohar. In the beautiful forest-covered hills to the north there is, or was, a fairly large population of Agaria, 198 being returned in 1891 and 870 in 1911. 'Iron-stone is met with near the village of Badpali while coarse grits are found in the river section.'[4]

Raipur District. We have already referred to P. N. Bose's survey of the Raipur District written in 1887,[5] though much of the territory he covered is now in Drug. He refers to the 'numerous furnaces' he saw, and says,

> The Agarias who work them are a very unsettled people, leaving a place as soon as the neighbouring jungle fails to satisfy their requirements, or the Zamindar enhances the duty levied on their furnaces.

Ranchi and Palamau Districts. These two districts form the extreme eastern end of what I have called the Agaria belt which stretches across the centre of India. In 1827, 29 furnaces were being worked in the Palamau pargana.[6] I do not know the present number of furnaces, but the Asur population numbered 2,024 in 1931, 1,940 being in Ranchi and 84 in Palamau. In 1911, the total was 3,716 and in 1921 it was

[1] *The Agricultural Ledger*, op. cit., p. 3. [2] *R.G.S.I.*, Vol. LXXIV, p. 408.

[3] Bourne, *Narsinghpur Land Revenue Settlement Report, 1923–26*, quoted in *Census of India, 1931*, Vol. XII, Pt. I, p. 35.

[4] *Gazetteer*, op. cit., p. 167. [5] *R.G.S.I.*, Vol. XX, pp. 168ff.

[6] L. S. S. O'Malley, *Bihar and Orissa District Gazetteers: Palamau*. Revised edition by P. C. Tallents, p. 137.

2,245.[1] The *Ranchi District Gazetteer* has a description of the Asur.

> The Asurs, a small non-Aryan tribe, are found in the north-west of the district and live almost entirely by iron-smelting. They also practise a form of cultivation akin to jhuming on the Pats or level hill tops. Extremely little is known about the origin of this tribe. Colonel Dalton was inclined to connect these with the Asurs who, according to Munda traditions, were destroyed by Sing Bonga, and it has been conjectured that they are the descendants of the original inhabitants of the plateau, who were driven out by the Mundas and of whom the only traces now to be found are a few scattered tumuli and occasional stone or copper celts. Another conjecture is that they are a branch of the Mundas, who, like the Turis, split off from the rest of the tribe on account of their profession. Whichever theory is correct, it is certain that the Asurs resemble the Mundas both in appearance and language, and, like them are divided into exogamous, totemic septs. . . At the census of 1911 there were 3,383 Asurs in the district, of whom 284 were classified as Hindus. The Agarias, who number only 250 persons, are probably akin to, and perhaps a sub-caste of, the Asurs.[2]

Sir G. A. Grierson believed on linguistic grounds that the Asur were closely related to the Korwa, a tribe which in Bilaspur has connexions with the Chokh and Agaria. He refers also to a language called Agoria or Agaria, which had been returned from the Ranchi and Palamau Districts. It had 1,616 speakers, but like Asuri and Birjhia was 'rapidly dying out' and its 'total disappearance can only be a question of time'.[3]

In 1880, when Ball wrote his *Jungle Life in India*, he was chiefly struck, in Palamau, by the iron work of the 'Aghurias', whom he considered to belong to the Munda family of aborigines.

Throughout the Ranchi and Palamau Districts, the Asur and Agaria appear to be abandoning their old profession.

[1] *Census of India, 1931*, Vol. VII, Table xviii.

[2] Sir M. G. Hallett, *Ranchi District Gazetteer*, (Patna, 1918).

[3] Sir G. A. Grierson, *Linguistic Survey of India*, Vol. IV, pp. 135ff.

Dr Reuben had the greatest difficulty in witnessing the process of iron-smelting. During my visit to the Neterhat plateau I found the Asur abnormally shy of exhibiting their work or even of admitting that they did it. Reservation of the forests and taxation are said to be the reasons for this. In some notes on the Latehar subdivision sent me by Mr W. G. Archer, he writes that the Agaria, Asur and Birjhia 'as with many other castes and tribes of that area, are now on a debased, non-descript level'. The Agaria of Latehar have given up iron-smelting for agriculture, and seem to have preserved few of the cultural features that would link them with the Agaria of the west. The Asur have also given up iron work and though they worship Asur-Asurin they say that they do not know who they are. The Birjhia have also given up their iron work owing to the difficulty of getting charcoal after the forests were reserved. Two Birjhia families of Kerakhar who still occasionally smelt iron make spades and ploughshares. They have a taboo on the sun and use salt and water to temper their iron.

Rewa State. The broad band of transition rocks running across the State parallel to and south of the Son River contains iron-ore.[1] There is a good deal of intermarriage between the Agaria of the Dindori Tahsil and those of the neighbouring areas of Rewa State. A number of Agaria migrated into Mirzapur, believing that they would have more freedom in British territory.

Saugor District. There are only a few Agaria left here, in the villages of Hirapur, Tingoda, Amarwow and Baraitha of the Banda Tahsil, where there is a supply of good red and yellow hematite. Here 'before the coming of what the villagers call the "Government" iron, the collection and smelting of the mineral supported a considerable non-agricultural population'.[2] There were in fact 189 Agaria in Saugor in 1891. Even as late as 1913 there were 19 furnaces in the District, though the number went down to 1 in 1930 and the industry is now apparently almost extinct.

[1] Watts, op. cit., p. 508.

[2] *Census of India, 1931*, Vol. XII, Pt. I, p. 237.

Seoni District. Seoni is now a subdivision of the Chhindwara District. 'The ore', says Sir Richard Temple, (1862), 'is worked out after the native fashion by a class of people called "Agree" chiefly at the villages of Ambagurgh, Pukhana, Dulall, Dourasee and Moondapur.'[1] At about the same period, Captain Thomson wrote that the best iron in Seoni was in 'Kuttunghee, in the drainage of the Hiree River and near the Dongurtal border at Jutama' but, he added, 'its true value is hardly yet known, as it has only been worked after the wasteful native method'. At that time a total of Rs.291 was being paid annually in royalties to Government. Thomson also thought that the iron near Dullal, also in the Hiree drainage, 'was worth working' as it was near a road and water-power was available.[2]

But such iron industry as there was entirely stopped in 1897 on the outbreak of the famine when 'the people left their houses and went to labour on relief works or elsewhere',[3] and it was never restarted.

Surguja State. This State forms the link between the Agaria Asur of Bihar and the Asur Agaria of Bilaspur; on the north it connects with Mirzapur. Iron-ores are found in the hills and forests of the State which were inhabited in 1911 by no fewer than 2,592 Agaria. 'In the Mainpat plateau on the south of the State the southern face is mainly composed of gneiss and iron-stone, while the northern side is a massive wall of sandstone, indented like a coast-line with isolated bluffs standing up in front of the cliffs from which they have parted.'[4]

In 1921 the Agaria population numbered 1,740. No returns were made in 1931, but in 1941 there were 2,643 Agaria and 683 Asur.[5] Many of these worship Lohasur and Jwala Mukhi—regarding both as goddesses. Some derive

[1] Sir R. Temple, *Report on the Administration of the Central Provinces up to August, 1862* (Reprinted, Nagpur, 1923), p. 96.

[2] W. B. Thomson, *Report of the Land Revenue Settlement of the Seonee District*, p. 11.

[3] *The Agricultural Ledger*, op. cit., p. 3.

[4] *Gazetteer*, op. cit., p. 227.

[5] From information communicated by Rai Sahib M. L. Varma, M.B.E., Minister of Surguja State.

their tribe from Asur-Asurin and say they came from Lohitpur or Tirhut. Most of them eat beef, make Virgin Iron and have a taboo on working in the sun.

Udaipur State. This small State, which was formerly part of Surguja, lies to the south of the great Mainpat plateau; on the west it is bordered by the Korba Zamindari and on the east by Jashpur. The main geological formations are of carboniferous sandstone, and iron is found in most parts of the State. Mr M. B. Bhaduri has provided me with a great deal of admirably documented and precise information about the iron-smelters of Udaipur. In 1911, 608 Agaria were returned from the State. Today, according to figures supplied by Mr Bhaduri, there are 352 iron-workers of all types, working 109 furnaces and 134 forges. These iron-workers are called by different names in different areas, but they probably fall into two main divisions:—

Chokh Agaria	41
Chokh	167
Mahali Chokh	53
Mahali Agaria	1
Chokh Asur	3

The majority of these are iron-smelters as well as blacksmiths. They consider themselves, the Agaria especially, as rather superior, and claim to have given up beef-eating and to use *kotri*- or *sāmbhar*-hide on their bellows.

Lohar	32
Mahali Lohar	22
God-dhuka Mahali Lohar ..	13
God-dhuka Lohar	5
Mahali	16
Chokh Lohar	1

With the exception of two Mahali Lohar, all these have given up iron-smelting, though many maintain small forges for the manufacture and repair of tools. They mostly eat beef and use cow-hide on their bellows. Although they use their feet for working the bellows, I am inclined to regard this group as distinct from the Agaria tribes with whom they have few cultural associations.

It is evident from the notes collected by Mr Bhaduri that there has been considerable immigration into the State from all the surrounding areas. Some have come from the Korba Zamindari and even the Jangjir Tahsil bringing with them the customs and traditions of the Chokh of Bilaspur. Kanpi Agaria of Dehidanr came from the Mainpat of Surguja. Chhertu Chokh of Kumarta came twenty-five years ago from Surguja. Thakur Chokh of Gersa came only two years ago from Raigarh. Seven generations ago Chamru Chokh of Gidkalo came from Jashpur. Burhao Chokh of Khargaon and Sahas Ram Chokh of Kurukela both came from the Korba Zamindari.

The taxation is low, Rs.1-8 for a forge and Rs.2 for a furnace, and other conditions seem also favourable. It is no wonder then that so many families should come to settle in the State in order to carry on their ancient occupation.

CHAPTER IV

ORGANIZATION

I. *The Divisions of the Agaria*

The Agaria tribes, as I have already shown, are made up of a number of more or less endogamous divisions; we must now study these in greater detail.

The first and the most characteristic of these tribes is the Patharia or, as they are sometimes called, the Mukhi or Mukhi-bansi after their hero Jwala Mukhi. These live in the Dindori Tahsil and the parts of Rewa and Kawardha States that adjoin it. The points that distinguish them from their fellows are not those that would immediately strike a foreign observer and would indeed often seem to him trivial enough. But they are very important to the villagers. When I go with a party of carriers taking my food and baggage into a new area, what are the things that they notice and report to their wives when they get home? They look to see how the bellows are fixed in the ground and the material of the cover of the bellows. They note the tattooing of the women, the kind of bangles they wear, whether or no they have an ornament in the nose, how they tie their saris. They are apt to be rather inquisitive about what the people eat and who they eat with, and whether they obey the menstruation rules properly or not.

None of these things seems of any great importance to the outside observer, but as they are obviously very important to the Agaria he must take note of them.

The Patharia fix their bellows in place, as their name implies, with a heavy stone. Their women do not wear a nose-ornament, they do not apply vermilion to the parting of their hair, they do not wear glass bangles. They are very strict about the menstruation rules. They eat beef, and make their own cow-hide covers for their bellows. In appearance, they are the best-looking of the tribes, and they dress themselves up in Baiga fashion for dances and festivals, when they sometimes are very attractive indeed. The typical Patharia is of medium stature, almost squat, very strong—he *looks* like a blacksmith—with smooth wavy hair, brownish-black skin, broad head, nose varying from heavy and thick to almost platyrrhine. He ties his hair in a bun on the left side of his head, though he sometimes lets it fall behind. The expression is amiable but unintelligent.

The Patharia live in Gond and Baiga villages and occasionally among the Dhoba. But except in Bhoira, where they have developed a small village on a typically Baiga model, they build their houses on the Gond pattern. Each home is a little settlement of three or four small huts round a central compound, with the smithy behind or some short distance away. In other ways, however, they follow the customs and habits of their neighbours and it is often very difficult to distinguish an Agaria in a group of Baiga or Gond.

There are far fewer Kalha Agaria. They live, as their name suggests, in Kalhoti, the lowlands of Chhattisgarh, and follow lowland ways. The women wear nose-ornaments, put vermilion down the parting of their hair, fix a spangle (*tikli*) on their foreheads, and wear glass bangles. They are said to be rather careless about the menstruation rules. They claim to have given up eating beef, and though they use cow-hide for their bellows they get the covers made by the Chamar. They fix their bellows with a stone. Probably they are Patharia who have migrated to the lowlands and settled there. The Patharia do not usually eat with the Kalha or intermarry with them, but if a Kalha comes to the hills, changes his habits and gives a small feast he can be admitted into their fellowship. Murwa Patharia of Karanjia married, by *haldi-pāni* rites, a Kalha girl, and very little fuss was made.

The Patharia never wear coloured clothes, for there are taboos on red and yellow, but the Kalha do not seem to mind this and often wear the characteristic Chhattisgarh red patterned sari—the most inartistic and unsightly cloth ever foisted upon a primitive people by the cotton mills. The

Patharia have a special affinity for the Baiga and eat from their hands, but the Kalha refuse to do this. The Kalha, in fact, regard themselves as somewhat 'civilized' and superior, though this fact does not prevent them from being generally despised by the highlanders.

The Khuntia Chokh live in the zamindaris of Bilaspur. The chief distinction between them and the Patharia is that they fix their bellows in place with two small bamboo pegs (*chingi khunti*) and not with a stone. I think too that although there are many Chokh who conform to the typical Agaria standard, others are taller, with longer heads and finer, sharper noses. But in a mixed population whose sense of endogamy is not very highly developed, physical features are an uncertain guide. For example, one evening in Nunera I was talking to three Agaria and I noticed that each had an entirely distinct type of hair. The first was clearly leiotrichous, the other two were cymotrichous—the one having wavy and the other curly hair. But all three belonged to the Khuntia Chokh division of the tribe. The truth probably is that the Patharia have a good deal of Gond and Baiga blood—within my own experience a Patharia of Karaujia married a Gond girl, Pandulal of Pungaon has married a Gond, and one of Mahatu's (Baiga) relatives married an Agaria. The Khuntia Chokh, on the other hand, live in a largely mixed population of Kawar, Pando, Dhanwar and Gond: some of their septs seem to link them with the Kawar.

What are the things an Agaria from Dindori would notice on coming into a Chokh village in Lapha? He would be struck by the fact that the furnaces were upright and not tilted as in his own home. He would notice that the bellows were covered with sambhar-hide or chital-skin instead of cow-hide. He would be astonished to see furnaces in the open air. He would mark the fact that there were no pigs in the village, and would learn that his hosts bought them when they were needed for sacrifice to Lohasur.

He would be particularly struck by the appearance of the women. The Chokh women do not wear the *choli*-bodice, probably because of the greater heat of Bilaspur. They put glass bangles on their wrists and heavy silver armlets on their arms. The unmarried girls tie the *kānch*[1] (slip of cloth between their legs), but not the married. They are not heavily tattooed. They have no hole in the nose for an ornament. They do not wear a red or yellow, but always a white sari. They refuse to eat from anyone outside the tribe (though their husbands may eat from Gond and Kawar), and observe the rules of menstruation and of exogamy very strictly.

The Khuntia Chokh build substantial houses after the style of Bilaspur. They are very clean and well walled and decorated, with good doors. They make many instruments that are unknown in Dindori, spades, the hubs of cart-wheels and meat-cutters.

The Mahali Asur or the Asur Agaria of Bilaspur are poorer, shyer and more primitive than the Khuntia Chokh. They say that they are called Mahali because they extract the *mail* (slag) from the iron.[2] Probably the name is taken from the Mahali caste, where it seems to signify some kind of craftsman. These Asur Agaria, who live to the extreme east of the Central Provinces, form a link between the Agaria of Dindori and the Asur of the Palamau plateau, though I have not noticed any special physical resemblance to either. In customs and mythology, the Mahali Asur are more closely related to the Dindori Agaria. Their own tradition is that they came from Surguja. 'Both Asur and Chokh came from Lohripur, beyond the sea. But we hid for a long time in the jungles of Surguja, and spread thence throughout the world. Those who went to Pendra became Patharia, those who went to Kalhoti became Kalha, those who fixed a peg in the ground and made the iron clean and white with sand became Khuntia Chokh.'

The full title of this branch of the tribe is Mahali Asur Tukutela Patharia Agaria. They are also sometimes called

[1] See *The Baiga*, p. 12.

[2] Mahali is the name of a sept of Lohar in Chota Nagpur. (Risley, op cit., Vol. II, p. 38.)

Guru or Karigar. They fix their bellows in place with a stone (*tuku*) and use cow-hide for their bellows-covers. In the forge they do not make a *danda* (wall to serve as a flue). They eat beef and worship Lohasur with a black cow. The women do not wear glass but only brass bangles. They wear red saris and put vermilion on the parting of their hair. They do not tie the *kānch*. They are allowed to put a *phulni*-ornament in the nose. Their women are chiefly distinguished by their very heavy tattooing. 'Wherever the *choli*-bodice could go, there is the *choli*-tattoo,' and indeed the tattooing seems to be a substitute for clothes.

The Asur allow cross-cousin marriage, but not the Khuntia Chokh: 'to marry the *phua-beti* (father's sister's daughter) would be a sin'.

The Agaria of Raipur, who are concentrated in the wilder country to the east of the District and in the Phuljhar Zamindari, call themselves Lohar. We were at first inclined to believe that the Agaria had died out or had migrated from the District. Further inquiries, however, showed that there were two entirely distinct classes of Lohar. The first were God-dhuka Patharia, who fixed their bellows with a stone and blew them with their feet. These were called Lohaparra. The Kathi Lohar fixed their bellows with pegs and blew them with their hands. We soon found that this distinction went very far indeed. The Hath-dhuka were clearly Hindus. I visited their forges in Sarangarh, in the Sambalpur District, in Phuljhar and in Raipur. Their appearance was entirely and strikingly different from that of the God-dhuka, as may be seen from a comparison of Plates 3 and 5. Their religion and mythology was different, they used a different type of bellows, and they did not extract iron from ore in clay furnaces.

The God-dhuka Patharia Lohar, however, were clearly aboriginals. They belonged to the class of society which included the Gond and Binjhwar. Look at their hair, their faces, the colour of their skin, their wretched little forges in the shade of trees. They admitted in the end that they were originally called Agaria, but had changed the name in order to get some social recognition.

The God-dhuka are, of course, very 'Hinduized'. Their smithies are indistinguishable from the Mandla smithies, but the women dress like ordinary low-caste Hindus, and the men—apart from their fine hair and sturdy physique—might belong to any of the craftsmen castes. Yet their mythology links them to the Agaria of Dindori; they worship the same gods and have the same superstitions and taboos about the furnace and the forge. They are not improperly classed as a branch of the Agaria tribes.

Miss Durga Bhagvat saw some families who admitted to being Agaria in the Bindra Naragarh tract, about three miles from Mainpur. But to the south, in Jeypore State, she found them 'ashamed to own the name', although they had furnaces, worshipped Agyasur, and took their 'names, language, septs and festivals' from the Gond.

When we move east from the Korba Zamindari into Udaipur State, and thence to Jashpur, we find the iron-workers still further divided into small groups, many of which regard each other with distaste.

Thus in Udaipur we find Chokh, Agaria, Mahali Chokh, Mahali Agaria, Chokh Asur, Mahali Lohar, God-dhuka Lohar, God-dhuka Mahali Lohar, Chokh Lohar, and Jharia Lohar. Of these the Chokh and Agaria living in the west and north of the State are apparently the same tribe. Some of the Chokh told Mr Bhaduri that they were really Agaria, but were called Chokh by the villagers because they smelted iron. In Khargaon, the blacksmiths said that Chokh was synonymous with Agaria and Asur with Mahali; the Agaria and Chokh intermarry. On the other hand Kharia Chokh of Chiknipani denied that he was an Agaria and claimed to be a Mahali Chokh. But this village is very near the Jashpur border, where the name Agaria appears to be less common. And in Kumarta, Raimer and other villages, the Chokh said that they were identical with the Agaria.

These Chokh and Chokh-Agaria claim to have given up beef-eating and say that they use *kotri-* or *sāmbhar*-hide on their bellows. They do not intermarry with the Mahali or Lohar, for these eat beef and use cow-hide. A similar tradition exists among the Agaria of Jashpur.

The Chokh and Agaria of Udaipur have the following cultural links with the Agaria of Mandla and Chokh of Bilaspur.

Their professional technique is similar. They use the same type of bellows, which they work with their feet, and build the same kind of clay furnace.

They have the same traditions of the magic Virgin Iron. They observe the taboo on working in the sun. They have the same legend of the origin of the tongs from observation of a dog sitting with legs crossed.

They have similar traditions of Logundi Raja who reigned in Lohrigarh. In the west and north of the State they worship Lohasur. Some identify Sabar Sai or Agar Sai with Logundi Raja, others identify him with Lohasur. They offer *sura-puja*, or pig sacrifice, to Logundi Raja before the kiln at the Nawa (New Eating) Festival. Some Chokh, however, say that this sacrifice is for the Asur-Asurin. As we have seen, these Agaria hold an intermediate position geographically and culturally. They are connected on the west with the traditions of Logundi and Lohasur, and to the east with stories about the Asur.

I have no doubt that the Chokh, Agaria Chokh, and Mahali Chokh of Udaipur are properly classed among the Agaria group of tribes.

I can only give the briefest account of the Asur tribes of Chota Nagpur. These attractive people have been studied in Reuben's elaborate monograph, but unhappily the author was unable to spend sufficient time among them for his researches to be of much authority. Mr S. C. Roy has written brief accounts of the Asur, and the Birjhia section of the tribe has recently been investigated by Mr Sailendra Bejoy Dasgupta.

Roy describes the Asur as divided into three sections, the Soika Asur, also called Agaria, who live in the forest and smelt iron; the Birjhia (the name is derived from *bewar* and means those who practise shifting cultivation) who also do iron work; and the Jait Asur, some of whom have taken to agriculture.[1] Reuben gives a list of four endogamous groups—the Birjhia Asur, the Bir Asur, the Agaria or Sankha and the Kodha or Thuppo. But Reuben found, what I also found myself, that there is a good deal of confusion among the Asur themselves about the names by which they should be known. In Kerakhair, for example, Reuben was told by the villagers that they were Birjhia, but the Catholic priest of the village and the local cowherd said they were really Agaria.[2] Similarly, I found some confusion between the Jait and Bir Asur, who appeared to form one group with the Thuppo and Kodha, while the Birjhia or Agaria and Soika regarded themselves as distinct and superior.

This confusion is probably due to the fact that these special names are new, perhaps often given the people by outsiders, and that many of them have become Christians. As far as I could tell from a brief tour on the Neterhat plateau the Asur have lost the greater part of whatever culture they once had. Many of them have turned to agriculture, and abandoned their old customs. The *sansri-puja*, in which a chicken is sacrificed on the anvil with a pair of tongs, is still generally observed. It will thus be best to quote one of the older descriptions of the Asur. I give an extract from Driver's account.

> The Asur appear to have considerable traditions in connexion with their former history. The following is the story regarding their origin, and general history. In ancient times they were a great people and inhabited the Dhauladir and Maingir Hills on which there were two large lakes. They were clever artisans, travelled about in palki, and used to eat red-hot iron. They did not cultivate the land, but had large herds of cattle. Then the Uraons, called Lodha, appeared and took all their cattle, and they had to go into the jungle. This drove them to desperation and they took to cattle-lifting and preying on the Uraons. These Uraons, unable to attack them in the jungles, called in the assistance of Bhagwan

[1] S. C. Roy, *Asurs, Ancient and Modern* in *J.B.O.R.S.*, Vol. XII, pp. 148ff.

[2] Reuben, op. cit., p. 40.

> who built a great fort and invited all the Asurs to attend. Being afraid to refuse, they all came at the summons, and were told to enter the fort of Bhagwan, who to allay their fears went in first. After they were all in, Bhagwan shut the gate and disappeared from the top. He then filled the fort up with charcoal. When he got outside he found two Asur (a brother and a sister) who had not gone in with the rest, and he made these two fix up a bellows and immolate the whole tribe. These two were then carried away by the Uraons, and left in the jungle, where their descendants are now found, being condemned for ever to use the bellows.[1]

I refer elsewhere to various aspects of the Asur's mythology, magic and professional technique. Their songs and dances, many of them most charming to watch, their dress and ornaments, their religious practices and festivals, their custom of sending the boys and girls to sleep in village dormitories resemble the Uraon. Many of them live in lovely upland country, with great views and open spaces. A visit to them is an unforgettable experience.

There are said to be a few other minor subdivisions of the tribes, but I have not personally been able to see any of them. Rowney, in a work that can hardly be regarded as authoritative, refers to the 'Tareemooks', a tribe of wandering blacksmiths, who from their name appear to be connected with the Mukhi Agaria. They are, he says, 'a poor and improvident race, living from hand to mouth. They are of a dark colour, though not quite so dark as the Gonds and some of the other tribes, and are a little taller and better formed than all of them. They are very laborious also, and are always loyally assisted in their labours by their women, who collect wood in the jungles to make charcoal for them, and work their forge-bellows; but they cannot, for all that, make the two ends meet, principally from being much addicted to drink. The life of the tribe, moreover, is very loose; there is no such thing as constancy among the men or chastity among the women; and married men make love to each other's wives almost openly, without

[1] Driver, op. cit., p. 7. A fuller, and rather different, version of this legend will be found on page 101 of this book.

fear or shame.'[1] The modern Mukhi are not nearly so enterprising. Russell also says that the Agaria 'move about from village to village with an anvil, a hammer and tongs, and building a small furnace under a tree, make and repair iron implements for the villagers'.[2] I have not myself met any example of this practice.

We may also briefly notice the Aghar and Agarwar who correspond in customs to the Kathi Lohar of Raipur, who now blow their bellows with their hands, fix them with pegs and do not extract ore. The Gondi Agaria are now a sub-caste of Lohar and have adopted Hindu customs. It is possible that they were never true Agaria, but simply Gond who adopted the profession of iron-work.

Although the Hindus and the other tribesmen look down on the Agaria, only the Bahelia and other 'impure castes' being willing to take food from their hands, they themselves make a good deal of fuss about their social relations with their neighbours. The woman who escaped from the destruction of Lohripur was saved by hiding in the house of a Gond: hence the Agaria eat in Gond houses and intermarry with the Gond. Kariya Kuar, according to one version of the myth, married the daughter of Nanga Baiga, and it is said that in the days of Sabar Sai, when there were only Baiga and Agaria in the world, the two tribes intermarried. So today, Patharia women dress in Baiga fashion and eat in Baiga houses; and when possible the men marry Baiga girls.

Pandulal of Pungaon (Motinala) added a Gond wife to a household which already included two other wives, and escaped censure, the other Agaria regarding it as something of an

[1] H. B. Rowney, *The Wild Tribes of India*, p. 20.

[2] Russell and Hiralal, op. cit., p. 7. There may be a confusion with the Hindu Panchal or Ghisari who are both castes of wandering blacksmiths. E. Balfour (in a note on 'The Migratory Tribes of Natives in Central India', *J.A.S.B.*, Vol. XIII, p. 8) says that 'the Taremook or wandering blacksmith' is called Ghisari in Dekhani, Lohar by the Mahratta and Bail-Kumbar by the Kanarese. He notes that their women collect wood for charcoal, work the bellows and sometimes help with the sledge-hammer. He also refers to their 'great name for gallantry'.

achievement—which indeed it was. Unhappily the compliment was not returned, and the Gond demanded a fine of Rs.140—over two years' income. The Baiga also regard it as a supreme disgrace for one of their women to marry an Agaria.

The Mahali Asur and Chokh of Bilaspur consider themselves related to the Kawar, and both men and women eat from their hands. It is probable that there has been a certain amount of intermarriage here. The Raipur Agaria, according to the doubtful authority of Russell, 'still intermarry with the Rawanbansi Gonds of the District'.

Between the different Agaria tribes there is very little social intercourse, for geographical conditions make that difficult. Marriage between Patharia and Kalha is tolerated. The Asur say that they marry Chokh girls, but the Chokh refuse to marry Asur girls. Yet the Asur regard themselves as the higher, and the Chokh admit it. Both tribes despise the Hindu Lohar and regard them as their servants.

II. *Totemism and Exogamous Groups*

Agaria society is divided into septs which are strictly exogamous, hereditary through the male line, and totemistic. Like the Baiga septs they are called *goti*, but they are much more important than in Baiga society. The institution is deeply rooted in Agaria mythology. Its totemism is still a powerful social and religious factor, and probably represents a highly developed system in antiquity. As the Agaria are a scattered people, living in very small groups in separate villages, their exogamous rules agree with the tradition that a man should marry outside his own village. This may be why, unlike the Baiga, they have no system of territorial exogamy—the *garh*—to supplement the *goti*, for it was not necessary.

As I have shown in *The Baiga*, that tribe regards clan-incest and even kinship-incest with some tolerance, and I have suggested that this may be due to the light hold their exogamous traditions have upon them and to the absence of totemism. The situation among the Agaria improves this argument, for both clan-incest and kinship-incest is very rare among them, though common among their non-totemic neighbours.

The names of the Agaria septs vary widely from place to place, probably—as we shall show—as a result of the influence of their neighbours. I will first give a list of the septs, and then proceed to examine them in detail.

Patharia of Karanjia Range (Mandla District)

Dhurwa	Masram	Ranchirai
Khusro	Pandro	Sonwani
Marabi	Parteti	Syam
Markam	Potta	Tekam

Patharia of Motinala Range (Mandla District)

Dhanchirai	Markam	Potta
Keram	Marrai	Syam
Khusro	Parteti	Tilam

Patharia of Rewa State

Baghel	Marabi	Sonwani
Dhurwa	Netam	Syam
Korcho	Parteti	Tekam

Chokh of Bilaspur District

Bagh	Gohariyar	Nang
Bare-chirai	Gorku	Parsa
Bhairat	Kumunjni	Ranchirai
Chhote-chirai	Mahto	Sonwani
Dudh-Kawar	Manjhi	Suri-saiyya-chirai
Ghet-kanda	Markam	Tekam

Asur or Mahali Asur of Bilaspur

Aind	Kerketa
Baghel	Munjni
Kachhuwa	Nonha

Sonwani

God-dhuka of Raipur District

Bans	Jal	Markam
Birrhi	Karri	Marrai
Dhoba	Kewachi	Nang
Gidhli	Kosmiha	Netam
Gorku	Kukra	Porre
Jagat		Sori

Agaria of Mirzapur District [1]

Banjbakwar (the frog)
Baragwar (*bar* tree)
Gidhle (vulture)
Goirar (probably the *gohariyar* tree of Bilaspur)
Markam
Paraswan (the *palas* tree, *Butea frondosa*)
Sanwan (*san*-hemp)

Agaria of Drug District [2]

Atyam Uika (6-god)	Kumara (5-god)	Netam (4-god)
Kowa (3-god)	Marai (7-god)	Syam (7-god)

Agaria and Chokh Agaria of Udaipur State [3]

Aenr	Gichrail	Lebri
Ahinda or Aind	Gidhri	Mahto
Deru (water-snake)	Gorear (tree)	Nang
Dudh-Kawar	Gorku	Pag gidhari
Garku (bird)	Koya or Bharewa	Ranchirai
Gentha		Sonwani

[1] *Mirzapur Gazetteer*, op. cit., p. 3.

[2] Reported to me by Miss Durga Bhagvat, who recorded the information at Bhatgaon, near Mohala, in Drug District. The Agaria here speak a dialect of Gondi.

[3] From information supplied by Mr M. B. Bhaduri, Udaipur State. The word Koya is a synonym for Koitur or Gond.

Mahali Lohar and Mahali Chokh (probably Mahali) of Udaipur[1]

Aind (a fish)	Kaint (the *chichinga* fish)	Kusura (fish)
Bagh	Kechua	Mudhni (fruit)
Baghen	Kerketa	Munjna
Barawa	Kowa (crow)	Sonwani
Bharewa or Koya	Kujri	Tirkhoi (bird)

Mahali Lohar of Jashpur State[2]

Aïnd	Gina	Kayest	Maghia
Baghela	Hanthi	Kerketa	Manjan
Bar	Hardi	Khalkho	Mund
Basara	Hundkera	Koro	Nang
Bharewa	Indwar	Kubra	Non
Bhawanr	Kachhuwa	Kusma	Pradhani
Biniya	Kadaku	Kusuan	Tigga
Gainth	Kaitwar	Latu	Tirkwar
Gelia	Kawa	Magahi	Toppo

Bir Asur of Palamau District[3]

Aind (eel)	Dhan (rice)	Lila (deer)	Suar (pig)
Bharewa (wild dog)	Kerketa (bird)	Munjni (*anjun* tree)	Titio (bird)
Bheng (frog)	Khusar or Khusro (bird)	Non (salt)	Toppo (woodpecker)

A study of these names immediately establishes a few broad facts.

In the Karanjia and Mawai areas of Mandla and in Rewa State, the Agaria live in villages inhabited mainly by Gond, Pardhan and Baiga, sometimes by Dhoba. Most of the Agaria septs in this area may also be found among the Gond, Pardhan

[1] From information supplied by Mr M. B. Bhaduri.

[2] From information supplied by Mr K. B. Le Patourel, Diwan, Jashpur State.

[3] Recorded by me at Jobhipath village on the Neterhat plateau. No other septs were discovered in the other villages I visited.

and Baiga. Thus among the Gond septs are Dhurwa, Marabi, Markam, Khusro, Tekam, Parteti, Potta, Sonwani, Syam, Masram, Marrai, Netam and Baghel. The Pardhan, who are a sub-tribe of Gond, have the same septs. Among the Baiga septs are all the above except Sonwani. The Dhoba, however, have the Sonwani sept, and pay much attention to its members.

Thus, in Mandla, Drug and Rewa, all except six of the Agaria septs may be found also among the Gond and Baiga, and even these may exist among them, but have not been recorded.

This close connexion with the Gond is recognized by the Agaria. 'We were saved by a Gond's pot of buttermilk, and so we eat from them and have their *goti*.'

But in Lapha and Uprora, the Chokh Agaria said, 'We have no bond with the Gond; our bond is with the Kawar and we have their *goti*'. Unhappily, out of 117 septs which were collected by Russell and Hiralal, only 25 were printed, and it is thus impossible to say how far this is true. The name 'Dudh-Kawar' however will be noted, and the Nang sept is common to many castes in Chhattisgarh, among them the Kawar and Lohar. The Sonwani sept has been recorded for Gond, Kawar, Dhanuwar and Panka—all neighbours of the Chokh Agaria in Bilaspur.

When we come to the Asur or Mahali Asur of Bilaspur, we find an entirely new set of parallels. Except for the Sonwani and Baghel *goti*, their septs are rare in the Central Provinces, and are connected with the Munda-speaking peoples of Chota Nagpur. Thus, during my visit to the Bir Asur of the Neterhat plateau, I found many people belonging to the Kerketa and Aind septs. These septs are also known among the Mahali of Chota Nagpur, the Rautia and Bhuinar of Jashpur, and the Kerketa sept is found among the Pando of Udaipur. The Nonha sept is recorded also for the Uraon, and the Bagh or Baghel sept, which is common among Gond and Kawar, is also known among the Munda and Uraon. The Asur Agaria believe that they came from the east through Surguja, and we need not be surprised to find this faint but definite connexion with the Munda tribes.

The Raipur Agaria have an almost completely new set of *goti*, and here again most of the parallels may be drawn with their immediate neighbours, the Gond, the Binjhwar, the Dewar and Solaha. The Jagat sept has been recorded for the Gond, the Jal for the Binjhwar, the Sori for the Gond and Solaha—a small occupational tribe of Raipur District, the Netam for Gond and Dewar. The Gorku sept, which has a horse-totem, is probably the same as the Binjhwar Ghodmaria, the horse-killer sept.

I doubt if it is possible to draw any conclusion from this beyond the broad and simple one that in this, as in many of their social customs, the small Agaria tribes have tended to imitate the neighbours on whom they depend for their livelihood. It would, I think, be unsafe to suggest that because the Mandla Agaria have so many of the Gond septs, they are therefore a sub-tribe of Gond, or even that they have taken many Gond into the tribe. They may have done, but this fact does not prove it. The Dhurwa sept, for example, is common to Gond, Baiga, Kolta, Kalar, Nat and probably several other castes; the Markam sept may be found among Gond, Baiga, Basor, Bhunjia and Solaha; the Tekam sept among Gond, Baiga, Bharewa and Binjhwar. I do not think anyone would seriously suggest that because a tiger sept, Bagh or Baghel, with a common totem and very similar rules of observance, is found among Gond, Panka, Ahir, Bhattra, Kawar, Teli, Turi, the Rautia of Jashpur and the Munda and Uraon of Chota Nagpur, there is any actual connexion between these widely dispersed tribes.

The great majority of the Agaria septs are totemistic, and their origin can be traced back to the classic heroes of the tribe. This is of great importance, for it means that the institution is guarded by sanctions deriving from the heroic and supernatural past. As among many other tribes, the septs originated during a journey or—among the Agaria—on the great flight from the stricken city of Lohripur. Thus, in one of the Mandla stories, we learn how

> After the war with the Sun, Logundi Raja's wife escaped to a Gond's house. She was pregnant and presently gave birth to twenty-four children. Six times she laboured, and there were born four at a time. The first group were born in the big cooking-pot called *marka*, and so they belonged to the Markam sept; the second group was born on the veranda (*parchi*) and were called Parteti; the third group was born among gold (*sona*) and were called Sonwani; the fourth group was born while the mother was cleaning an earthen *tilai* pot, and became Teka or Tekam; the fifth was delivered in the dust (*dhur*) and was called Dhurwa; and the sixth at sunset (*shām*) and was called Syam.[1] When Lohasur saw all these children he fainted, but when he recovered his senses he thought and thought how they could get married. There were twelve boys and twelve girls, so he said that each of the six groups belonged to different septs, and he told the mother how they could marry, sept with sept, without doing wrong; but that if they married within their sept, worms would attack their bodies and they would die miserably.

Another story, from Motinala, connects the origin of the septs with the destruction of Lohripur by Bhimsen. According to this story some of the Agaria brothers escaped—or perhaps they were the sons of the woman who escaped—and wandered through the jungle, living where they could.

> One settled in Raigarh and worshipped Lohasur there; from him came the Marrai sept[2] (*Raigarh mē*). Another hid in the hollow of a *parsa* tree and lived on air, whence sprang the Parteti sept. A third brother lived in a tree in which a *khussera* bird had its nest, and the bird stole his iron tools. His was the Khusro sept. A fourth lived in a *mahua* tree, and became the father of the Markam sept, which worships Marra Mua, the ghosts of men killed by tigers. The fifth lived under a *tilai* tree, and he founded the Tilam sept, a sixth in the *khair* tree, whence the Keram sept which does not eat plantains (*kera*). A seventh brother went to Samaliya

[1] Actually the names Markami, Tekami and Syam are derived from the Gondi words, *marka-marra*—the mango tree, *teka-marra*—the teak tree and *soi*—the porcupine.

[2] According to Russell, Marai is a name for the goddess of cholera, who is called Marai Mata. (Russell and Hiralal, op. cit., Vol. I, p. 388.) But the *Census of India, 1931*, Vol. XII, I, p. 408, says it means a cobra, and that the Gond sept of Mandla of this name honours the cobra and will not kill it.

Pahar, and founded the Syam sept, and an eighth lived under a *dhanbahar* tree, where a *dhan* bird lived, and thus started the Dhan-chirai sept.

In Raipur, the septs spring from the son of Logundi Raja's wife, the woman who escaped from Lohripur and hid in the house of Ghunsi Gond. It will be remembered that she gave birth to twins, a brother and sister; these married and had five sons.

When these five too had children, Angarmati was born in the furnace, and spoke from it saying, 'My name is Angarmati; the names of the five brothers will not die'. So saying, she disappeared.

Then the five brothers went to the jungle, the eldest leading.[1] They came to a river, and began to cross it. The eldest brother saw a tortoise: it said, 'Don't touch me', and dived into deep water. The second met a cobra, and it said, 'You must honour me, or you will do great wrong'. The third crossed while the cobra and its wife were quarrelling, and they said, 'Don't come here: if you do, you'll fall ill'. The fourth brother went to pick the *kewāchi* fruit, and the fruit also said, 'Don't come near me, don't touch me'. The youngest brother got nothing at all, and they laughed at him saying '*Jagat*'. After this they all went home. When they kindled fire in the furnace, Raja Loha-barran Sai appeared and said, 'From now on, you are no more kin-brothers, but sib-brothers. He who saw the tortoise is called Netam,[2] he who saw the cobra is Nang, the third is Marai, the fourth is Kewachi, the fifth is Jagat.' So saying, he disappeared.

Yet one more story, from the Samnapur police-circle of the Dindori Tahsil, attributes the origin of the septs to Jwala Mukhi.

From Jwala Mukhi's left shoulder were born five daughters, and they stood in a row on his shoulder. The twelve Agaria brothers came to marry them, but Jwala Mukhi gave his five daughters to only five of the brothers, and sent the other

[1] A similar story is told by the Gond of Betul (Trench, *Grammar of Gondi*, Madras, 1921, Vol. II, p. 8).

[2] In Gondi Netam means the 'dog' sept, from the Gondi *nei*, a dog, but in some districts the members of the Gond sept of this name have the tortoise as their totem.

> seven to roam over the world and marry whom they would. From that time the Agaria have been a tribe separate from the rest. The five brothers who married Jwala Mukhi's daughters were called Marabi, Markam, Netam, Dhurwa and Korcho, and these were the fathers of the five chief Agaria septs.

In such stories as these, the Agaria can see how the institution of exogamous totemistic septs arose in the dim antiquity of his favourite myths. But many other septs have a later origin, some arising almost casually, others as the result of a crime or an accident. For example, the ancestor of the Gorku sept of the Chokh was bitten by a horse; the first members of the Sori sept stole food from a neighbour's house; the first Karri carried off his friend's wife, but was caught, tied up and thrown into a river where a *karri* fish went into his mouth.

Among the Chokh Agaria, the Dudh-Kawar trace their origin to the fact that 'they were born among the Kawar', probably meaning that at some time there was a union between a Chokh and a Kawar; the Kumunjni sept say they were born under a tree of that name; the Bhairat sept that their ancestor was born under a *bar* tree, the Gohariyar that their ancestor was born under a *gohariyar* tree; the Suri-saiyya-chirai sept that they originated beneath the nest of this bird. The Ranchirai people say that one of the first Agaria brothers, from whom they claim descent, was as quarrelsome as this bird, and they are named after it. The Manjhi sept is named after the middle Agaria brother from whom they are supposed to be descended.

Some of the septs, however, have a more elaborate theory of origin. One of the most interesting is the story which accounts for the existence and customs of the Potta sept in Mugdara village near Mawai in Mandla. Here is undoubtedly a placenta-totem, apparently confined to the Agaria, for the Gond Potta sept does not have the tradition.

> Four Gond and an Agaria went out hunting. They grew hungry and camped by the roadside to cook. The Gond had some *ghī*, and the Agaria asked them to give him a little. They refused, and the Agaria got very angry. He cooked his food quickly, ate it, and went on ahead. He

reached a great river. There was a creeper growing across from bank to bank, and by its aid he crossed over safely. Then he broke the creeper. The Gond came to the bank of the river and found the creeper broken. But a crocodile carried them across. They wanted to kill the Agaria, but he ran away and hid in the house of a Gond. The man was away, but the Agaria told the wife his story and begged her to save him. She killed a goat, and put its stomach [to represent the placenta] on a winnowing-fan, and covered the Agaria's body with blood and made him lie down beside her.

Then the four Gond came and asked, 'Where is our enemy? He must be hiding here'. The woman said, 'How should I know? Look! I have just given birth to a child'. 'Where is this child?' they shouted. 'Here it is, you may see it', she said, and showed them the Agaria covered with blood and the goat's stomach lying in the winnowing-fan. 'I have not yet washed the blood, and here is the flower [placenta].' The Gond were frightened. 'It is a monster,' so they said in their minds. 'It will be a giant when it is grown. We had better not offend it.' They said, 'But where is the father?' 'O he has gone to make a hole in the sky.' Then they were still more frightened; perhaps, they thought, the clouds will fall through the hole and kill us. So they ran away.

Thus that Agaria's sept is the Potta sept, and they eat the goat, but not its stomach. They take the stomach and give it to Lohasur, and then bury it in a hole in the ground inside the house, just as if it was the flower [placenta] of a child.

Another story from the Mawai area explains why certain members of the Parteti clan can marry within their sept.

Kariya Kuar had four sons and one daughter. He called the eldest Markam, the next Tekam, Dhurwa and the youngest Parteti. He also called the girl Parteti. Kariya Kuar died, and the four brothers quarrelled. The three eldest wanted to take the property and give none to Parteti, but kill him. So Parteti ran away and hid in a Baiga's house. When the girl grew up, the three brothers went to find her a husband. They took a sack of the grain of the *sukla* grass to the bazaar, and said, 'Whoever can tell what kind of rice this is, to him we'll give our sister'.

To that very bazaar came the boy named Parteti whom they had driven away. He was wearing shoes made of rat-skin and a hat made of monkey-skin. He kicked the sack and hurt his foot. He said, 'Will you really give me this girl?' The brothers said, 'Certainly, if you can tell us what this is'. He said, 'It is grain of *sukla* grass'. So they gave him the girl, and when they were married, he told them who he was, and that they both belonged to the Parteti *goti*. So they said he was Sadabadha Parteti, and that members of this sept could always marry one another.[1]

In the Mawai area, the members of the Khusro sept trace their origin to this incident:—

There was an Agaria boy named Khusra. He was being married. The marriage party started out, but he forgot to worship Dulha Dee. On the way back from the marriage, when he wanted to cross the threshold of his house, there was a tiger waiting, and it seized both bride and bridegroom. Everyone ran to save them but it was useless, the tiger carried them off. But one old magician there realized what had happened, and he silently offered sacrifice to Dulha Deo.

Dulha Deo was pleased and sent a *khussera* bird to wait on the road. When the tiger came by, it fought the tiger and saved the girl. But the boy was already dead. The bird took the girl back to the house. The people there said, 'This bird is *sahinām* (of the same name) as the dead boy, we must keep it as the girl's husband'. So they did, and from their union a child was born and became the ancestor of the Khusro sept.

The Bagh or Baghel sept, the tiger sept, is—as we might expect—one of the most famous and most widely diffused of all the septs. In Mawai, the Agaria have an elaborate story to explain its origin.

You ask why it is that those who belong to the Bagh sept, and worship Baghesur Pat, do not wear bangles. Listen, and I will tell you the true story.

There was a Baiga and his wife. The girl was pregnant. They went together to dig for roots. There in the jungle a boy was born. The Baiga had gone on ahead, a load of

[1] In Rewa, however, the origin of the Parteti sept was given differently. The Agaria brothers were crossing a river; one of them caught hold of a creeper, but it broke. He was drowning, but a tortoise came, and he sat on its back. In the middle of the river it sank. The Agaria promised to worship it as a god if it took him over. So it did, and this clan therefore has a tortoise totem. But among the Gond, the Parteti totem is the crocodile.

roots on his shoulder. He shouted to his wife, 'Come along, why are you so slow?' She cried, 'What can I do? I have just given birth to a boy'. The Baiga said, 'What's the use of a boy? We will have to pay bride-price for him, and he will bring us nothing. Put him down there and come along.'

So they went home with their roots. Then came a tiger and his tigress. They found the child weeping. The tigress took him and fed him with her milk. After a few days he asked for a bow and arrows.

One day four Agaria and their wives came to make charcoal. They cut the *sarai* trees, and were burning them. As the smoke rose to the sky, the tiger seized the youngest Agaria, and took him to its cave. The others ran away. On the tenth day they performed the ceremonies for his death.

But the Agaria was alive. On the eleventh day, he said to the tiger, 'If you want to eat me, eat me; otherwise let me go'. The tiger said, 'Make me twelve loads of bows and arrows, and I'll let you go, otherwise, I'll come and eat you.'

So the Agaria went home, and everyone was terrified of him till he explained what had happened. Then they were very happy. He made the bows and arrows, and put them on a path in the jungle. As he was running away, the tiger caught him, and forced him to carry the load to its cave.

Now the Agaria's wife's bangles had been broken, because they thought her husband was dead, and the tiger said to the Agaria, 'You must not put new bangles on your wife's arms, or if you do you must put them in my name'. But when he got home, he forgot all about it, and put new bangles on the girl.

The tiger's boy used to hunt daily, and brought many a fine meal for the tigers. There was a Baiga Raja there, and the tiger caught his daughter and brought her to be married to the boy. She cooked very well. One day as she was bringing water, she heard the tiger say to the tigress, 'If the flesh she cooks smells so good, how sweet would be her own'. The boy and girl decided to run away. They killed a pig, and hung up its fat, lighting a fire below. Soon there was a delicious smell. While the tigers ran to see what it was, they escaped and ran away to the Agaria's house.

The tiger followed them there, but they had hidden somewhere. The tiger saw that the Agaria's wife had put on new bangles. 'Why was not this done in my name?' It was very angry, and ate the Agaria. Since then our women do not wear glass bangles and we offer a goat to Baghesur Pat at weddings.

The Asur Agaria of Matin Zamindari derive their septs from Logundi Raja.

Logundi Raja had many pets. He had a pair of *kerketa* birds, a pair of jungle dogs, a pair of tigers. One day, from the jungle dogs a boy and a girl were born. From the tigers a boy and a girl were born. The birds laid two eggs, and they cracked and a boy and a girl came out. One day Logundi Raja went to kill fish, and got an eel (*aind*) and brought it home. Before cooking it, he cut it into bits, and out came a boy and a girl. Logundi Raja and all his pets died, and only the children were left. They took the names of the septs, Kerketa, Baghel, Sonwani and Aindhar according as they were born from the birds, the tigers, the jungle dogs and the eel. They got married. Logundi Raja himself had a son and a daughter, and these ground *haldi*, and anointed the others for their marriage, and were known as Haldi-Sonwani.

Another version of the origin of the Aind sept was given us in Pachra village of Matin.

An Asur girl gave birth to a snake; it was like a child, it drank her milk and lived in the house. There were two brothers. The girl married the elder; when the younger brother married, the snake called his wife *bhai bahu*. That girl wore *bichhia*-ornaments on her toes and they tinkled as she walked. The snake used to sleep in the hearth, in the inner oven: when it heard the ornaments, it knew fire would be lit and it escaped. One day the girl was making mud and she took off her ornaments. When she brought fire that day there was no warning sound. The snake was burnt to death. She had killed her *jeth* [husband's elder brother]. Since then those of the Aind sept do not wear *bichhia* and only make a simple hearth without an inner chamber.

The God-dhuka of Raipur have their own version of the origin of the Gorku sept which differs from that given by the Chokh of Bilaspur. In Raipur they say:

Long ago, our ancestors went to the jungle to burn wood for charcoal, and a horse was caught by the flames and died.

The people took it home with them and said it was sambhar flesh. A man picked up a bit of the flesh and tasted it. A friend saw it and laughed at him, 'You are eating horse-flesh!' Then they threw it all away. But the man who had tasted the flesh became the father of the Gorku sept which does not ride on horses.

In these stories, the Agaria find the origin, the reason, the theory of their totemism, and because it is vitalized by a theory, this institution, which must often be inconvenient enough, survives.

We must now consider the rules governing the different septs. The first of these is, of course, that there must be no marriage within the sept. We have seen that one section of the Parteti *goti*, the Sadabadha, has a sound mythological reason for ignoring this rule. There may be intermarriage between all the septs, except between Marabi and Tekam who are considered to be *bhai-bhai* or related as brothers. I have not yet been able to discover the reason for this.

What we may call the second rule governs the reverence to be paid to the totem plant or animal. These totems are sometimes, as we have seen, based on a direct connexion between the sept ancestors and the totem object—as when the first Gorku ate horse-flesh by mistake. They are often based on a curious punning relationship, sometimes fantastic and far-fetched. In Rewa, for example, the Dhurwa sept is regarded as connected with the *dhauhara* tree, and its members make a wooden sword of its branches, and use it to kill any pig or goat offered in sacrifice. The Marabi sept in Rewa has an equally far-fetched etymology: it is supposed to be derived from *maruka garh*, the fort of the dead, and when an animal dies of its own accord, they do not eat it. When they offer any animal to their godlings, they do not eat it. It is said that in the old days when any member of this sept gave rice to a sacrificial animal, it died of its own accord. But now, owing to 'sin', that is, plough-cultivation, the godlings are defiled, and this no longer happens. In Uprora, the Gorku sept do not make grain-bins standing on wooden posts called *goda*, for their first ancestor hid under a horse and was bitten by it. Even more fantastic are the derivations I have already quoted—the connexion between *mahua*, Markam and Marra Mua, or between *khair*, Keram and *kera*, or between *marka* and Markam, or *parchi* and Parteti.

In other cases the connexion is more obvious. In Raipur, members of the Jal sept must not eat any fish that has been caught in a net (*jal*). The Kewachi sept do not pick the flower of that name, the Kukra sept do not eat the cock (*kukra*). The members of the Nang sept never kill a cobra, and at Dashara make a small image of a cobra out of mud, and offer it milk and a speckled hen. The Karri sept must not eat the *karri* fish or steal other men's wives, for reasons given in the story of their origin. The Marrai sept do not go where there is a quarrel (*marrai*). The Kosmiha sept avoids the *kosam* fruit: 'it is our god'. The Kerketa sept of Asur Agaria must not eat the *kerketa* bird, nor the Aindwar sept the eel, nor the Kachhuwa sept the tortoise. Members of the Asur Munjni sept must not cut or sit below the tree of that name. The Nonha sept could hardly avoid salt altogether, but they have a rule that when a man dies or a feast is given salt is taboo.

Among the Chokh Agaria, members of the Parsa sept must not cut or injure the *parsa* tree, and those of the Kumunjni sept must not eat the leaves or use the oil extracted from the *kumjun* or *anjun* tree. The Ranchirai sept must not kill a *sursa* bird or a sparrow.

The Potta sept of Mawai, as we have seen, may eat goat but not the stomach which represents the placenta, and this must be buried, as if it were a placenta, inside the house.

Most of the septs have the rule that if their totem-object is killed or damaged, they should observe some of the signs of mourning. If a Kawar neighbour dies, members of the Dudh-Kawar sept break their pots as a sign of kinship and sorrow. The Parsa sept do the same if they hear of any *parsa* tree being injured even by accident. When a tiger is killed, members of the Bagh or Baghel sept break their pots, fast, and sometimes

Photo by G. C. F. Ramsden, I.C.S.

10. Scene on the River Hasdeo in the Uprora Zamindari.

11. Chinnibinni, Agaria girl of Pandpur, Mandla District, in dancing-dress.

shave their heads. The Markam sept mourns for the tortoise, the Tekam sept for the fallen teak tree, the Parteti generally for the crocodile.

Various other rules attaching to different septs may be noticed. The Sori sept of Raipur originated when its ancestor stole food from a neighbour's house. So now whenever anyone sends them food, they put a little on the fire before eating. The Netam sept of Raipur (though not elsewhere) also believe that they originated when their ancestor stole fire and *urad dāl*, rice and water from a neighbour's house. So now they must grind *urad* and rice to make *chila roti* and offer it in sacrifice.

The Baghel sept in Mawai must not wear glass bangles, for reasons given in the story already quoted. The Baghel generally believe they have a special affinity with tigers, that no tiger will injure them, and that at weddings Baghesur Pat, the Tiger-Spirit, comes upon one of them. Extraordinary scenes may be witnessed at weddings of this sept, when a man possessed by the Tiger-Spirit leaps upon a goat, tears its throat with his teeth and drinks the hot blood.

The Chhote-chirai sept of the Chokh Agaria has a special rule for marriages. Instead of putting the vermilion mark along the parting of the hair, as other people do, the bridegroom takes a little dust from his heel and puts it on the forehead of his bride. She then does the same for him. The reason is said to be that once a man fell dead while applying the vermilion mark.

The Sonwani sept has special duties. Among the Agaria I have recorded three divisions of this sept, the Son Sonwani, the Haldi Sonwani and the Kari Sonwani.[1] The special duty of the Sonwani, which exists in many Chhattisgarh tribes, is to admit back into social communion those who have been temporarily excommunicated. The following account was given in Daldal (Karanjia):—

[1] The Dhanwar, who are the Agaria's neighbours in Bilaspur, have a Rakat Sonwani sept in addition to these. Their duty is to give, at a re-admission ceremony, a little of the blood of the sacrificed fowl to the penitent.

> When a man is outcaste he does not go to the river. He shaves his head, and prepares bread in his house. Then one of the Son Sonwani sept brings a pot of water in his hand and a coconut. He puts the coconut down, offers fire and incense, and 'feeds' it with pulse and rice. Sometimes the coconut breaks of its own accord: then we know that the man has done a great wrong and we run away. If it doesn't break, we put a gold ornament in the water, and the Son Sonwani sprinkles the water over the offender and the house. The Sonwani must first eat from the offender's hands; it is he who eats the sin.

The Haldi Sonwani also has an important social function: he gives *haldi* water to the mourners at a funeral. The Kari Sonwani sept has a black cow as its totem animal.

Many attempts have been made to explain the origin of totemism. Herbert Spencer thought that it arose from a misinterpretation of nicknames—and some of the punning totems given in this chapter tend to support his view. Haddon considered that totems were originally the animals or plants on which groups of people lived and were so named by their neighbours. One of Frazer's discarded suggestions was that totemism originated in the belief in the 'external soul', whereby a person puts his soul in some external object for safe keeping.

A later theory of Frazer's is that totemism originated in a primitive explanation of conception and child-birth, the totem being the object which overshadowed the mother and made her pregnant. This might possibly be true for such aborigines of Australia and the Trobriand Islanders as have no knowledge of physiological paternity, but it throws little light on the Agaria mind.

In all discussions about totemism I think insufficient attention has been paid to the Indian evidence and to the light which folk-tales can throw upon the subject. In India everywhere, and certainly among the Agaria, we can see the strength of the fears which may so easily gather round inanimate objects. In the folk-tales we see these objects endowed with life and speech and acting in a sometimes hostile, sometimes friendly, way on human affairs. It is very common for a house which has been the scene of ill-luck or death to be deserted: a bed on which someone has died must not be used again; a stream by which someone has fallen ill is afterwards avoided.

The Agaria stories suggest some such quite obvious and simple origin for totemism. Someone is bitten by a horse and he and his children first avoid and then honour the horse so that they will not be bitten again. Probably the many sections of the Bagh or Baghel sept are composed of the descendants of people who, long ago, were killed by tigers.

But whatever the origin of the totems, they are still important to the Agaria mind. They keep him free from kin- and clan-incest, and link him closely with the animal and material world. How close that union is may be seen in a study of the folk-tales, of which many incidents have a totemistic basis.

CHAPTER V

MYTH

I. *Introductory*

The mythology of the Agaria seems to me of quite unusual interest, both for itself and because it so obviously directs and vitalizes the life of the tribe. These legends are not a mere interesting addition or decoration, an optional subject which we might omit; they are the root and life of the religious and economic structure of Agaria society.

One myth, for example, gives the economic basis for the cult of the godlings or demons of the smithy, establishes a tariff of sacrifices and suggests reasons for possible failure of the iron. Probably one reason why the tribe has clung so long to a faulty technique of iron-smelting is that this is fully established in the myths, and without a new mythology it may be difficult to persuade the smelters to adopt new methods. The making of fire and charcoal, the manufacture of bellows, tongs and hammer, the use of a charge without flux, the importance of the fine *kodon* chaff, are established and explained in ancient myths.

Religious observances find their sanction in these stories. The worship of each of the special Agaria demons originates in historical moments and practical necessities: the Wind must be honoured, or the bellows will not work; Fire must be worshipped, or the coal will remain dead and black. The duty of ancestor-worship is established in a vivid story from Raipur.

Social relations also depend on the myths: the sole survivor from Lohripur took refuge in a Gond's house, and ever since the Agaria have eaten from the Gond. Through Kariya Kuar, who married the daughter of Nanga Baiga, the Agaria have a link with the Baiga and many of their women (in Mandla) dress and adorn themselves in Baiga fashion. In

Raipur, the God-dhuka attribute their change of name to an incident in their legendary past. Like the Baiga, the Agaria attribute their poverty to an actual moment in history. But where poverty was a blessing and an honour to the Baiga, given them by God himself, it was a curse to the Agaria, the curse of their old enemy, the Sun.

The story of Creation follows the Baiga pattern,[1] but adds a number of new details. From the very beginning, the Sun appears as the enemy of man and withers the great lotus-leaf with which God tries to make the world. The incident of the crow sucking two-and-a-half drops of the Creator's milk does not occur in the Baiga myth, nor do we read there of the baby Nanga Baiga playing on a fiddle stringed with his own hair. The Agaria version of the first driving of the nail attributes to Nanga Baiga great sacrifice and courage, for he cuts off his own finger and drives it into the ground.

The Agaria myth admits the priority of the Baiga. Nanga Baiga was born from the side of a great crab, and Agar Sai was created to make him nails. In another story, Nanga Baiga broke open the rock from which emerged the Agaria godlings. The creation of the Gond and Hindu races occurred much later.

The most significant thing about the Iron City of the Agaria is its destruction. God gets the better of the simple Agaria king by deceit, as he later tricks the simple Agaria magicians. The treachery of the Gods is also a feature of Baiga mythology. We have already mentioned how the age-long war between Deva and Asura began with a similar act of deceit on the part of Vishnu.

It is interesting to note how the first Agaria kings ate iron and apparently enjoyed it. There was a strict taboo on water, the introduction of which brought the first kingdom to its ruin. The struggle with the Pandava brothers for the possession of the *sarai* tree may reflect ancient conflicts with Hindu zamindars over the right to make charcoal from its

[1] See *The Baiga*, pp. 308ff.

wood. There is another echo of the Pandava (or is it a relic of some tradition of fraternal polyandry?) in the story of Angarmati who was sister and wife to the twelve Agaria brothers.

The myths give tantalizing glimpses of an earlier technique of iron-smelting: there are many references to leaf-covered bellows; one description, of a bellows made from leaf-baskets with bamboo sticks in the sides, sounds like an experimental piston-bellows. We read too of a process by which ore and coal were piled together, plastered with mud and fired without blast. Sabar Sai apparently extracted iron from ore in an open hearth. The first Agaria, we are told, used their knees as anvils and hammered the iron with their fists. The invention of hammer and tongs is ascribed to Hindu influence—in other words, to Mahadeo—who, curiously enough, also teaches the use of cow-hide instead of leaves as a covering for the bellows.

I need not draw further attention to the many points of interest in these myths. The student of human sacrifice, of the origin of fire, of primitive notions of religion will find many things to remark and note. Along with the stories given in this chapter, there should also be studied the myths relating to the origin of totems and the exogamous septs, and one account of the origin of magic in Chapter VI.

The Agaria myths are confused and contradictory. Their heroes blend into one another and change their character and even their sex—Lohasur, for example, is sometimes male and sometimes female. But they are alive. And so long as they live, the primitive smelting industry cannot altogether die. Lohasur must have his temple, and Agyasur be honoured in the virgin fire.

II. *The Creation of the World*

The Agaria Creation myth as told in Mandla follows with certain variations the outline of the Baiga story. In Kareli village near Mawai, we were told how

> God first made the world by laying a great lotus leaf on the face of the water. But the Sun arose and withered that leaf with his heat.

Then God made the world of lac. But when he climbed on it, it broke into a thousand pieces.

At last, from the dirt of his breast God made a crow, and allowed it to suck his milk two-and-a-half times, saying, 'Now you've drunk my milk, you'll never hunger nor thirst; you and I will search for the earth together'.

So away, away, away went that crow, till it grew weary and thought, 'My father is my enemy: he created me only to kill me'. So thinking, she fell on the body of Kekramal Chhatri, the great crab. Kekramal Chhatri went down below the water and found Nal Raja and Nal Rani sleeping. They had slept for twelve years. He shook them awake. Nal Raja said, 'Nizam Raja has the earth, not me'. But Kekramal Chhatri squeezed his throat till he vomited up the earth in little balls. So the crow took the earth back to his father, and God made the world.

Five years passed, then Nanga Baiga and Nanga Baigin were born out of a crack in the ground. Nanga Baiga said to Mother Earth, 'Mother, where is my fiddle (*bāja*)?' She said, 'Child you are yet but a navel and a cord; what need is there of a fiddle?' So said Mother Earth. But on that day Basin Kaniya (the Bamboo Maiden) was born, and Nanga Baiga went to cut the bamboo, in one breath, above and below. So he made his fiddle with his own hair for strings, and played it, and God's seat shook with the sound. Then God knew that the Baiga were born, and sent to call them. But his messenger found Nanga Baiga asleep in a winnowing-fan. Mother Earth said, 'Don't go, my son', but Nanga Baiga took his fiddle and went. God said to him, 'Drive your nails into the earth to make it steady'. But Nanga Baiga had no nails, so he cut off the little finger of his right hand and drove that into the ground. But God was not satisfied. 'I want strong pillars', he said.

So Nanga Baiga called Agyasur and worshipped him, and Agyasur flamed up with great flames, and from the fire an Agaria was born. Since we Agaria were born from fire, we never fear it, and can beat the slag from the glowing iron with our hands. Then that Agaria made twelve pillars of Virgin Iron and set them at the four corners of the world, and it became steady, and God sowed seeds everywhere.

In a village near Karanjia, however, we heard how Nanga Baiga first tried to fix the earth in place with a bamboo nail, but without success. 'So he went to look for iron, and in a far corner of the earth, he found Sabar Sai blowing leaf-bellows and making iron in a great fire. "What are you doing?" asked Nanga Baiga. "I had a dream", said Sabar Sai, "that you couldn't steady the earth with a bamboo nail, so I am making you an iron one". He gave five nails of Virgin Iron to the Baiga. When God heard of it, he was very pleased, and gave Sabar Sai the city of Lohripur.'

A variant of this story comes from a Chokh Agaria of Chhuri Zamindari—and it is important to note that the story in its main outline is known as far east as this. After relating the adventures of the crow and the discovery of earth below the sea, our Chokh informant went on to say how

> when God found the earth was still unsteady, he went to Kekramal Chhatri the crab. This crab brought Nanga Baiga out of its right side and Nanga Baigin out of its left side saying, 'These two will worship the earth as their goddess, and fix it in place with nails'. But as God did not know how nails were made, he created Agar Sai from the dirt rubbed from his skin, and gave him all the implements for his smithy. Agar Sai blew his bellows, but the iron did not flow. A shower of sparks flew up, and from the sparks appeared a girl. She began to weep. Agar Sai said, 'This is Tilmati'. But God said, 'If this girl blows your bellows, the iron will flow, and it will be Virgin Iron fit for the nails we need'.
>
> Then Tilmati blew the bellows, and the iron came. Agar Sai made five great pillars,[1] four for each corner of the world, and one for the middle. Nanga Baiga drove nails from above through the earth into the pillars, and the earth was made steady.
>
> Then God went again to the crab and said, 'Now the earth is ready, but there are no living creatures for it'. Kekramal Chhatri pulled five living creatures (*jiv*) out of his side. The first was called Gond, and the others became all the tribes living in the world.

In Dawalpur (Mawai) the Agaria say that when Nanga Baiga needed the Virgin Iron for the nails, he got a great stone

[1] Early Egyptian mythology describes the sky as a rectangular plate of iron, supported at each corner by a pillar. The throne of the supreme God is also made of iron. See Budge, *History of Egypt* (London, 1902), p. 136.

and broke it. Out of the stone came Lohasur, and out of the spark came Agyasur, and then as they broke the stone again and again, came Koelasur and Dhua Dharni. Lohasur himself made the nails of Virgin Iron, and Nanga Baiga drove them into the earth.

In Lapha Zamindari, among the Chokh Agaria, I found a similar cycle of tales, but there the fish called Raghuman took the place of Kekramal Chhatri the crab. When the crow asked the Fish Raghuman for the earth, it said, 'There is no earth here. You must go to Dhurrapur (the City of Dust) where the King-Worm is and get it from him.' The Crow said, 'I cannot go there; you must get it for me'. At that the Fish went to Dhurrapur and caught the Worm, and squeezed the earth out of its body. Then the Crow took the earth to God who sprinkled it on the waters and the earth was made.

An Asur Agaria story of Singia village in Uprora Zamindari also mentions Dhurrapur, but preserves a wholly different account of the Creation.

> At first there was no city but Dhurrapur. There lived Dhundi Rakshin and her daughter Hiraman. Hiraman swung to and fro in a golden swing. She kept as a pet a mud parrot in a golden cage.
>
> One day a sadhu cursed her. 'When Rama comes and touches your parrot, it will be turned into the earth.' So said the sadhu.
>
> In the sea was the Fish Raghuman. From its belly a boy was born. But the boy could not live under water, and said, 'Mother, take me somewhere where I can live and eat and breathe'. So Raghuman sent the boy to Dhurrapur.
>
> Hiraman was twelve years old and very beautiful. She was swinging in her golden swing. The boy caught it and stopped it. She tried to go on swinging, but he stopped her. She said, 'Why have you come here? If my mother sees you, she will eat you'. The boy said, 'My life is in your hands'. So she hid him in a golden grain-bin.
>
> Above the waters the great lotus blossomed, whence Rama was born. Presently a dream came down to the hidden boy that Rama was born and coming to Dhurrapur. After a few days Rama did come and fought with the

Rakshin and conquered her. She said, 'Don't kill me, and I'll give you anything you want'.

'Then give me the mud parrot in the golden cage', said Rama. But when Rama touched the parrot, it turned at once into the great world. There were only these living creatures, and from the boy and Hiraman all other creatures were born.

An Agaria living near the Udaipur-Surguja border recalled a tradition that when Mahadeo created all living beings out of earth, some earth remained uncreated and unshaped. Out of this earth, he created the Agaria. He then breathed life into all creatures and they began to move.

III. *The Kingdom of Logundi Raja*

Of the origin of the Agaria, we have no very clear account; they were born from fire, or from the sparks of a broken stone; in one myth we are told that Agar Sai was created from the dirt rubbed from the skin of God. But there are many stories about the kingdom of the first Agaria Raja, Logundi,[1] and his city Lohripur.[2] There is also much detailed, if conflicting, information about its destruction. The old kingdom was a golden age for the Agaria; there was little work; the smiths

[1] Logundi, as Raja of Lohrigarh in the hill of Dhoragaon, is known in Udaipur State. He was the founder of the Agaria or Chokh tribe. His queen was Tingamati. He is regarded as identical with Lohasur by some, with Agar Sai by others. In Kumarta village, Chokh Agaria immigrants from Surguja believe that Agar Sai reigned in Lohitpur. He built a fort and many tanks. He was a great iron-smelter and the first of the Agaria.

[2] There is an iron village in the Krishna legend called Lohaban, where the demon Lohajangha is killed by the god. He is represented by an ancient red-sandstone image and has offerings of iron made to him. (Penzer, Vol. I, p. 139). In Beal's *Buddhist Records of the Western World* (London, 1884), Vol. II, pp. 240ff., Hiuen Tsiang describes how 'in the midst of a great iron city of the island Ratnadvīpa was the dwelling of the Rākshasi women (Lo-t'sa)', who used to allure mariners to their fate, 'sharing all sorts of pleasure with them, then shutting them up in an iron prison and devouring them at leisure' This iron city was at last destroyed by Simhala, and the island became Simhala or Ceylon. So too in the Celtic tale of the voyage of Mailduna, the adventurers approach an island inhabited by gigantic blacksmiths. One throws with his tongs a bit of glowing iron at the curragh, but misses. *Folk-Lore*, Vol. XIX, p. 174.

lived on red-hot iron; they had vast supernatural powers. The fall of their kingdom is attributed to different causes. Some say it was due to the jealousy of Bhagavan; others that it came about as a result of a war with the five Pandava brothers —an obvious echo of the long conflict between the Aryans and the aboriginal tribes; others again that it was due to the enmity of the Sun. But, however it was caused, the old kingdom collapsed, the ancient glory departed, the Agaria lost their superhuman powers. It is significant that it was a Gond, a fellow-aboriginal, who saved the sole survivor of Lohripur.

The Mandla myth refers the conflict to God himself.

Agar Sai was the father of Sabar Sai, who was the father of Logundi Raja, who was the father of Jwala Mukhi, who was the father of Kariya Kuar. God gave Sabar Sai the city of Lohripur; it was a city of blacksmiths. Logundi was the eldest of twelve brothers, but there was only one girl: she was Angarmati, she was most beautiful, she was the wife of them all. After Sabar Sai died, Logundi became Raja of Lohripur.

Lohripur was a city twenty-four miles long and twenty-four miles broad. For twenty-four miles the road was made of iron plates. When the brothers blew their bellows, the road glowed red, and they used to pick up the glowing iron that was liquid as rice-water and drink it. There was no food or water in Lohripur and because of the fire no traveller could approach.

Now all over the world there is a twelve years' famine: Annadeo (god of grain) hides in the jungle of *sukla* grass. God has a store of food to last two-and-a-half years; he gives this to the world. Everyone goes to him for food. But no one goes from Lohripur. Then God thinks, 'Everyone but Logundi Raja has come to me. This Raja must be greater than I.' Thus thinking he falls asleep and sees in a dream that Logundi Raja is eating iron, and when he awakes he thinks and thinks what he can do with such a man.

At last he goes to Sukhi Chamarin the Witch and consults her. The witch says, 'Well, I have magic that will cool hot iron'. So God goes with the witch to Lohripur, and she makes the glowing road dark and cold so that they can go along it safely. God takes the form of a beggar and goes first to Logundi Raja's youngest brother, and asks for something to eat. The boy brings out a great pile of red-hot iron bars and a dish of iron shavings (this was their rice) and sets it before him. It is Virgin Iron; Sukhi Chamarin has no power over it: it glows red; it is very hot. But God says 'I can't eat without washing my hands'. The Agaria asks, 'What is this "washing"?' 'What? Don't you wash?' asks the beggar-God. 'Of course not,' says the Agaria. 'O ho!' says God. 'This is a disgraceful thing! What a filthy fellow you must be! Go and wash and bring me some water too.'

So Logundi Raja's youngest brother goes for water—for the Agaria will always do as they are told, provided it is to their disadvantage, so foolish are they—and directly he touches the water, his body loses its power and he is no longer able to eat hot iron.

Then God plays the same trick in turn on each of the Raja's brothers, until at last he comes to Logundi himself. The Raja is seated on a great iron chair, but God persuades him to come down and fetch him water.

But when Logundi Raja returns with the water, he finds that the beggar has disappeared. Then the twelve brothers themselves feel hungry, and blow their bellows till the iron runs red and liquid like gruel (*pej*), but when they put it in their mouths it burns them and they are killed. But the girl who was their wife, and pregnant, only took a little of the burning iron and she ran and ran and ran burning with the fire till she came to a Gond's house. There on the verandah was a big pot full of buttermilk, and the girl jumped into it and was cooled and saved. So now whenever an Agaria is burnt he puts buttermilk on the wound. And because we were saved by the Gond's pot, we have always eaten from the hands of the Gond.

Such is the myth most commonly known in the neighbourhood of Bajag and Karanjia. But in Mawai as well as in the Chhuri, Korba and Lapha Zamindaris of Bilaspur—and possibly elsewhere—it is Bhimsen and the Pandava [1] who destroy the ancient kingdom. This is the Mawai version of the story:—

[1] While the Agaria regard the Pandava as their enemies, the Lohar of Garhwal 'regard as the founder of their caste one Kaliya Lohar, who is supposed to have supplied the Pandava with their fighting weapons, and he is now propitiated before each smelting operation with an offer of five pieces of charcoal'.—*R.G.S.I.*, Vol. XLVI, p. 120. It is tempting to compare Kaliya Lohar with the Agaria Kariya Kuar, but both names—each meaning literally blacksmith—are sufficiently obvious to have an independent origin.

12. (*a*) Mahali Asur woman from Singhia showing characteristic tattoo marks on the arm.

(*b*) Married Agaria woman from Gaura, Mandla District.

13. Khuntia Chokh girl from Nunera, Bilaspur District.

As Lohasur and Dhua Dharni were blowing their bellows, Agar Sai was born in the furnace. After him was Sabar Sai. Then Kankalin Mata was born in Kalkapur and she married Sabar Sai, and from them were born the twelve Agaria brothers, the thirteen Tamesur brothers and fourteen Kansasur brothers. Of these Logundi and Bhoirgundi were the eldest. They made a kingdom of seven forts, in the very heart of which they hid the *sarai* tree. The first fort had a river round it, the second was of iron, the third of mud, the fourth of cow-dung, the fifth of brick, the sixth of stone, the seventh of wood. Inside the seventh was the *sarai* tree.

Now came Bhimsen [1] and his brothers to find the flower of the *sarai*. They fought the Agaria and broke down the seven forts, driving the Agaria south to Mandla. For where there are *sarai* trees there will you find Agaria; where there is no *sarai*, there are Lohar who make charcoal even from bamboos.

This is a version of the story from the Patharia Agaria; the Khuntia Chokh Agaria of Chhuri and Korba have a similar myth.

At first the twelve Agaria brothers made a kiln like the kilns in which bricks are made; they put the coal and the ore together in a pile and plastered it over with mud and set fire to it. There was no blast. Nor was it charcoal, but the coal they use in the railway.

The two eldest brothers were Logundi Raja and Bhoirgundi, they were sons of Sabar Sai, the son of Agar Sai. In those days, wherever there was coal in the country, there was Logundi Raja's furnace. Much of the liquid iron sank into the ground, and was wasted. What remained

[1] Bilaspur and Mandla are full of stories about Bhimsen. In Chhuri, the Dhitori Hill is Bhimsen's *dhitori*-basket. He had stopped up a river and a great fish jumped out and fled from him across the land. Near Deori-Chicholi he killed it and cut it into sixteen pieces: the great stones may still be seen. In Lapha, Bhimsen killed a *gaur* with his spear. One of the *gaur's* testes broke and turned into stone. The spear too stuck in the earth and though they tried to pull it out with elephants, nothing would move it. Near Nunera I saw a shrine to Bhimsen. In Mandla, the Gond tell how Bhimsen again and again tried to stay the current of the Narbada River, and near Karanjia two remarkable hills Lingo and Dhuti represent loads from his shoulders. At Bhimkundi, his huge footstep may be seen in the rock.

was red, and people used to eat it, hot as it was. Iron was then made for food, not for weapons.

The excreta of the Agaria was fiery like their food, and when they relieved themselves in the jungle they started great fires. So the twelve brothers thought, 'If we spread iron all over the ground near our city, an iron floor, then our excreta won't start fires'.

Logundi Raja had the flower of the *sarai* tree; he kept it with honour and love. This was desired by Bhimsen. But he couldn't enter the city for fear of being burnt by the red-hot iron floor all round it. There was no water there. So he dug under the ground, and brought up springs of water that cooled the floor; then he entered the city and killed all the brothers. Only a woman escaped. As he passed by, the shadow of Bhimsen fell on her, and she became pregnant, and her child got all the strength of Bhimsen. That child was Kariya Kuar.

Of Kariya Kuar we shall hear more presently. I will add one other version of this story, a Khuntia Chokh tale from the village of Dumarkachhar in Lapha Zamindari.

God created Aginjhar to make iron nails for Rikki Muni. They built a furnace and made bellows of leaves, and made five nails of Virgin Iron. Rikki Muni married Aginjhar; it was the first of marriages, and they had two sons. Their eldest son was hungry; he said, 'What can I eat?' Aginjhar said, 'Eat that red stuff in front of you'. It was molten iron from the furnace. He dipped his fingers into it as if it were honey, and sucked them. Then he was called Lohasur. The younger son made a *sabar* (iron bar) to dig with and was called Sabar Sai.

God came to see what the two boys were doing. But Sabar Sai had laid great iron plates all round their city, and God could not approach. But from afar he saw one brother picking up the red-hot iron bars and chewing them, and the other bending the iron with his bare hands. He called that city Lohripur.

Each brother had twelve sons. They shut up Rikki Muni in an iron grain-bin to stop him eating iron. Now came the five Pandava brothers to get the *sarai* flower, for it was only with this that they could win Ahibarran as their bride, but the iron floor was too hot for them. So Bhimsen caught a *tareli* rat, as big as a hill, and sent it to make a burrow from the sea to Lohripur. The rat made a hole up to the city and all round it, and presently the water rushed in and cooled the iron, so that Bhimsen was able to go and fight the brothers. He caught six of the Asur brothers and six of the Sabar brothers, and put them into the furnace and stamped on the bellows till they were consumed by the heat. The rest escaped.

Bhimsen took the *sarai* flower to his brothers, and they returned rejoicing. But Lohripur was a ruined city, and the waters flooded it.[1] The iron floated away to every corner of the earth. To this day there is an island where once Lohripur was; it is black and called Kalapatpar. So we always consider the rat our enemy, and when we see one we try to kill and eat it. Lohripur is in Raigarh.

God went to find the scattered brothers. He found them hiding in the jungle. He said that Lohasur's sons were to be Asur, and Sabar Sai's sons were to be Chokh.

These incidents are mentioned in a Karma song from the same village.

The twelve brothers are working at the furnaces,
But the red iron will not cool.
Twelve, twelve, twenty-four *kos* they hammered the iron-plates.
O Logundi Raja Ho!
The twenty-one iron rafters! The twenty-one iron doors!
O the iron nails Ho!
There's a channel for the sea.
O Logundi Raja Ho!
Bhimsen broke that nail of iron.
Then was Lohripur flooded.
O Logundi Raja Ho!

IV. *The War with the Sun*

We come now to another cycle of stories, practically confined to Mandla, which attributes the destruction of Lohripur to the great war with the Sun. A taboo on working iron under the direct rays of the sun is known in Africa. It is stringently

[1] Murray (op. cit., p. 80) traces Munda tradition back to Azamgarh and adds, 'by the reign of Ram Chandra of Ayodhya the Raj Bhars appear to have been the only tribe left at Azamgarh and before the departure of the Savaras, or Asuras, as they were then called, both Hindu and Munda traditions record a deluge'.

enforced by the Agaria of Mandla, less so in Bilaspur and Raipur. The Chokh of Udaipur State often make their kilns facing west so that the sun's rays will not fall on them. 'The shadow of the sun spoils the iron. The sun does not like the work of the Asur.' In Mandla it is believed that if the sun shines on the kiln, the kiln will burst; if it shines on iron while being worked on the anvil, the iron will prove brittle or mis-shaped. 'Midday iron' is always useless.

In Mandla, therefore, it is Narayan Deo or Suraj Deo, the Sun God, who is the enemy. The sun was originally the great round pan of red-hot iron that surrounded Lohripur. This was lifted up by God and set in the sky to shine there. The sun itself, therefore, is iron. [1]

This cycle of stories attributes the destruction of Lohripur not to water, but to fire. Some say that the fire was started as the great burning plate was being lifted off the earth; all the trees and grass caught fire as it passed. Others trace the disaster to a direct conflict between the Agaria brothers and the Sun.

> The Sun went to Logundi Raja's house at Lohripur. There was an iron door, but it broke to pieces at the Sun's approach. All the iron houses turned to ashes as the Sun went by. Logundi Raja came and begged him to spare them. 'I am less than you', he said, 'I admit it'. But the Sun smote him with his rays, and as the Raja lay dying, he cursed the iron that had betrayed him, saying, 'Before the Sun you will always have to bend'.

Another version describes how Logundi Raja had one daughter who was very beautiful. There was a great battle between the Sun and the Agaria on her account, and Logundi Raja put out one of the Sun's eyes. Then the Sun took his full fiery shape and burnt Logundi Raja and destroyed his kingdom with fire. The wife of the twelve brothers, who was pregnant, had gone to another village. When she returned, she was caught by the Sun and burst into flames. But she

[1] So too the stars are sparks from Logundi Raja's anvil. The moon is the *tarki*-ornament from Logundi Raja's wife's ear. Lightning falls from the sun: it is the excreta or slag of the sun.

ran to a Gond's house; there was a pot of buttermilk there, she jumped into it and was saved. The next day she gave birth to a son under a *chhindi*-palm tree, and he was called Jwala Mukhi in memory of the rescue of his mother.

The story goes on to describe how Jwala Mukhi[1] avenged his father's death, and brings us into that widely-spread complex of stories which explain the Sun's eclipse, and in which Jwala Mukhi the Agaria plays the part of Rahu the Asura who devoured the Sun.

Jwala Mukhi grew up and played with the boys of his village; they shot birds and hares with their arrows. When the boys killed anything, they used to cry 'Good for father', but when Jwala Mukhi killed anything he cried 'Good for mother'. Presently the other boys began to say, 'Jwala Mukhi has no father: we shouldn't eat with him'. When Jwala Mukhi heard this he was very angry and went to his mother and asked her what it was about. 'Son, you have no father?' she said and told him of his twelve fathers who had been killed by the Sun.

'Where does this Sun live?' then asked Jwala Mukhi. 'Beyond the seven seas and the sixteen rivers, my son, live the Sun and Moon; every day at dawn they play with the sand on the shore of the great ocean.'

That night Jwala Mukhi did not sleep; he built a great furnace; he made a mighty lump of *kuāri lohā* (Virgin Iron) and from this he fashioned an iron net and an iron cage—it was like a seven-storied house of iron. In the morning he said to his mother, 'Give me food for twelve years, and in the thirteenth year I will return'.

And then he went away towards the east, across the seven seas and the sixteen rivers till he came to the shore of the great ocean. There he hid among the sand and waited.

[1] Jwala Mukhi means 'Mouth of Fire' and is the name of a pilgrim-place in the Lower Himalayas, where fire comes from the ground. Sati, wife of Siva, is said to have created this and burnt herself in it. Abbott records a Hindu charm against cold or fever from Bombay: the word

JVA
LA
MUKHI

with a certain combination of minerals is tied to the neck of the sufferer. J. Abbott, *The Keys of Power*, p. 521.

At dawn the Sun came to play with the Moon, and Jwala Mukhi caught him, as fishermen catch fish, in his net, and shut him up in the iron cage. So the whole world was dark and everyone went to look for the Sun, but they couldn't find him.

Then they called for the blind Pawan Daseri, the Wind; he found a tiny crack in the iron cage, and crept inside and there was the Sun.

When the Sun came out and saw Jwala Mukhi, they cursed each other. 'Go to your wife', said Jwala Mukhi. 'You will only meet her during her period.' And so it is that only when the Moon is full and red that the Sun can meet her. And the Sun said to Jwala Mukhi, 'All the wealth you earn from iron shall disappear like ashes'. Therefore the Agaria have always been poor. When the Sun said that, he went away full of anger. He saw an Agaria with his wife, and kicked them and knocked them over. That Agaria also cursed him, saying, 'If you ever go to your wife, you will die'. Thus the Sun only sees his wife in her period and he can never go to her. And he hates the Agaria who gave him this curse.[1]

[1] The Agaria stories are full of picturesque details about the Sun. In a Chokh tale from Lapha, Ashtangi Mata is impregnated by his rays. 'As I rose into the sky, my seed fell hot upon her, and boils arose in her hands whence the five gods (i.e. Rama, Sita, Brahma, Mahadeo and Parvati) were born.' The Agaria of Angai in Mandla tell how the Sun and Moon used to play together as children, and how after their marriage they used to travel together, the Sun on a *hiran* deer, the Moon on a hare. For half the year the Sun rides on his deer, for the other half on an elephant: as the elephant goes more slowly, so the days are longer then. In Mawai I heard a story of how the Sun, the Wind and the Moon were children of Chuchu Raja and lived below the sea. The Sun married Bhaiyan Rani, but she said 'I want air, and light and darkness: take me out of the water'. So they went up out of the water, and the Sun lived in the sky. But he was so fond of the beautiful Bhaiyan that he could never leave her in the mornings, so she changed her appearance to that of an old woman covered with flies and clothes knotted together, and after that he went quickly to his work.

In one story from Motinala, it is the Agaria who offends the Sun. Kariya Kuar carries off the Sun's daughter Suraj Mukhi, and keeps her as his wife. The Sun comes to take her back, and abuses the Agaria. But Kariya Kuar invites him to have a smoke before he goes, and as he sits on his threshold catches him and shuts him up in an iron grain-bin. This is the origin of eclipses.

The Agaria take this quarrel with the Sun very seriously, and it is not uncommon to hear them refer to their happier past as 'before the war'. The same tradition of an earlier age before the flood or fire had ruined them exists among the Asur of the Neterhat plateau in Chota Nagpur. In Jobhipath, a Bir Asur village, we were told this story, which affords a cultural parallel of some interest.[1]

In Rohidasgarh, the twelve brothers Asur Asurain lived and worked; day and night they blew their bellows. They ate the iron and thought the slag was rice-water. Night and day they smelted their iron.

Bhagavan had two horses, Ankhraj and Pankhraj. Since the Asur were always making their furnaces hot, there was no water or fodder for these horses, and they began to wither. So Bhagavan sent his white crow-messenger to tell the Asur-Asurin not to work day and night, but only by day. But the Asur said, 'Who is this Bhagavan? We are Bhagavan, we are rulers'. They caught the crow and made him black with charcoal and sent him away.

The crow went home to Bhagavan and told him what had happened, so he sent Dichua the King-crow. But the Asur caught this bird also and made it black, and with hot pincers from the forge divided its tail into two.

When the Dichua also returned, Bhagavan changed his form and went and sat by the road as an old man covered with sores. To everyone who passed by, he said, 'Keep me as your servant'. But each wife of the Asur said, 'You

[1] A similar story is given by S. C. Roy in *The Oraons of Chota Nagpur* (Ranchi, 1915), pp. 470ff., and another version in *The Birhors* (Ranchi, 1925), p. 402. Yet another version is reported from Jashpur State, in which Mahadeo is said to have created the first Asur and Asurin out of curd (cf. p. 94) and taught them the art of iron-smelting. It is difficult to resist a reference to the well-known folk-tale motif of the Arrogant Smith. A stranger shoes his horse by cutting off its legs, throwing them into the furnace, and blowing the bellows. The smith tries to imitate him and fails. Then the stranger changes a number of old hags into one beautiful one by roasting them in the furnace. The smith tries to do the same with his own mother and mother-in-law, and fails again. Marstrander has summarized forty-eight versions of the tale in different parts of Europe, where the story is specially associated with the Flemish saint Eloi who boasted that he was Master of all Smiths until Christ humbled him as in the tale. See K. Jackson, '*The International Folktale in Ireland*' in *Folklore*, XLVI, pp. 277ff.

are covered with sores, how can you work for us?' But at last an old widow kept him as her servant.

Then Bhagavan stopped the iron-food flowing from the furnace, and the Asur-Asurin, growing hungry and afraid, went to find a magician.

But there were no magicians then in the world. At last they went to Bhagavan. He said, 'Well, I may tell you'. He went with them to the furnaces. He said, 'First a man must be put into the furnace and burnt; then your iron will be good'. But no one was ready. So Bhagavan said, 'Very well, I am an old man, I'm certain to die tomorrow, why shouldn't I die today instead?' He went into the furnace, and the twelve Asur plastered it well, and blew their bellows for seven days and seven nights. All the time from the flue flowed gold and silver. At last they opened the furnace, and there was Bhagavan in his glory. And they said, 'We put you in an old man covered with sores; how did this happen?' Bhagavan said, 'This too can be done for you'. They said, 'Put us also in the furnace'. So Bhagavan took them one by one, Asur and Asurin, and dropped them into the furnace. Two were left, brother and sister. They plastered the mouth of the furnace and blew the bellows. The roar of the fire silenced the cries of their brothers. They blew the bellows for seven days and seven nights, but no gold or silver came out. Then when all was still they opened the mouth of the furnace and there fell out many rattling bones.

Then said Bhagavan, 'Put stones of ore into the furnaces, and take out the hot iron and make tools and you will live'. So saying he went away.

But that brother and sister became man and wife, Asur and Asurin, and we are their descendants, the true Bir Asur.

V. *The Origin of the Gods*

We have seen how, according to the central tradition, there was one survivor from the disaster that fell upon Lohripur. This was the woman who cooled herself in a Gond's pot of buttermilk. She became the mother of the later Agaria. From her were born twelve sons and twelve daughters, the youngest of whom was Jwala Mukhi. The Mandla stories centre round the figure of Jwala Mukhi, and the Agaria in that District are sometimes called Mukhibansi on that account. In the Bilaspur Zamindaris, among the Chokh and Asur Agaria, the hero is Kariya Kuar, the eldest of the sons of the woman who escaped.

We will give the Mandla legend first. The brothers and sisters of Jwala Mukhi were divided into septs—we have given a full account of this in the chapter on exogamy—and married.

They began to work. Some got bullocks and ploughed, some opened shops, some made baskets. Then came Jwala Mukhi and said to those who were ploughing the land: 'Brothers, this is not your work, please stop it.' And to those who bought and sold, and to those who made baskets, he said: 'Brothers, this is not your work, please stop it.'

Then the brothers were angry, they came to their mother, and asked her what they were to do.

'We are children of iron,' she said, 'and our work is in iron. Your father had an iron-pit on Nanga Pahar. Go there and dig for iron.'

So the twelve brothers went to Nanga Pahar and they searched for eight days and nine nights, and at last Jwala Mukhi took his bow and a red arrow and shot it through the jungle. Where it fell, there was the pit. Then the eldest brother said to the others, 'Go down into the pit'. But each in turn said, 'No, I am afraid'. At last Jwala Mukhi said, 'I will go. But you must wait for me till I return.' So saying, he went down into the pit.

Now in that pit were piled up all the instruments of iron made by Logundi Raja—tongs, hammer, anvil, punch, tewel poker, bellows, chisel. And there among them sat Lohasur deep in thought, disconsolate, wondering if any would worship him. When Jwala Mukhi saw Lohasur, he slapped his face. 'Wake up, you old fool, why are you sitting there with your eyes shut?' Thus said Jwala Mukhi.

Lohasur opened his eyes. 'I am very hungry,' he said, 'why shouldn't I eat you?' Jwala Mukhi said, 'If you eat me, who will there be to worship you?'

Lohasur said, 'Well, you shall be my first worshipper. But you must give me plenty to eat, and in return I will give you all these iron things.'

'How can I get food in this pit?' said Jwala Mukhi, 'I will give you half my own body.' Lohasur said, 'Then you yourself must cut it and give it to me'.

Jwala Mukhi picked up an axe that was lying there and struck himself as hard as he could. But the axe would not cut him. One drop of his blood fell to the ground. Lohasur licked up this drop and cried, 'Aha! My stomach is full. I need no more.'

Then Jwala Mukhi picked up all the iron tools. But whenever he touched them, they turned to earth in his hands. When he saw that, Lohasur cried, 'Stop! I have a sister. She is not yet fed. That is why the iron is turning into dust.'

FIG. 1. Light hammer
1/7 actual size

Then came Koelasur and Jwala Mukhi fell at her feet. She said, 'Go, call your brothers and tell them to bring me a black cow that has not yet calved'.

So Jwala Mukhi climbed out of the pit and found that all his brothers had run away. He began to weep. There was no sign of man or bird or animal in that place. He went weeping along the road, and in one day he reached home. There his brothers were waiting for him. They took food offerings and went to the pit. Jwala Mukhi climbed down again and said to Koelasur, 'I've brought your offerings. Come and take them'. But she said, 'If I leave this pit, you'll never get your iron. Go up and throw the cow down to me.'

Then Jwala Mukhi carried up all the iron tools one by one out of the pit. He found the bellows very light, for the lower half was made of mud and the upper part of lotus leaves. The pipe was a lotus stalk. But some people say that the bellows were covered with *mohlain* leaves stitched together as you make leaf-plates. Then they sacrificed a black goat and twenty-one kinds of cock to Lohasur. And for Koelasur they killed a black cow and cut off the ears, and threw the carcase into the pit. For Koelasur lives in the furnace and the ears of the cow must be offered there.

After that they went home and began their work. Koelasur lived there in the charcoal, and Pawan Daseri, the Wind, in the bellows, and Dhahu Dhukan in the twyer. First of all, Jwala Mukhi's mother sat on the bellows. She was light as a flower and no wind came. They all tried but it was useless. Then came Lohasur and said, 'Here is

Pawan Daseri in the mouth of the bellows. He is hungry; give him a black hen.' So they gave him a black hen, and now when they pressed the bellows the air came, but very soon the leaf covering broke. Then the twelve brothers were frightened and began to weep. But Lohasur said, 'This is Dhahu Dhukan's fault. Give him a black goat and the bellows will mend of their own accord.' And so it was.

Then for eight days and nine nights they blew the bellows, but the coal remained dark and cold. And once more Lohasur said, 'Why didn't you come first to me? You must give a black virgin she-goat to Koelasur: then the coals will turn red. With her lives Dhua Dharni who was born in the smoke: give him a black chicken.'

They did as Lohasur had told them, and now the furnace burnt red and hot, and the iron came.

In those days they used to take a bit of red-hot iron, lay it across their knees and hammer it with their fists.

So passed twelve years and thirteen ages. Then said Mahadeo: 'These men use their hands, they will never want tongs or hammers.' So he cursed them and the bellows burst. As they were blowing them, they burst. The brothers went weeping to Lohasur, but he had nothing to say. Presently Mahadeo came in the form of a Gond to the smithy, bringing a sickle to be sharpened, and they wept before him and told him their trouble. He made them bellows of wood, and sent them to fetch a black cow, which they killed in the smithy. He covered the bellows with its skin and they had no more trouble.

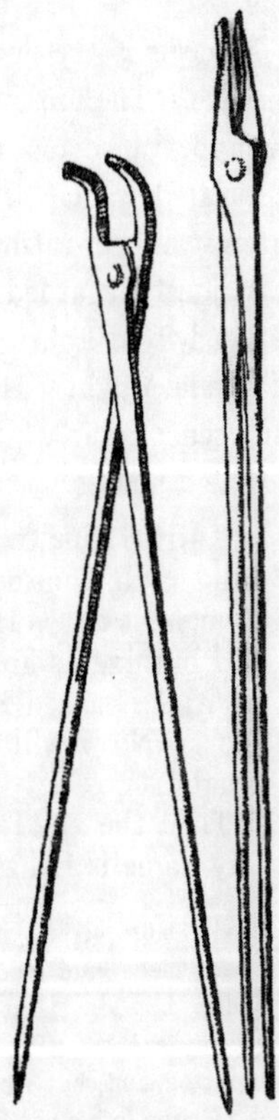

FIG. 2. Tongs
1/5 *actual size*

As they were sitting in the smithy, a *tak-taki* bird (woodpecker) flew on to the tree that shaded them, and pecked at the wood. Thus they learnt how to make a hammer, and an anvil like the wood the bird was pecking. And presently a dog came by and sat before the forge with its forefeet crossed. And they made iron pincers like the crossed feet of a dog.[1]

This myth gives the economic basis of the cult of the godlings of the furnace and the forge. It establishes the correct offerings that should be made, and suggests reasons why the work of the smithy should be a failure.

VI. *Lohasur*

Lohasur is the godling, or perhaps even the demon, of the furnace. The most popular of the stories about him describes his appearance as a child inside the kiln. The first of these is associated with Kariya Kuar, who is specially noted for his interest in beef-eating and the sacrifice of cows. Kariya Kuar is variously regarded as the eldest son of the Agaria woman who escaped from Lohripur at its destruction, or as the eldest son of Jwala Mukhi. He married the daughter of Nanga Baiga, and hence Agaria girls follow Baiga fashions in dress and eat in Baiga houses.

Kariya Kuar was blowing his bellows when he heard a child crying inside the furnace. He put in his rake and brought it out. He took the child in his lap, but it was red and burning as fire and he could not hold it. 'Will you eat or drink?' asked Kariya Kuar. 'Yes, I will eat your eldest son.' 'No, I will not give him to you.' Thus said Kariya Kuar.

Then the child grew very angry; he stood up and said, 'My name is Lohasur. Give me a black cow or I'll eat not

[1] In a more or less parallel story among the Asur Agaria of Uprora, Mahadeo made mud models of the various tools, first of the heavy, then of the light, hammer. But he did not know how to make the *tongs* until a dog came and sat with its feet crossed. Mahadeo then made a model of this out of mud, but when Lohasur picked it up it broke. Then Lohasur took red iron in his hands, and made all these implements himself and gave them to the brothers. A similar legend is reported from Udaipur State.

The Angami Naga still use hammers 'made of smooth oblong or egg-shaped stones . . . bound tightly to a short stout stick by means of a sort of cane cradle, which leaves the nose of the stone free for use. A split and flattened bamboo serves for pincers.'—Hutton, *The Angami Nagas* (London, 1921), p. 63. Green sticks were used as tongs until recently in the Southern Sudan.—Garland and Bannister, *Ancient Egyptian Metallurgy* (London, 1927), p. 107.

one but all your sons.' Kariya Kuar ran to the cattle-shed and brought the cow. Then said Lohasur, 'Give me a place to live in'. Kariya Kuar was angry and he said, 'Your place is the place you came from'. As he said that, Lohasur disappeared.[1]

Kariya Kuar tied the cow by the furnace and went to his house to smoke a pipe with his gossip. When he returned to the smithy, he found the cow standing there headless. He was very frightened; he hit the cow and made the blood flow. He took a little of the blood on the fourth finger of his right hand and put it on his own forehead and on the kiln and sprinkled it over the forge. Then he buried the cow.

That night Kariya Kuar had a dream. Lohasur came to him saying, 'You have buried my food. Now I shall eat you.' That is why we Agaria eat beef.

This story, from Daldal (Karanjia), establishes cow-sacrifice in honour of Lohasur. I recorded a slightly different version from Indri in the Motinala Range of Mandla District.

When Lohasur was born in the furnace, he cried like a baby, but no one understood what was the matter. The twelve Agaria brothers were lying drunk with the charcoal smoke. At that time Lohasur was crying *Kaon kaon*, but no one understood. Then he became angry and went to where the *kodon* chaff was heaped up on the ground and played there. An old Gondin was passing by, a pot of buttermilk in her hand. She saw Lohasur playing with the *kodon* chaff. She went into the smithy and gave each of the drunken brothers a little of the buttermilk to drink, and when they had recovered she said, 'Lohasur has been born. Bring a black cow and tie it by the kiln, and put *kodon* chaff in your kiln, and cry, "Come, Lohasur Bhavani. I give you food. I give you a home. Come and live here." If you do this Lohasur will come. Then you must kill the cow.' Thus said the old woman.

They did as she said. Lohasur came and sat on the *kodon* chaff within the kiln. They killed the cow and put some of the blood on their foreheads and on the kiln. They

1 A similar story in Mandla tells how Bura Deo, or Bara Deo (the chief Gond godling) appeared in Jwala Mukhi's furnace, but declared: 'I cannot live here: I belong to the Gond family, and I must live in a Gond's house. However, whenever you are in trouble, make me an offering, and I will help you.'

cooked a little of the flesh for Lohasur, and ate the rest themselves.

The importance of the *kodon* chaff, hinted at in this story, is further stressed in the next tale, from Dadargaon (Karanjia).

> The twelve Agaria brothers put iron stones in the furnace, and for eight days and nine nights they kept up their fire, but the iron did not come. The iron used to go out secretly to a pile of *kodon* chaff and play with it. Then came an old woman, and said, 'What are you doing, my sons? The iron is over there. It is playing with the *kodon* chaff.' They laughed at her, but she said again and again, 'No, it is over there, in the pile of chaff'. So at last one of the brothers went and saw that Lohasur really was there. That brother picked up Lohasur, but his hands broke; then all the brothers came, and somehow they put Lohasur back into the furnace, but he again crept out and went to play with the *kodon* chaff.
>
> Then Lohasur came in a dream and said, 'Make a place of *kodon* chaff within the furnace where I can sit'. When they did that, Lohasur remained. Lohasur wanted to marry the Virgin Kodon Chaff. For love of her he used to go to play with her. And to this day, if the *kodon* chaff is not put in the furnace, the iron does not settle properly.

Here, of course, is an elaborate mythological basis for a detail of the Agaria's technique of iron-smelting. The bloom of iron must have a proper base on which to rest, and the *kodon* chaff, being very fine, is the best for the purpose. The Agaria of Mandla invariably use *kodon*, but in Bilaspur, where I have not found this story, paddy chaff is also used.

One more story about the relations between Kariya Kuar and Lohasur may be given, this time from a Chokh Agaria of the Chhuri Zamindari. The tale is also known in the neighbourhood of Korba, and no doubt elsewhere. As generally in Bilaspur, the hero is Kariya Kuar rather than Jwala Mukhi.

> Kariya Kuar had four brothers. 'What shall we eat?' they said. Kariya Kuar saw many cows everywhere. His mother said, 'Whatever you see, eat that'. So he began to eat the cows. He took some to his brothers, but when they tasted the flesh they were sick. Those four brothers thought, 'He is poisoning us: one day he will kill us'. So thinking

they ran away. But Kariya Kuar continued daily to kill and eat cows.

Then thought Guru Mahadeo, 'If he eats a cow every day, soon there'll be none left in the world'. So he came and showed Kariya Kuar how to make a furnace and bellows of leaves. But Kariya Kuar was so strong that he broke the leaf-bellows. He had a great heap of cow-hide and used that instead.

Mahadeo put chaff into the furnace, and said, 'Here is your Bara Deo; his name is Lohasur. He too eats cows.' 'Will he eat them all, or will there be some also for me?' asked Kariya Kuar. Then Kariya Kuar killed a black cow in honour of Lohasur, and sat watching the road for him to come. But there was no news of him. So many days passed.

Then Mahadeo came and said, 'Lohasur has already come and eaten the cow. As you killed it, he ate. When the blood does not flow, then you know that Lohasur is drinking it. When it flows freely, then you know he has not come. When that happens, cook a little for him and put it aside. Then your own family, but not others, can eat of that cow.'

When the four brothers who had run away heard that Kariya Kuar had begun to make iron and was rich, they returned. But they were afraid to touch the cow-hide. One day Kariya Kuar said to them, 'You blow the bellows, I want to smoke my pipe'. But only one brother obeyed. The rest ran away. Kariya Kuar said to his brothers, 'You take your share and work separately'.

In those days, Kariya Kuar used to temper the iron with flour and not *chirona* dust, and the iron looked like silver. But Mahadeo being jealous came secretly, and put dust in the place of the flour and the iron turned black.

When Kariya Kuar made sickles and axes, he didn't make them sharp; the other brothers did that, and were called Chokh. Kariya Kuar was called Asur Mahali. The Chokh brothers do not eat beef.

VII. *The Raipur Myth*

The Agaria of Raipur District, including those of the Phuljhar Zamindari, now deny that they are Agaria, and call themselves God-dhuka Lohar. In a previous chapter I have given reasons for believing them to be real Agaria, and I add two stories to show how far their mythology runs parallel to that of Mandla and Bilaspur. Although there are new features in the Raipur myth, and it is obviously trying to explain a situation that does not exist in Mandla (that is, the distinction between the Lohar who work the bellows with their hands and do not extract iron from ore, and those who work with their feet and do extract iron), the general atmosphere is the same. There is a similar account of the Creation of the World, similar also is the story of Lohripur and the escape of one pregnant woman. The differences are no greater than occur in Mandla itself where at least three different reasons are given for the destruction of the Iron City.

The Raipur myth is an obviously Agaria myth: it even has a faint echo of the Neterhat Hills in its account of the burning of the old parents in a furnace. Compare it with the real Hindu Lohar stories and its primitive character becomes immediately apparent.

> In Lohagarh lived Loha-barran Sai Raja. He married Raja Indra's daughter Angarmati. In Lohagarh there was neither food nor water. The Raja used to make iron soft in the fire and eat it. Many years passed, for twelve years and thirteen ages he lived thus, and he never approached the beautiful Angarmati.
>
> Owing to the Raja's work in his furnaces, the fire spread twelve miles long and twelve miles broad. For eight days and nine nights he would work his bellows and take no rest. Because of the fire, no one could approach his kingdom.
>
> His Rani lived in a seven-roomed palace. One day she said in her mind, 'I have been married all this time, and not once has the Raja been to me. How can I bear a son?' She went for help to Bhagavan. One day Bhagavan sat in the mouth of the bellows. The Raja began to work the bellows, but no air came. He tried for eight days and nine nights, but there was no blast and no fire. Then came the Rani and said, 'O my Raja, why do you distress yourself so much? I have been your wife all these years, yet you never distress yourself for me, and we have no sons. Stop this blowing of bellows and come to me.'
>
> Hearing this, the Raja was very angry and tried to beat her. But Bhagavan had given her a gourd full of water,

and she threw this over her Raja. He had never seen water before; when it touched him, he lost his power, and could no longer eat iron.

The Rani then went to her palace, and Bhagavan hid himself. The Raja returned to his work. But now he could not bear the heat of the iron. Bhagavan came to him and said, 'Go to your Rani and you will have twelve sons and thirteen daughters'. The Raja went to his palace, and soon he had twelve sons and thirteen daughters. When they grew up, they married each other, and the one girl who was left became wife to all twelve boys. After this the Raja and Rani died. Before her death, Rani Angarmati had planted a gourd, and from its stem there grew twelve gourds. When they were ripe, the sons took one apiece. They opened their gourds and made seven rooms in each, putting food and water and all they needed. Those gourds were big as houses. Then came a great flood.

The world is now completely destroyed by water, and the myth follows the main outline of the Creation story that we have already given. Then

when the earth was ready, the twelve gourds were found lying on its surface, huge as mountains. The crow saw them and called Bhagavan. He came and looked at them. They were all shut, so Bhagavan tapped on each of them and one of them broke open and out came twelve boys and one girl and all kinds of iron tools. The second gourd broke open and there came out thirteen boys and a girl and all kinds of bronze things. And a third gourd broke open and there came out fourteen boys and a girl and all things made of bell-metal. In the other gourds there was nothing at all. The first they called the Lohasur brothers, the second the Tamesur brothers and the third the Kansasur brothers.

These now lived in Lohripur. They made bellows of mud and bamboo fans. Their Raja was Lohasur's elder brother. His name was Logundi. The twelve brothers worked at their bellows so hard that there was fire everywhere. They made great iron plates and covered the country for twenty-four miles round. When they blew the bellows very hard the plates got red-hot and the brothers were burnt to ashes. But their wife escaped, and came to Ghunsi Gond's house in Binj Pahar. There was a pot there full of *pej*-gruel three days old, and the girl jumped into it to cool herself. When Ghunsi's wife saw this she was frightened and ran away.

That girl was pregnant and soon a boy and a girl were born to her. They went to Karipatpar and lived on jungle roots and leaves. The children grew up. The boy made leaf-baskets and closed their mouths and put bamboo sticks into the sides, and used them as bellows to make the iron soft so that he could eat it. Thus he became strong and wise.

The mother married him to his own sister. Then afterwards he took a second wife, a girl of another tribe. From the first wife he had five sons, from the second three. Then he died, and the five brothers and the three brothers quarrelled. Bhagavan gave a dream to the five brothers, 'Make a circle of wood and put hollow bamboos into that'. They asked their mother what work they should do, and she told them that their father used to make things of iron. They went to the jungle and found a dead sambhar and used its skin for their bellows. Thus the five brothers started their smithy.

They worked their bellows, but at first no blast came. Then their mother came to help, and all was well. The five brothers drove the three brothers away. The three brothers could not extract the iron ore from the ground.

The five brothers went to look for wives. On the Gadasur Mountain there were five girls living with their parents. They too were ironsmiths. The five brothers put the parents into their own furnaces and burnt them to ashes, and carried away the girls. Therefore we are the highest of all castes.

But the poor three brothers could not get wives among the blacksmiths, so at last they married girls of other tribes, and began to work the bellows with their hands.

But the God-dhuka Lohar who are the sons of the elder wife are the higher. The Hath-dhuka Lohar who are the sons of the younger wife, who was of another tribe, and who cannot extract the ore, are lower than we are.

The second story, which is much shorter, shows how the cult of Lohasur arose in Raipur, and again affords a close parallel to the Mandla myth. It was recorded in Sapos village.

In Lohripur, Logundi Raja had eleven brothers who worked their bellows before the furnaces. One day Lohasur came out of the furnace and sat down beside Logundi Raja. Logundi's daughter was Jhilmili Kaniya, and Lohasur fell in love with her. One day Logundi Raja caught them together, and was very angry. In his house were seven kinds of things—gold, silver, iron, bell-metal, brass, stone, wood—in one store-bin. He shut Lohasur up in this. But now no iron came from the furnace.

Lohasur had four wives, Lohakutin Loharin who lives in the heavy hammer, Pathar Paherin Saorin who lives in the bellows, Gangi Gohanin who lives in the anvil and Loharin Bai who lives in everything in the smithy. They sat watching the road, waiting for their lord's return. When he did not come they went to find him. They met Logundi Raja's wife, and she told them where Lohasur was imprisoned. So the four wives went and danced before Logundi Raja who was very pleased and forgot everything. While he was thus drunken Lohasur came out burning and black in a cloud of smoke, and killed him and his brothers. None escaped save Logundi Raja's wife who hid under the sari of Loharin Bai.

Then Logundi Raja's wife ran away to a Gond's house and gave birth to a son. When he grew up, his mother taught him how to make iron things. When he could not get covering for his bellows, he brought a cow and killed it and made his bellows in the names of the four wives of Lohasur. They all came and lived in his smithy.

And then at last, inside his furnace he heard a child weeping. It was Lohasur and he worshipped him.

VIII. *The Origin of Fire*

To the Agaria fire is naturally a thing of absorbing interest and romance. The great red flowers of fire that come tumbling out of the furnace when the iron is ready, the mysterious flames that dance above it lighting the hut by night with uncanny beauty, the deep red glow of the coal in the blast of the bellows, the showers of sparks that spring out beneath the hammer, in this is the beauty and poetry of the Agaria's life. 'Fire is the Agaria's friend, he knows no other' is a common proverb.

The Agaria were born from fire, their heroic ancestors ate and excreted fire; Kariya Kuar used to dip his fingers in the burning liquid iron and suck it 'as if it were honey'; the ancient blacksmiths drank blazing iron as if it were rice-water. And as they were born from fire they have never feared the sparks that fall upon them or the heat of the furnace. Fire is both god and servant, a co-worker and a friend. A proverb describes the conduct of fire through the varying seasons.

> In the rains, it makes us weep.
> In the cold, it gives us *mohini* (love-charms).
> In the heat, it terrifies us and wanders blazing through the jungle.

That is to say, in the rains the fires are smoky and make men's eyes water. In the cold weather, fire is so comforting and homely that all men love it. And in the summer, fire becomes a danger that burns the smithy and destroys the jungle.

There are many versions of the myth of the origin of fire. Aginjhar was created in order that the first Agaria could make the iron nails required to fix the earth in place. Another story tells how Nanga Baiga, in order to get the iron for these nails, broke open a great stone, and out of the crack came Lohasur and from the spark was born Agyasur, the demon of Fire. Some attribute fire to the Sun [1] and say it was when the great plate that surrounded Lohripur was being raised off the earth to shine in the sky that the trees and grass caught fire and rocks turned red with the heat. Since then fire has been made from stone and from wood—probably a reference to the flint and steel and the fire-drill. In Hindu thought also the Sun is a form of Agni which the gods set in the sky.

Another story tells how Kariya Kuar was digging iron-stones out of a pit and breaking them into pieces. Near by was the cotton of a *semur* tree. As he threw out bits of iron-ore from

[1] 'Certain natives of Victoria relate that once upon a time a man threw a spear, with a string attached to it, at the clouds; the spear stuck in the clouds, the man climbed up the string, and brought down fire from the sun to the earth. A tribe in Queensland told how men obtained fire from the sun in a different fashion. They went westward to the setting sun, and just as the glowing orb was sinking beneath the horizon they adroitly chipped a piece off it and bore back the burning fragment to their camp. The Gilbert Islanders say that fire was procured from a sunbeam which a man caught in his mouth . . . According to one account, Prometheus procured fire for men by lighting a torch at the sun's fiery wheel.' Frazer, *Myths of the Origin of Fire* (London, 1930), p. 206.

the pit, they struck against each other, and some of the sparks fell on the cotton and fire was born.

This story comes from Bilaspur as does the following, longer, tale which also has Kariya Kuar as its hero.

> A sadhu did penance for twelve years without food or water, meditating on Fire. He had no fire. Save for the fires in the sky he had never seen fire nor felt its warmth. At last Fire in the form of a Virgin[1] stood before him and said, 'I am very cold: make a fire for me'. The sadhu said, 'I have nothing, I have never made a fire'. The Virgin said, 'Bring a bit of cow-dung and some wood, and put them into a small pit in the ground'. So saying, she disappeared.
>
> The sadhu dug a hole in the ground, and put the cow-dung and wood as the girl had said. The dry dung and the wood burst into flames of their own accord. When he saw the fire, the sadhu's nature changed; he gave up his penance and went to the nearest village. There was no fire there: the villagers ate raw meat and uncooked rice. The sadhu went back to the forest to fetch fire for the people, but he found that it had once more taken the form of a Virgin and run away.
>
> Bhagavan was going to kill a great Dano. He saw the Fire Virgin and said to her, 'Come and help'. She said, 'Certainly I'll help, but what will you give me?' He said, 'I'll give you an offering of *ghī* and *gur*'. Bhagavan went to Sabar Sai and said, 'I am going to kill the Dano, come and help me'. Sabar Sai said, 'I have this great kingdom, and no fire. How can I come with you?' When Bhagavan promised to give fire to the Agaria, Sabar Sai went to the battle.
>
> During the great fight, Sabar Sai was killed and with him his son Logundi Raja. Logundi's son, Kariya Kuar, escaped. He went home and wanted to work in his smithy, but he had no fire. He went to the iron-pit, and killed a black cow there in the name of Lohasur. As he did so, all the implements and tools of iron rose out of the pit and came to him.

[1] 'The notion that fire was elicited from a woman's body, and particularly from her genital organ, finds a ready explanation in the analogy which many savages trace between the working of the fire-drill on the one hand and the intercourse of the sexes on the other.' Frazer, op. cit., p. 220. In many myths, from Australia, the Murray Islands, Melanesia, the Caroline Islands, South America, etc., women are represented as being in possession of fire before men.

> Logundi Raja also returned to life and said, 'My father's name was Sabar Sai, and Bhagavan promised fire as a reward for his help'. Thus said Logundi Raja and returned to the pit.
>
> So Kariya Kuar made his smithy and prepared his furnace in the Kajli-ban-pahar. There were many bamboos there. As the dry bamboos rubbed against one another in the wind, they caught fire. Kariya Kuar found a blazing bamboo and brought it home. This was the Virgin Fire, and from this the first charcoal was made. So fire began in the world.

Fr Schmidt suggests that while the younger cultures 'report that in the beginning fire was zealously guarded by the gods who would not give it to man and that man was therefore forced to steal it by cunning or take it from them by brutal force, the oldest, the primitive tribes relate that the Creator himself had given fire to man and instructed him in the art of making fire'. He illustrates this from the Maidus of Central California and the Great Andamans; he might have added the Agaria, whose legends clearly belong to the primitive cultures.[1]

For all the mythological setting, however, the Agaria actually give fire a thoroughly practical and natural origin. It came from the rubbing together of bamboos—a sight the Agaria must often have noticed in the forest; it sprang into being from the breaking of a stone, from the friction of iron pyrites against each other, or from the sun's rays.

In the last story, there is a reference to the Virgin Fire which has considerable importance in Agaria magic. Virgin Fire must be used to kindle the wood for charcoal: 'Only a true virgin bears the best charcoal and iron; with violated fire the coal is spoilt.' It is an essential item in the ritual for the extraction of Virgin Iron from a new furnace. It is always better to use Virgin Fire for the manufacture of any kind of iron implement.

Virgin Fire is generally simply the fire that is freshly kindled, preferably by the fire-drill or fire-saw, but if need be by flint and steel. It stands in sharp contrast to 'fire leåvings',

[1] W. Schmidt, 'The Oldest Implements of Man', *Jubilee Volume of the Anthropological Society of Bombay*, 1938, p. 78.

fire that has been used for some other purpose before being brought as kindling for a new fire. The only exception to this is fire brought from the Holi bonfire: a flaming brand is carried from the bonfire to the smithy and fires at the furnace and forge are kindled with it. This is also called Virgin Fire. At the same time a bit of iron is thrown into the bonfire in the belief that the fires of the smithy will then burn as well as the Holi fire. This is called 'warming the iron at Holi'.[1]

The god of fire is Agyasur or Agin Deo, and every year at the Deothani (which according to the Asur falls at Divali, according to the Chokh at Hareli) a red cock is offered in his honour. Special reverence is always due to fire: it must not be kindled for some days after a death; it is dangerous to swear by fire; if a man urinates on fire, his penis may become swollen and covered with sores. This happened to an Agaria boy in Bhanpur (Karanjia). He tried many remedies without effect: at last he gave food-offerings to Agyasur and recovered.

It is equally dangerous to walk over fire; this may result in a nasty attack of gonorrhoea. If a man kicks the fire, when he next goes out walking his feet will burn under him. It may even be fatal to throw 'living fire' into running water, as the following story shows.

Long ago an Agaria died and they were taking fire to light his pyre. On the way, the brand burnt the hand of the man who was carrying it and he got angry and threw it into the river. They brought fresh fire, but the wood would not catch: there was smoke but no fire. Then the dead man spoke from the pyre and said, 'Because he threw the living fire into the river, he will be carried away by the river'. So they ran to see, and there was the stick blazing on the surface of the water. That very man went into the river to fetch it, and the river carried him away and he was drowned. The stick came to the bank, and they took it and lit the pyre.

[1] Compare such European customs as, for example, in Germany on Easter Eve, when a bonfire is kindled before the Church by the new fire which lights the great Paschal: the people take burning sticks home to light their own fires. Frazer, *Balder the Beautiful* (London, 1913), Vol. I, p. 121.

Agaria are not allowed to play *luki* with burning sticks. If they do, then at night Fire comes in the form of a *bhut* (ghost) and marks the players on the back of the neck (just as they burn a child with a hot sickle) and the boys wet their bed in fright. To cure this, a burning stick should be taken and every place should be marked again: then the ghost will not return. It is interesting that Freud has traced a connexion between 'playing with fire' and bed-wetting: 'The interpretation of dreams of fire justifies a prohibition of the nursery, which forbids children to "play with fire" so that they may not wet the bed at night. These dreams also are based on reminiscences of the *enuresis nocturna* of childhood.'[1]

Another taboo is on red clothes.[2] It is thought that if a man or woman dressed in red enters the smithy, it will catch fire. In fact this has actually happened. Chandia Agaria of a village near Karanjia went into his smithy wearing a red cloth, and fire immediately broke out of its own accord. Another reason for not wearing red is that it is the colour of the cock offered to Agyasur.

The importance of fire to the Agaria is evident from their dreams, for nearly one quarter of the dreams I have been able to collect (with far more difficulty than among the Baiga) have been dreams about fire. The fire-dream is one of the 'type-dreams' that have been fully studied by Seligman,[3] and found by him to be almost universal. He thinks that fire in a dream means reproductive energy or creative energy. In India, the symbolism of the fire-stick (a method of making fire still common among the Agaria) has always been sexual. 'The making of fire,' says Held, 'has been closely associated in the

[1] S. Freud, *The Interpretation of Dreams* (London, 1932), p. 372. See also his 'Fragment of an Analysis of Hysteria' in *Collected Papers*, Vol. III.

[2] On the subject of colour-symbolism, see W. H. R. Rivers, 'Primitive Colour Vision' in *The Popular Scientific Monthly*, Vol. LIX, No. 1, pp. 44ff. and D. A. Mackenzie 'Colour Symbolism' in *Folk-Lore*, Vol. XXXIII, pp. 136–169.

[3] See Seligman, 'Anthropology and Psychology', *J. of R. Anth. Inst.*, Vol. LIV, p. 46 and Seligman, 'The Unconscious in Relation to Anthropology', *B.J. of Psych.*, Vol. XVIII, Part IV, pp. 314ff.

Indian mind from ancient times with the physical act of generation, and is, as a result, accompanied in the prescribed ritual by a number of traditional sayings bearing upon sexual life. The two fire-sticks represent man and woman. . . . The very bringing of fire to men is connected with the advent of the first man.'[1]

We have already seen how the first Agaria was born from the fire, and how fire was itself created by the intercourse of two bamboos. An Agaria riddle gives a sexual meaning to the making of fire by the flint and steel—'Father beats mother and the child springs out'. The latent meaning of fire as 'creative energy' is clearly seen in this dream of an Agaria of Mawai.

> I made my forge and began to fashion iron tools. A spark fell on me. I got up and waved my hands to put it out. My wife threw water on my penis. 'There is the fire,' she cried.

Unfortunately, I was unable to obtain from the Agaria their own associations to these dreams, and beyond a statement that 'to dream of fire means a quarrel on the morrow',[2] I was also unable to get interpretations of their meanings. But I think that even from the little material I have been able to obtain, it is possible to say that in the manifest content of Agaria dreams fire is an unusually prominent ingredient (in Freud's *Interpretation of Dreams* there are only two references to fire, in Ella Sharpe's *Dream Analysis* only three) and that probably the fire symbolism represents either a normal anxiety-conflict or a sexual conflict. I have already pointed out that the Agaria are exceptionally timid and anxious about their future: not only are they in a constant state of fear about their suppression by the Government or a possible increase of taxation, but the danger of fire is a very real one, and the

[1] Held, *The Mahabharata*, p. 140.

[2] In Central Africa, to dream of a great bush fire means war. Artemidorus of Ephesus (2nd century A.D.) interprets war in the sky as meaning war or famine. See H. J. Rose, 'Central Africa and Artemidorus', *Man* (1926), p. 211.

ruin of the smithy by a menstruous woman or a witch is equally possible.

The following dreams have an obviously sexual content :—

'A girl was blowing the bellows in front of the furnace, when fire caught the smithy. I went to put it out and caught the girl and went to her, putting fire in her vagina. Then a man came and pushed me into the fire.'

'I was making charcoal in the forest. The trees caught fire. I ran away. Two women with very big teeth came, and one said, "I'll swallow him", and the other said, "I'll put him in my vagina".'

In the next dream we can trace an obvious anxiety lest certain religious duties have been unfulfilled.

'Lohasur came to me in a dream saying, "Fill my belly, you have forgotten me. When your smithy is burnt then you'll realize your folly." So I made a sickle and an axe, and in front of the furnace a ball of fire flew up into the air and fell upon me. My hand broke open, and the whole smithy caught fire. A sadhu came by and asked for food. "Give me something," he said, "and your smithy will be all right".'

Here the sadhu obviously symbolizes the forgotten religious duties towards Lohasur. The myths are full of stories about the penalties which non-fulfilment of such duties may incur.

It is possible that fear of official interference with the work of the smithy (fully described in Chapter IX) is at the bottom of the conflict in the dream: 'My brother was working in his shop. He was making an axe. I was burnt by his fire and a big sore appeared on my hand. Then a policeman came and pushed me out of the house.' And again: 'I was working in my forge. A chaprasi came and ordered me to make him a spear quickly. Then a fire broke out in the thatch.'

But the next two dreams may be simply anxiety dreams of a general character: 'My house was on fire. I shouted for help. A *bhut* came and seized me by the throat and squeezed me till I choked.' 'I went for iron to the jungle. I brought it and put it in my furnace. When the iron came out, I was burnt. I threw water on the furnace and it broke. Then the whole smithy collapsed.'

Perhaps this last dream may be connected with the belief, clearly indicated in the myths, about the danger of water, and how the original Agaria lost their supernatural power of eating iron and handling it when they touched water. In both dreams there is a suggestion of the constant fear of unseen supernatural forces.[1]

IX. *Legends of Charcoal*

'Where there are *sarai* trees, there you will find Agaria,' for the *sarai* gives much the best charcoal. The Agaria are expert charcoal-burners, and with reason, for good charcoal greatly lessens their labour. They make it usually of *sarai*, though *dhāmin* and *sāja* are sometimes used. I think they enjoy making charcoal; the tribesmen generally delight in anything that takes them into the jungle.

Let us follow a party from Daldal as it goes along a pretty winding stream towards the forest. There are two men and a woman and some children. The woman is carrying a large bamboo basket, the children have smaller leaf-baskets, the men have their axes. As they go along, excited by the beauty of the early sun touching the green tops of the trees, they sing a Karma song.

The twelve Rikkimuni brothers are stamping on their bellows.
How slowly cools the iron!
The charcoal's made from wood, the iron from ore.
How slowly cools the iron!

They reach a clearing in the forest: the ground is already black with charcoal-dust, showing that they have been here before. The woman clears a patch of ground, removing stones

[1] The Lhota Naga interpret the fire-dream as being prophetic of children. 'A fire which burns up well when the dreamer lights it means a big family, but a fire that goes out foretells deaths in the home ... Anything red, such as a red spear or red goat's-hair, represents man's blood and means that someone will get hurt.'—J. P. Mills, *The Lhota Nagas* (London, 1922), p. 172. The Manipur Naga regard the fire-dream as meaning a hot summer and ruined crops. Hodson, *Naga Tribes of Manipur* (London, 1911), p. 130.

and refuse, and the men pile faggots and half-burnt branches into a sort of pyre. Then, as they have heard that the Forest Guard has gone into Karanjia to draw his pay, they cut fresh green *sarai* [1] above it. On this again, firewood is placed. The pyre is built with the care and after the pattern of a real funeral pyre, carefully but with some haste for 'it must not be done at midday, for then there is warfare between the Sun and Fire, and both are destroyed'.

The 'pyre' is lit with new (*kuāri*) or virgin fire which should be made with the bamboo drill or saw, though nowadays it is sometimes made with the steel and flint. 'Then the fire is truly a virgin and bears the best charcoal: with violated fire the charcoal is spoilt.' The wood begins to burn, and the company sits down to watch it, the men filling their leaf-pipes and puffing contentedly: the woman and children fill in the time by collecting broad *mohlain* leaves for plates. After an hour or two, the men scatter the wood. They drive their axes into the logs and pull them apart, then beat out the fire with long branches. Sometimes they throw earth on the burning wood, but never water, for that would spoil the charcoal. The woman comes to help and gradually they sort out the cinders, first with heavy poles, then with sticks and branches, till it is ready to be collected. After a short time for cooling, they put the coals into the big bamboo basket and the leaf-baskets which the children have brought. The woman hoists one of

[1] I do not think the Agaria use different kinds of charcoal for different purposes in the manner of the Maria Gond. 'Having collected the ore, the smith collects a supply of bark for roasting the ore before smelting, and makes a supply of charcoal (*bugi*). For the former purpose he prefers the bark of the sacred *sāja* tree . . . For smelting he makes charcoal from *karra* wood, unless he can get tamarind, and for refining from *mahua* wood.' Grigson, op. cit., p. 176.

In the Garhwal District, charcoal of the *buran* (rhododendron) and *ayas* (oak) or, in the lower hills of the *chir* (*Pinus longifolia*) is used in the primitive 'bloomeries'. *R.G.S.I.*, Vol. LVII, p. 163. The Agaria of Palamau used *sāl* and *bija* (*Pterocarpus marsupium*) for charcoal (Ball, *Jungle Life*, p. 479). The Panchal Lohar used 'as fuel the roots of thorn bushes, which they battered out on the ground with the back of a short-handed axe'. *Census of India, 1891*, p. 199.

these onto her head, the men take the others, the children carry the bundles of leaves, and they set out for home and the midday meal.[1]

The bamboo basket is called *ghandri* (Fig. 3). It is 2½ by 1¼ feet, or even larger, with an open mesh as shown in the drawing. The leaf-baskets called *patli* are smaller. In Bastar, baskets are sometimes made of branches and leaves. The *dādu* baskets, normally used for bringing home the ore, may also be used for charcoal.

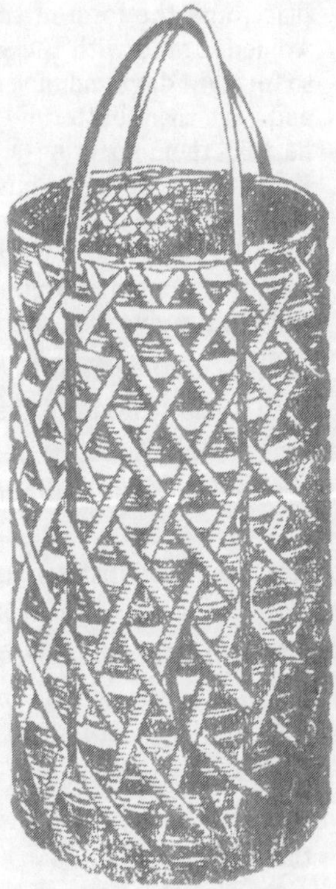

FIG. 3. *Ghandri* basket
1/8 actual size

The godling or demon of charcoal is Koelasur, and the Agaria have a number of stories about him, as about everything in which they are interested. But there do not seem to be any ceremonies or *mantra* connected with charcoal-burning or with the cult of Koelasur, beyond, of course, the customary offerings.

One of these stories describes the origin and birth of the godling.

[1] Where wood is scarce, the Chokh Agaria sometimes make *gār-koela*. A pit is dug, dry and green wood are thrown into it and lit, and then covered with earth. Charcoal made this way is not considered good, and is only used in the forge. In Bastar, however, they first burn the *karra* wood, and then 'plaster wet mud over the heaps to prevent the escape of smoke, and leave them all night. Meanwhile they make the *mahua* charcoal, burning the heaps of dry logs and pouring water over the glowing embers; this can be collected overnight, but the *karra* charcoal is not ready till the morning'.—Grigson, op. cit., p. 177. Reuben (op. cit., p. 13) describes how the Asur put green *sāl* branches 'thick as an arm' into a pit and, after firing them, cover them with leaves and earth.

The youngest of the Agaria brothers went to make charcoal in the jungle. He cut wood and piled it up and set it on fire. Then out of the smoke a terrible form appeared, black, with long hair and gaping mouth, and swallowed the Agaria boy alive. His wife was with him and she ran weeping home and told the other brothers. They all ran to that place, and the form of smoke swallowed all the men. The women, drunk with the smoke, fell senseless, and remained so for eight days and nine nights. Then came Guru Mahadeo and gave them buttermilk to drink, and they recovered. So he told them to bring a black cow, and kill it saying, 'O Koelasur, release our husbands. We will honour you and give you food-sacrifice'. Then Koelasur gave them back their husbands, and they too fell at his feet saying, 'Our ancestors honoured you. We had forgotten. But now we will always give food-sacrifice.'[1]

In the myth recorded on page 104, it is Jwala Mukhi himself who initiates the cult of Koelasur. When he picked up the first tools of iron they turned into dust in his hands, and Lohasur told him to offer a black cow in honour of his sister Koelasur. The bewildering changes of sex in the myths need not distress us unduly. Lohasur is sometimes regarded as a woman, and Koelasur as both male and female. The truth is that the Agaria do not attribute ordinary sexual activities to their special godlings and demons: they reserve that for Mahadeo and Parvati or for Rama and Sita.

Another story, from the Motinala Range, gives a curious picture of the relations of the Agaria to the great war described in the *Ramayana*.

After Rama had killed Ravana, he said to Sita, 'Now there is not one left'. She said, 'But there is another Ravana with a thousand heads down in hell'. Rama wounded this Ravana in the foot, but he pulled the arrow out, saying to it, 'Whoever sent you, go and kill him'. The arrow flew back and struck Rama in the chest and he fell senseless. Sita was frightened out of her wits, and ran to Lohripur and said to

[1] The following dream may be a recollection of the myth. 'I was making charcoal in the jungle. I had turned black from the smoke. When I came home and the neighbours saw me black, they all ran away, and my wife fell at my feet and waved a lamp before me in my honour.'

Logundi Raja, 'Send Agyasur and Lohasur and all the gods you have, with half an earthen pot filled with charcoal.'

Logundi Raja only had two gods, but he sent these and the charcoal, and Sita turned black with the smoke of the charcoal. She carried the pot of charcoal in one hand and a sword in the other, and so cut off Ravana's head. As she did so, Agyasur and Lohasur licked up the blood.

There Dhua Dharni and Koelasur were born and asked Sita to give them somewhere to live. 'Otherwise we'll devour you', they said. Sita took them to Logundi Raja and said, 'Put these in your furnace: they will drive away witches'. Then she lit the charcoal in her earthen pot and the smoke rose and Logundi Raja fell drunk at her feet and she went away. So now we always avoid the smoke that rises from the furnace. Formerly it killed men, now it makes them drunk, but it is best to avoid it.[1]

Throughout the Gond and Baiga country there are scores of such stories illustrating the first reactions of the aboriginal mind to Hindu teaching.

X. *The Mythology of Beef-Eating*

The custom of eating beef, which has been abandoned by many tribes under Hindu pressure, is firmly established in Agaria mythology and, probably for this reason, survives. Earlier in this chapter I have recorded stories in which Jwala Mukhi offers a black cow to Lohasur in the pit, and Kariya Kuar makes a similar sacrifice in the smithy. In another story, we see how the division between Asur and Chokh Agaria arose on the question of beef-eating and the use of cow-hide for bellows. A few more stories may be given here. My first is from a Patharia Agaria of Dadargaon (Karanjia).

When Lohasur was born, he said to the Agaria, 'Whenever you go anywhere, take my *prasād* (sacrament) with you'. But the Agaria said, 'What can we take?' At that moment, the Agaria's little boy came crying, 'Father, I am hungry'. The Agaria picked up the child and took him home. He

[1] The danger of charcoal gas is very real to the Agaria, and for this reason they ignite the smoke that rises above the furnace.

gave him *pej* to drink, but the child said, 'I don't want *pej*'. He gave him bread to eat, but the child said, 'I don't want bread'. He gave him rice, but the child said, 'I don't want rice'. 'Then what do you want?' asked the father. 'I want my mother's milk.' So the mother took him and he was content.

Then Lohasur came as a child and wept. 'I too am hungry.' So said Lohasur. The Agaria gave him *pej*, but Lohasur said, 'I don't want *pej*'. Then the Agaria gave him bread, but Lohasur said, 'I don't want bread'. The Agaria gave him rice, but Lohasur said, 'I don't want rice'. 'Then what do you want?' asked that Agaria. 'I want meat.' So the Agaria gave him a chicken, but Lohasur said, 'I don't want chicken'. The Agaria gave him a pig, but Lohasur said, 'I don't want a pig'. The Agaria gave him a goat, but Lohasur said, 'I don't want a goat'. There was a black cow grazing there. The child Lohasur caught it by the neck and dragged it to the smithy. The Agaria thought, 'If I don't kill this cow, my own son will die'.

So he killed the cow, and Lohasur came in his own form, blazing like fire and in a cloud of smoke, and drank its blood. He said, 'Every three years offer me a black cow here and in the pit, and eat its flesh. Whenever you go to visit any of your family, take a little bit of beef with you. If you don't, a tiger or a snake will kill you on the way.'

Another very interesting story was told by a Chokh Agaria of Thanakar village in the Uprora Zamindari. The Chokh generally deny to outsiders that they are beef-eaters, but there is no doubt that they continue the practice, perhaps with a little secrecy.

An old Agaria and his wife had five sons. Every day they got up early and worked in the smithy. Gradually the boys were married, and when the last was married, the parents died. In the smithy there were light and heavy hammers and tongs made by the old man's own hands. At night these used to talk to one another. When the old man died, the heavy hammer said, 'Now who will do us honour? There are five brothers, but we do not know them.' The tongs said, 'Let us hide somewhere.' The light hammer said, 'I'm small and have no brains, but I'll tell you what to do. When they come for work and lift you up to hammer, break in half of your own accord.'

The heavy hammer said, 'Good, but you too must break in half. Then they'll take some notice of us.' The kiln said, 'But what shall I do? I am the biggest of you all, I am your mother.' The others said, 'When they light the fire and blow the bellows, let your mouth break open'.

Next morning, the Agaria came to the smithy to work. One brother raised the heavy hammer above his head, and it broke in pieces. The other struck with the light hammer, and it too broke. Another lit the fire in the furnace, and its mouth fell open of its own accord. Then the brothers were very frightened, and said, 'Our parents have become ghosts and are breaking our things.' They went to the pit to dig out iron-stones, but found the earth had fallen in and the pit filled with rubbish. They said, 'Our parents are destroying us. Let us dig up their bodies and cut them into pieces.'

When they went to the grave and began to dig, the dead man spoke to them from the ground. 'Do not trouble me,' he said. 'Give food-offerings to Lohasur in the smithy and the pit, and then if you have trouble, come here and break my bones.' So the brothers took grass and offered it to Lohasur. But it was no use, and they came filled with anger to break their father's bones. But he spoke again from the ground, 'What did you give, my sons?' 'We gave grass,' they said. 'But I used to give a cow. You too sacrifice a cow.'

When they did that, the broken things came together of their own accord. And ever since we have done cow-sacrifice and honoured our dead parents.

The next story illustrates the process of change and 'reform' among the tribesmen. It was recorded from a God-dhuka Lohar (Agaria) in Patandadar village of Raipur.

In the old days we called ourselves Agaria, and killed bullocks with our own hands, and ate the flesh. Then Guru Mahadeo came by in the form of a Brahmin, and we offered him a seat. But he said, 'No, I will not sit with you. You are great sinners.' 'Tell us what we have done,' we said, falling at his feet, 'and we will give up our sin'. Mahadeo said, 'You must stop killing living cows. You may eat dead cows. If you don't get enough cow-hide, buy it from the Chamar.' So saying he disappeared, and we stopped killing living cows.

Some time afterwards, an Agaria was marrying his daughter. The Dhimar were there carrying her in a litter, and the Ganda brought drums and sang. After the marriage, the party was resting by a tank under a pipar tree. Some small branches fell from the tree. The bridegroom saw them and cried, 'Look father, these branches will be very good for the springes for our bellows'. Then the Dhimar and Ganda got up and said, 'We will not carry your litters or play for you. You are Agaria. The true Lohar do not eat beef or use springe-poles' [that is, the Lohar use hand-bellows only and thus do not need the springe-poles]. The Agaria replied, 'No, we are God-dhuka Lohar'. From that day we stopped eating pig. We only eat jungly pig.

In this story we see very clearly the scorn with which the Hindus normally treat the tribesmen. In deference to this and in order to raise their social status, many tribes are abandoning their old customs. The Agaria have actually changed less than many others, for even the Raipur section of the tribe continues to eat the flesh of dead bullocks and cows, though it no longer uses cow-hide for its bellows. The Chokh Agaria of the Korba and Chhuri Zamindaris and of Udaipur State deny that they eat beef, and use sambhar skin for their bellows. The Mahali and Asur Agaria openly eat beef and use cow-hide. The Mahali Lohar of Udaipur and Jashpur do the same. The Chokh and Agaria of this area say that the original bellows of Agar Sai were covered with sambhar hide. If a Chokh eats beef he is outcasted and becomes a Mahali or Lohar. In Mandla, there is a certain reticence, not amounting to actual denial of the practice, and cow-hide is generally used. But it is not easy to generalize, for even within the same subsection of the tribe the customs vary; for example Agaria living in or near large Hindu centres will naturally be more inclined to follow Hindu ways.

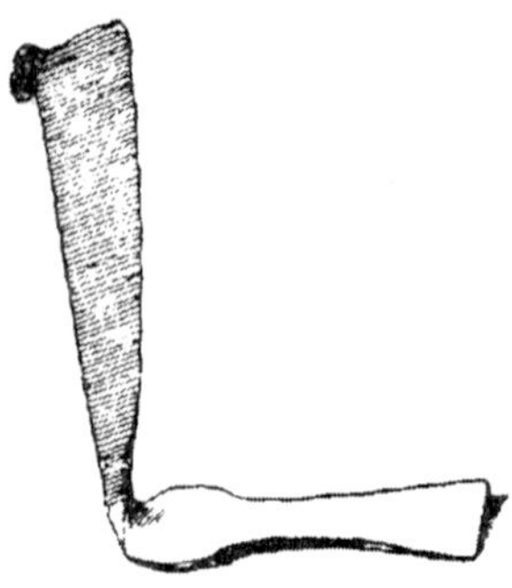

FIG. 4. Meat-cutter
1/4 actual size

4. Polygamous
agaria family.
Pandulal with
is two wives
and children,
rom Pungaon,
Mandla District.

15. (*a*) Bir Asur youth from the Neterhat Plateau.

(*b*) Bir Asur youth of Jobhipath.

Except for sacrifice, however, it is rare nowadays for an Agaria to kill a cow or bullock. But in most places, when a cow dies in a village, the nearest Agaria goes to claim it. Many Chamar have now abandoned beef-eating, but if there happens to be an unreformed Chamar there, he shares the flesh and part of the skin. The owner is paid one or two axes, or is excused from giving his *jewar*, the annual payment to the blacksmith for all his minor services. But sometimes nothing is given to the owner, who is glad enough to get rid of the carcase.

The Agaria summons his friends and relatives from all the surrounding villages. He himself keeps the skin and the larger portion of the flesh; the rest is divided. A scrap of the liver is offered to Lohasur. For distant relatives, long strips of meat called *sukhri* are set to dry, first in the sun and then hung from a pole above the hearth so that they are smoke-cured. They are then cut into bits and stored in a *jhāpi* basket. Very rarely, the Agaria sell the flesh, and then only to members of their own tribe.

A curious custom, established in the story we have already quoted, compels the Agaria to carry a bit of beef with rice and bread when he goes to visit his relatives. This is called *tola*. He presents it on arrival, and when he leaves he too is given a bit to carry home.

Men believe beef to be good for sexual potency.

In the Mawai area I was told that even so recently as ten years ago, the Agaria used to steal other people's cows for sacrifice to Lohasur in the pit. The practice then stopped, but a year or two ago, Lohasur appeared to an elderly Agaria called Doharkur and said, 'If you don't offer me a cow, you'll die and your children'. Doharkur stole a cow and killed it, but he was caught, and punished.

CHAPTER VI

MAGIC

I. *Position of the Blacksmith*

All over the world primitive people regard the blacksmith with a mixture of fear and reverence. In ancient Egypt iron was believed to convey some moral taint to the user. In Africa, the Nandi clans, who share the general Hamitic attitude of contempt for smiths, will not generally intermarry with those of the tribe who work in iron. They will not let their cattle herd or breed with the cattle belonging to the smiths, and whenever 'a Nandi picks up anything new which a smith has made he first spits into his hand'.[1] Other African tribes object to the introduction of iron hoes which they say keep away the rain,[2] an objection shared by the Bhadawi of Java,[3] the Eastern Rengma of Assam[4] and the peasants of Poland. Among the Caribou Esquimaux, iron, a new material to them, was not worked during the musk-ox hunting.[5] On the coasts of Connacht, Ireland, the blacksmiths—against whose spells there is an invocation in the ancient charm, St Patrick's Breastplate—are greatly feared, for they have the fatal power of cursing by turning their anvil or making a hole in a coin laid upon it. Near Canra too an uneasy fear of the blacksmith's magic protects the forge from theft.[6]

The blacksmith is not only feared and despised socially; he is also regarded as sacred and even worshipped. Among the people of the Lower Congo, 'the native forge of a blacksmith was considered sacred and they never stole from it. If anyone did so he would be punished by contracting "mpiki" or scrotal

[1] A. C. Hollis, *The Nandi* (Oxford, 1909), p. 36.
[2] R. U. Sayce, *Primitive Arts and Crafts*, p. 194.
[3] Frazer, *The Golden Bough: Taboo* (London, 1911), p. 232.
[4] J. P. Mills, *The Rengma Nagas* (London, 1937), p. 87.
[5] Sayce, op. cit., p. 194.
[6] *Folk-Lore*, Vol. XXXIII, p. 393.

hernia. Any person who so far forgot himself as to sit on the anvil would get swollen legs.'[1]

The Zulus regard the smith with respect: his art is a secret and confined to one family: the workshop is in a secret place.[2] In Irish folk-lore, the dreaded blacksmith Cullann, who lived not only by the art of working in metals but also by the wealth which prophesy and divination brought him was originally a deity of the lower world. He was the enemy of Cuchulainn, whom Rhys identifies with the Sun, and killed his war-hound.[3]

In England, too, the calling of a blacksmith has a 'long tradition of magic and power. He was associated with the most potent of charms—fire, iron and horseshoes: he was the servant of the sacred horse.'[4] In Berkshire, under the White Horse, is Wayland's Smithy. If anyone put a coin on a stone here, his horse would be magically shod by Wayland—who was once a god of the Scandinavian pantheon. The great number of people called Smith and the tradition of marriages in a smithy—as on the anvil at Gretna Green—testify to the honoured and even sacred nature of the profession.

There is a blacksmith deity in Japan, but he is one-eyed,[5] and in Burma a coconut, surmounted by a piece of red cloth, still hangs in every house in honour of Min Magayi, the mighty blacksmith who watches over the home. This blacksmith, who was called Maung Tin De as a man, was so strong that when he struck his anvil the whole city shook. This angered the king who had him burnt alive in a champac tree; his sister followed him into the flames. After their death, the spirits or Nats ate everyone who came near, and at last an annual festival had to be instituted to appease them.[6]

So also in India we find iron-workers generally occupying an inferior social position, although at the same time their

[1] J. H. Weeks, *Folk-Lore*, Vol. LXX, p. 311.

[2] E. Krige, *The Social System of the Zulus* (London, 1936), p. 209.

[3] J. Rhys, *Lectures* (London, 1888), pp. 445ff.

[4] C. Hole, *English Folk-lore* (London, 1940), p. 41.

[5] *Folk-Lore*, Vol. XIX, p. 73.

[6] *Folk-Lore*, Vol. XXXII, pp. 86ff.

magic is feared and they are sometimes honoured. Ibbetson writes of the Lohar of the Punjab that 'his social position is low even for a menial. Although not an outcaste, his caste is impure.' He quotes Colebrooke as saying that 'the Karmakara or blacksmith is classed in the *Puranas* as one of the polluted tribes'.[1] Whenever a Jat or Rajput, driven by poverty, or a member of the Suthar tribe of carpenters, turned to iron work, he was at once separated from the rest of the caste. In Bengal, those of the Barhi who took up iron work had to separate as the Kokas Lohar. Sonar who did the same thing were at once degraded and became the Kamarkalla Lohar.[2] In Champaran, the Kamia Lohar are regarded as ceremonially unclean.[3]

Russell quotes a saying which may be translated 'Beware of the Lohar, Teli and Dhobi, for they are of evil omen'.[4] When a Maria or Muria takes to iron work he has to move outside the village, and his former tribes-fellows no longer eat with him.[5] Of the five divisions of the Kamsala, the occupational caste of the Telugus, the blacksmith ranks as the lowest and the goldsmiths will not intermarry with them.[6] The Irumbu Kollan, the iron-workers of Malabar, are regarded as inferior.[7] The Tamil goldsmiths also now refuse to intermarry with the Karuman blacksmiths, though both belong to the same great occupational caste, the Kammalan.[8] Among some of the jungle tribes of South India, the iron-workers seem to be immigrants and are thus isolated as a foreign caste or guild.[9] The Lhota Naga regard the blacksmith's trade as very unlucky. 'It is believed that no blacksmith lives long after he stops work.' No house is ever built on the site of an old forge. If a piece of dross from the forge is brought into a house, the inhabitants will fall ill.[10]

[1] D. C. Ibbetson, *Outlines of Panjab Ethnology* (Calcutta, 1883), p. 327.
[2] ibid., p. 328.
[3] Risley, op. cit., Vol. II, p. 22.
[4] Russell and Hiralal, op. cit., Vol. IV, p. 122.
[5] Grigson, op. cit., p. 175.
[6] Thurston, op. cit., Vol. III, p. 143.
[7] ibid., p. 305.
[8] ibid., p. 107.
[9] Cammiade, 'Iron Smelting by Kois', *Man*, April 1931, p. 66.
[10] Mills, *The Lhota Nagas* (London, 1922), p. 41.

On the other hand, in India as elsewhere, the blacksmith is sometimes regarded with respect and awe. In Bengal the Lohar ranks with the Koiri and Kurmi, and even Brahmins take water from his hands. So also all Hindus take water from the Mahur Lohar.[1] In Chhattisgarh, at a Binjhwar wedding, someone belonging to the Lohar sept must always be present. Russell suggests that the reason is to be found in the estimation in which this craft was held when the Binjhwar first learnt it from their Hindu neighbours.[2] In Garhwal, it is believed that Kaliya Lohar had the honour of making weapons for the five Pandava, and he is worshipped accordingly.[3]

In the same way, although the Agaria are despised socially, they are regarded as having considerable supernatural value. Their power to make the Virgin Iron necessarily sets them apart from all others. I doubt if those who have abandoned beef-eating and use goat-hide or sambhar-hide instead of cow-hide for their bellows have done themselves much good by such reforms. The fear of the blacksmith does not derive from such superficialities but goes back, as we shall see, to a fundamental antagonism. The Agaria remain the lowest, socially, among the tribesmen proper. Baiga sometimes sell their children to the Agaria for a pice, Gond or Bharia call their sons Agaria in order to deceive hostile spirits as to their true value. It is a supreme disgrace for any family if a son or daughter marries a blacksmith. If a Hindu touches an Agaria bellows, he is penalized. The Agaria house is usually apart, away from the rest of the village. Yet the very people who so carefully segregate the Agaria come to them to have their babies touched with the red-hot sickle and call them to drive nails of Virgin Iron into the doors of their houses.

What is the meaning of this curious attitude? Ibbetson thought that the blacksmith's impurity was due to the dirty nature of his employment, or because he used bellows of cow-hide, or because black was ill-omened.[4] The Ages have, of

[1] Risley, op. cit., Vol. II, p. 22.

[2] Russell and Hiralal, op. cit., Vol. II, p. 332.

[3] *R.G.S.I.*, Vol. LVII, p. 163.

[4] Ibbetson, op. cit., p. 327.

course, degenerated in Indian thought from white, red, yellow, to the black Kali Yug. Black is the colour-symbol of the lowest, Sudra, caste.[1] Abbott thought that one of the reasons why the blacksmith was considered so unlucky was that he put an iron pipe or a bellows with an iron nozzle into the fire which the Brahmins considered holy.[2]

In Bastar State, some of the Dantewara Maria have rationalized their dislike of the blacksmith. In one village they explained their feeling by the fact that the originator of the Naiko Lohara had intercourse with a corpse. In another village they said that long ago a Lohara removed the brains from a dead Maria and put them into the furnace to improve the iron. Since then the Maria have not eaten with Lohara, even though most of them are members of the Maria tribe. But probably this explanation is intended to cover a piece of snobbery of which the people are really somewhat ashamed.

A curious parallel, however, to the Maria tradition has been recorded among the Achewa of the Sowa District of Nyasaland. When members of this tribe want to make a furnace, they get a doctor to put 'medicine' in a maize cob and throw it at a pregnant woman. This causes abortion and the foetus is buried. But the doctor digs it up at night, mixes it with more medicine and burns it in a hole in the ground. The furnace is then made by working clay into a wall which rises above this hole.[3]

Gunnar Landtman has discussed the low social position of the blacksmith in some detail. He considers that it is his association with iron, a magical substance, that suggests his possession of uncanny powers and thus sometimes causes him to be despised and sometimes feared and honoured.[4]

[1] Muir, *Sanskrit Texts*, Vol. I, p. 140. While organizing the Census in Bastar State, I found that many Hindus objected to having numbers painted in black on the walls of their houses. Throughout India, I believe, the house-numbering is usually done in red.

[2] Abbott, op cit., p. 217.

[3] A. G. O. Hodgson, *J.R.A.I.*, Vol. LXIII, p. 163.

[4] Gunnar Landtman, *The Primary Causes of Social Inequality* (London, 1933).

I have no doubt that this is the cause of the Agaria's low social position. The other reasons suggested are not sufficient. The Agaria's house and smithy are generally kept clean enough; he very rarely uses bellows of cow-hide; black is not specially ill-omened among the tribesmen. But iron is charged with a mysterious and dangerous power, which is specially potent against ghosts and evil spirits. 'Why iron has been regarded as a scarer of demons,' says Crooke, 'has been much debated. Natives (*sic*) of India will tell you that it is the material out of which weapons are made, and that an armed man should fear nothing. Others say that its virtues depend on its black colour which is obnoxious to evil spirits. Mr Campbell[1] thinks that the explanation may be that in all cases of swooning and seizures—which are, of course, generally regarded as due to attack or possession by evil spirits—'iron is of great value, either applied in the form of the cautery or used as a lancet to let blood'.[2] It has also been suggested that observation of the magnetic power of iron caused primitive peoples to think that it was possessed by a spirit and therefore had magical and powerful qualities.[3]

But the classical explanation of the power and danger of iron is that of Tylor, who is followed by Crooke and Westermarck. This is that the fairies and elves of Europe, the *jnūn* of Morocco, the *deo* and *bhut* of India, are creatures of the Stone Age surviving to a later time and entertaining a great hatred for the new metal which brought their kingdom to an end. As I suggest elsewhere, it may be that the war between the Gods and the Asura reflects this conflict, the Asura representing an iron-using people who first assailed and destroyed the customs of the Age of Stone. So Westermarck[4] accepts Tylor's[5] explanation of the spirits' fear of iron for the *jnūn* of Morocco, that they are essentially creatures

[1] J. S. Campbell, *Notes on the Spirit Basis of Belief and Custom* (Bombay, 1885), p. 34.

[2] Crooke, op. cit., Vol. II, p. 12.

[3] W. Ridgeway, *Report of the British Association for 1903*, p. 816.

[4] E. Westermarck, *The Belief in Spirits in Morocco.*

[5] E. B. Tylor, *Primitive Culture*, Vol. I, p. 140.

belonging to the ancient Stone Age and the new metal is hateful and hurtful to them. On the other hand, Canon J. A. Macculloch thought that the spirits' dislike of iron was simply a human dislike transferred to them—what men feared, spirits would also fear.

'Look now', he says, 'at the fairy dislike of iron, a dislike shared by ghosts and spirits. This is certainly primarily a human dislike, transferred to them, for what man feared, spirits would also fear . . . The discovery and working of metals was surrounded with mystery. This, and the suspicion connected with its early use and the supposed ill-luck following on that use contributed to the ideas regarding it in folk-lore. Its discovery was bound to be revolutionary to men whose ancestors had used stone weapons and tools for thousands of years; and as it was at first bound to be rare, magical ideas were easily connected with its use. Those who found it used against them would be struck with terror and easily conquered, just as in New Guinea, the possession of a single little piece of iron, out of which they would fashion a rude but terrible weapon, increased the repute of a single tribe. For such and other reasons, and for the fear of metal by those who did not possess it, men now regarded it as obnoxious to supernatural beings and effective against their inroads. Thus this dislike of iron by fairies need not prove that they are an early iron-metal using people transformed into elfins, but only that a well-known human fear of metal was transferred to supernatural beings by those who used it.'[1]

But there is very little sign of this supposed dislike of iron among the Indian aboriginals[2]; and the fact that a thing is mysterious does not, at least in India, cause its owner to be socially despised. I have little doubt that Tylor's view is

[1] J. A. Macculloch, in *Folk-Lore*, Vol. XLIII, pp. 372ff.

[2] Nor indeed elsewhere. Iron is usually eagerly sought by primitive people. When, for example, Captain Cook discovered the Hawaiian Islands in 1778, the islanders bartered their women for the new metal with the result that syphilis also was introduced among them. T. A. Rickard, 'The Knowledge and Use of Iron among the South Sea Islanders', *J.R.A.I.*, Vol. LXII, pp. 1–22.

right: the fear of the blacksmith, the power of his iron, the ambivalent attitude of avoidance and reverence, must have a very deep and ancient root. In the mythology of the Asura we have a symbolical picture of the whole position. And indeed there is a remarkable incident in a Birhor legend that directly links the iron-working Asur with the spirits. After Sing Bonga had succeeded in trapping the male Asur in their furnaces and destroying them, he 'hurled the female Asur in different directions; and their spirits still haunt rocks and woods, pools and streams and springs on which they fell. Such is the origin of some of the Elemental Spirits.'[1]

It is, I think, an important point in support of Tylor's view that the extraction of iron from ore is considered much less respectable, in the social sense, than simple iron work at the forge. The Agaria who brings iron out of the womb of the earth is the real enemy of the gods and spirits of the Stone Age.

II. *Taboos on Iron*

We are now in a position to examine the vast accumulation of folk-lore that has gathered about this truly precious metal, iron. We will begin with a discussion of the many and varied taboos that have been placed upon the metal. This subject has been elaborately considered by Frazer in *The Golden Bough*,[2] and from him I take the following examples. In antiquity no iron might touch the body of a king. In China, for instance, King Tieng-tsong-tai-oang died of a tumour, for no one dared lance it with a knife. Roman and Sabine priests might not be shaved with iron. The sacred wooden Pons Sublicius in Rome was kept in repair without use of iron or bronze. When an iron graving-tool was taken into the sacred grove of the Arval Brothers at Rome, a sacrifice was offered. As a general rule iron could not be taken into Greek sanctuaries. The Archon of Plataea was not usually allowed to touch iron. The Hebrews used a stone knife for circumcising

[1] S. C. Roy, *The Birhors* (Ranchi, 1925), p. 402.

[2] Frazer, *The Golden Bough*: *Taboo*, pp. 226ff., where all the authorities are given.

children, their altars might not be hewn, and Solomon commanded that neither hammer, nor axe, nor any tool of iron should be heard while the Temple was building. In more recent times, Frazer refers to the Hottentot priest who must not use iron to sacrifice an animal or circumcise a lad. In Uap of the Caroline Islands, hibiscus wood must not be cut with iron. The use of iron implements was forbidden to the Esquimaux of Bering Straits for four days after the slaughter of a white whale and an iron axe must never be used where salmon were being dressed. The negroes of the Gold Coast remove iron from their person before consulting their fetish. In Scotland the makers of a need-fire had to divest themselves of all metal. No Scottish Highlander would put iron into the ground on Good Friday.

We may add a few more examples to this impressive array. A writer in *Folk-Lore*, commenting on Frazer's list of taboos, remarks that 'my grandmother was not allowed by her midwife to touch knives, scissors, etc. I remember hearing my grandmother say how much annoyed she was at having all her food cut up for her, and when later she objected, she had to have the handles of the knives and scissors tied up in flannel bags.' [1]

Although iron is constantly used as a demon-scarer in pregnancy and confinement, yet 'according to an idea spread all over South America, the umbilical cord must not be cut with a knife or any other iron instrument, but with a bamboo knife or a snail's shell, for otherwise the child would die'.[2] There is a similar taboo among the Antandroy and Tanala of Madagascar.[3] Many tribes in India always used a bamboo knife or bit of broken earthenware for this purpose, though some have now taken to the use of knives. In Sind and Gujarat, according to Abbott, the cord must not be cut with iron. The Brahmins of Karnatak first touch the cord with the sacred thread of the child's father, and it is this which is supposed to do the actual cutting.[4]

[1] M. C. Paddon, in *Folk-Lore*, Vol. XXXII, p. 211.
[2] R. Karsten, in *Folk-Lore*, Vol. XLII, p. 196.
[3] Frazer, op. cit., p. 227.
[4] Abbott, op. cit., p. 218.

We have already seen how dangerous it is to steal anything from a smithy—a belief that may account for the casual way the Agaria leave their tools about near the forge—or to insult the iron. In England, in Hereford, it 'is considered most unlucky to hide iron: if the person who has done so dies, his spirit cannot rest, but haunts the place until the iron is found. A man called "Bill o' the Mill" in Witney Parish was haunted by someone who had hidden iron: he grew pale and ill and at last died. Another man was haunted by an apparition which obliged him to go and find some iron which had been hidden.'[1]

We have seen the taboo on the iron hoe. In a tenth-century collection of precepts known as the *Geopanica*, a Byzantine work on husbandry, it is advised that a young plant should always have superfluous leaves plucked off by hand, not cut with a knife, for it will be paralysed if it is touched with iron.[2] Vergil had long ago given the same advice.[3]

In India, the Magahiya Doms 'place iron under a stringent taboo, and any Magahiya who breaks into a house with an iron implement is not only put out of caste, but it is believed that some day or other he will lose his eyesight'.[4] The Lhota Naga regard the blacksmith's trade as very unlucky. No house is ever built on the site of an old forge. To bring a piece of dross from the forge into a house makes the inhabitants fall ill, and it is believed 'that no blacksmith lives long after he stops work'.[5]

The Sindhi Mussalman will not allow his *matar* crop to be reaped with an iron instrument, and in Sind iron may not be taken on to the threshing floor. In Kanera the turmeric root may not be uprooted by iron. The Mussalman refuses to use iron for pounding antimony. When a Hindu offers *bel* and *tulsi* leaves to a god, he must not cut them with iron.[6]

[1] E. M. Leather, *The Folk-lore of Herefordshire* (1912), pp. 33ff.
[2] H. J. Rose, *Folk-Lore*, Vol. XLIV, p. 76. [3] *Georgics*, ii, 366.
[4] Crooke, op. cit., Vol. II, p. 12. See also *North Indian Notes and Queries*, Vol. V, p. 63. [5] Mills, *The Lhota Nagas* (London, 1922), p. 41.
[6] Abbott, op. cit., pp. 217ff.

A different application of the taboo was seen in the prohibition of a nineteenth-century Raja of Vizianagram, who forbade the employment of any iron in the construction of buildings in his State, because this was believed to be followed inevitably by small-pox and other epidemics.[1]

So also, even at the present day the Clavie at Burghead is prepared for the New Year celebrations with stone tools only. It is still thought unlucky, in parts of England, to accept a knife from anyone without paying for it.[2]

III. *'Iron is Lucky'*

If a subconscious dread of the new metal has induced mankind to impose certain taboos on iron, a more conscious instinct has driven him to use the same metal as a protection against the hostile denizens of the world he has now left long behind him. Iron may be taboo, but iron is lucky. Iron is the symbol of the safe, convenient, mobile world we know. Iron is our defence against all human foes; it may surely be turned against those supernatural relicts of the past which assail us with the clumsy missiles of the Age of Stone.

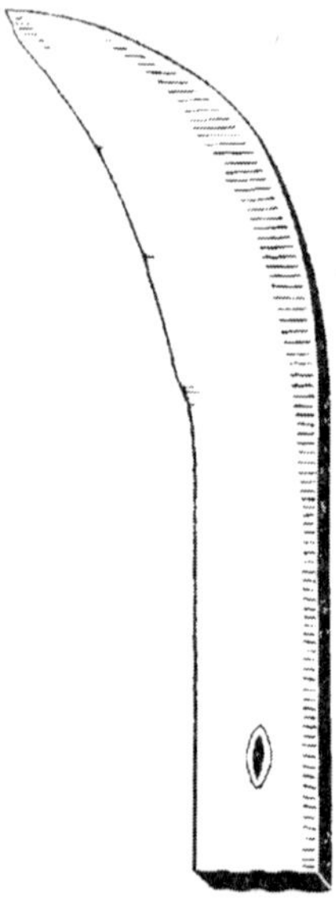

FIG. 5. *Bāki* knife
1/3 actual size

Iron is lucky. In England, chauffeurs are said to carry a nail which has caused a puncture as a mascot.[3] On the Irrawaddy River in Burma, boatmen carry iron pyrites as a protection against alligators.[4] In English Worcestershire, it is considered lucky to tread on a bit of iron with the left foot.[5] In Norway, a knife or other bit of iron dropped into the brewing-vat will improve the quality of the Yule-ale—

[1] *Indian Antiquary*, Vol. X (1881), p. 364. [2] Hole, op. cit., p. 127.
[3] *Folk-Lore*, Vol. XIX, p. 292. [4] Penzer, *Ocean of Story*, Vol. III, p. 168.
[5] *Folk-Lore*, Vol. XX, p. 345.

and what better luck is there than that?[1] In France, where it is considered unlucky by non-Catholics to meet a black-clad Catholic priest, there is a custom of touching iron, such as a bunch of keys, or even a railing or lamp-post.[2] In fact, 'to touch iron has the same protective value as touching wood'.[3]

This so lucky iron is humanity's best weapon against the other, or the ancient, world. R. U. Sayce,[4] discussing the origin of fairies, compares them with the Moroccan *jnūn.* Both fear salt and iron. In Fez many people wear a steel ring on the finger to keep them off. Swords, daggers and needles are often used at weddings and guns are fired to drive them away. He quotes Campbell for the story that in Scotland a man once aimed with his gun at an enchanted deer which was really a beautiful lady in disguise. It was only when he looked through the iron sights that he saw what it was. Another man shot a deer from his hip, because on looking over the sights it looked like an old man. But when the hunter came up to his quarry he found nothing but the body of a very old man crumbled into dust. The iron sights had told the truth.[5]

Iron is everywhere a protection against witchcraft. In the Isle of Skye a piece of old iron buried near the gate keeps witches from the house. On the coasts of Connacht, Ireland, charms of fire, iron and salt are used against the *pūca* spirits.[6] A report from the west of England describes how a certain Vicar 'was scandalized to see an old lady hammering a large nail into the footprint of another woman who had just passed down the lane and was informed that the maker of the footprint had overlooked the operator, and that this proceeding would counteract the spell'.[7]

Among the Catholics of Salsette, iron was believed to be efficacious against the mischievous spirit called *gira*, who is

[1] *Folk-Lore*, Vol. XX, p. 322.
[2] *Folk-Lore*, Vol. XIX, p. 205.
[3] Hole, op. cit., p. 127.
[4] R. U. Sayce, in *Folk-Lore*, Vol. XLV, p. 130.
[5] *Folk-Lore*, Vol. XXXIV, p. 92.
[6] ibid., p. 335.
[7] ibid., Vol. XIX, p. 88.

afraid to touch anyone carrying a knife or nail. 'It is believed that if anyone can manage to drive a nail in the *gira's* head, he again becomes a man,' and a useful servant. Horseshoe nails were driven into the threshold to stop spirits entering the home.[1] Similarly in Rumania, iron alone can stop a vampire turning a living brother, who was unfortunate enough to be born on the same day or month of the year, into another vampire. The process is called 'taking out of iron'. An iron chain, such as is used for hanging the pot over the fire or in bullock carts, is put round the two brothers, the living and the dead. The ends are solemnly closed and opened three times and the living brother is free.[2]

In Norway, it is believed that the *huldre*-folk, the underground people, have large herds of cattle. But they are afraid of steel, and the cattle may be caught by its help.[3]

Many Esthonians of Oesel Island will not eat bread baked of new corn till they have taken a bite at a piece of iron.[4] So too the Mahakam Dyaks of Central Borneo bite on an old sword or set their feet on it, as a protection against the spirits of the other world.[5]

IV. *Iron at Birth*

The protective power of iron is specially evident at the great crises of human life, birth, marriage and death, when mortal man lies specially exposed to the malice of his enemies. In the Isle of Skye, a bit of iron should be put in the baby's cradle.[6] In Rumania, the Serb women of Moldavia put a needle with a red thread on the threshold during pregnancy; in Macedonia, they put a twisted red and white thread over the door and a knife at the threshold; in Bukovina, the midwife drives a nail with a red tassel over the door during the birth.[7] In Galicia, 'in order to facilitate delivery it is

[1] C. F. D'Penha, 'Superstitions and Customs in Salsette', *Indian Antiquary*, Vol. XXVIII (1899), p. 114. [2] *Folk-Lore*, Vol. XXXVIII, p. 62.
[3] ibid., Vol. XX, p. 324. [4] Frazer, op. cit., p. 481.
[5] Frazer, *The Golden Bough: The Magic Art*, Vol. I, p. 159.
[6] *Folk-Lore*, Vol. XXXIV, p. 92. [7] ibid., p. 359.

customary to place the front-door key under the pillow'.[1] In Norway a bit of steel was tied in the swaddling-clothes of a new-born baby.[2] The Toradjas of Celebes set the feet of a new-born child on a bit of iron to strengthen it.[3] Among the Italian peasants of the Abruzzi in the Central Apennines, it is believed that it is dangerous for the mother to comb her hair till eight days after delivery; then she must have a piece of heated iron, such as a spit, pick or hatchet, under her feet or she will lose all her hair.[4]

In the Philippines, the husband is said to strip himself naked and stand on guard in the house or even on the roof, flourishing a sword continually till the child is born. When a child is born in Upper Burma, the Kachins fire guns and brandish knives and torches over the mother.[5]

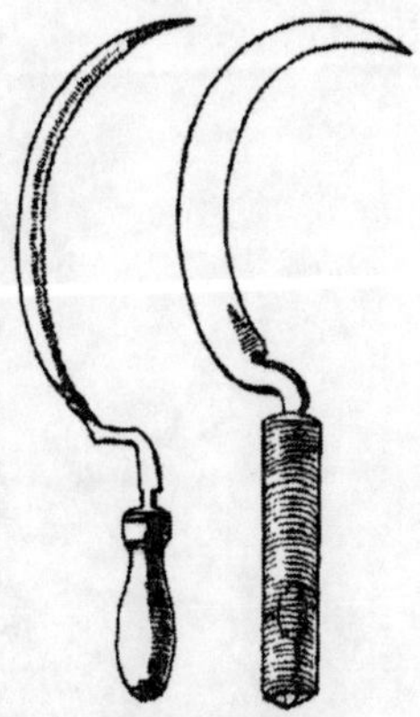

FIG. 6. Sickles
Blades 1/5 actual size

The Mala of South India keep a sickle and *nim* leaves in the child-bed to drive away evil spirits, and the child is branded with a hot needle in twenty places.[6] In the Deccan nails are driven into the ground at the four corners of the mother's bed; in Sind arrows are often used instead. Iron nails are driven in the threshold. Lingayat women wear an iron needle in their hair and Vaddar women keep a knife tied in the arm-pit at this time.[7]

The Vadval of Thana (Bombay), in order to guard against a spirit which attacks the child on the sixth day after birth, place an iron knife or scythe on the mother's bed, and an iron bickern at the door of the lying-in room. This has also been observed for the Panjab, and probably occurs throughout

1 *Folk-Lore*, Vol. XL, p. 386. 2 ibid., Vol. XX, p. 320.
3 Frazer, op. cit., p. 159. 4 E. Canziani, *Folk-Lore*, Vol. XXXIX, p. 214.
5 Penzer, op. cit., Vol. III, p. 167. 6 Thurston, op. cit., Vol. IV, p. 369.
7 Abbott, op. cit., p. 223.

India.[1] I have myself noticed how Gond and Pardhan women with young babies always carry an iron sickle when they go abroad. An iron betel-cutter may also be kept near the child's head.

The Catholics of Salsette put iron in the dress of a young mother dying in child-bed. Such a woman in other parts of India, or a woman dying in pregnancy, is supposed to turn into a *Churelin*—and this can only be prevented by the use of iron nails.[2]

Crooke suggests that the reason why mothers are particularly exposed to supernatural influence at this time may be inferred from the fact that the Scotch fairies are very fond of milk, and try to gratify their desires on 'unsained' or unchurched women.[3] I know of only one case where the magic qualities of iron are used for contraception. Himes quotes a report from the island of Nias, near Sumatra, that 'a woman who does not wish to become pregnant is obliged to rub a knife on a grindstone; then to pour some water on the knife and grindstone, and subsequently to drink this water

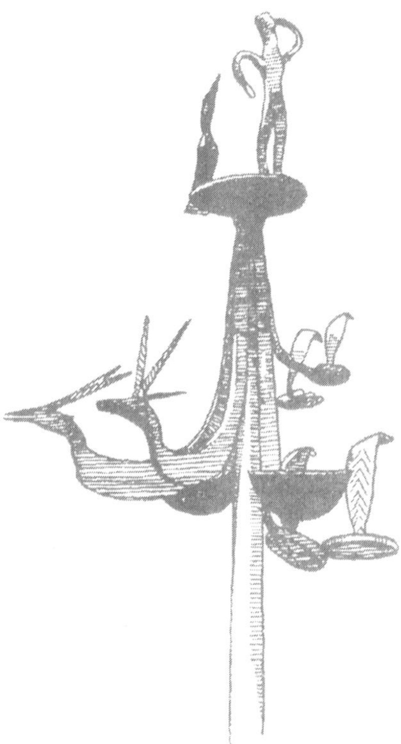

FIG. 7. *Hiranoti* lampstand
Height, 3' 5"

[1] Penzer, op. cit., Vol. III, pp. 166ff.

[2] D'Penha, op. cit., p. 114.

[3] Crooke, op. cit., Vol. II, p. 13.

16. (*a*) Patharia Agaria house at Pungaon.

(*b*) Khuntia Chokh house at Nunera.

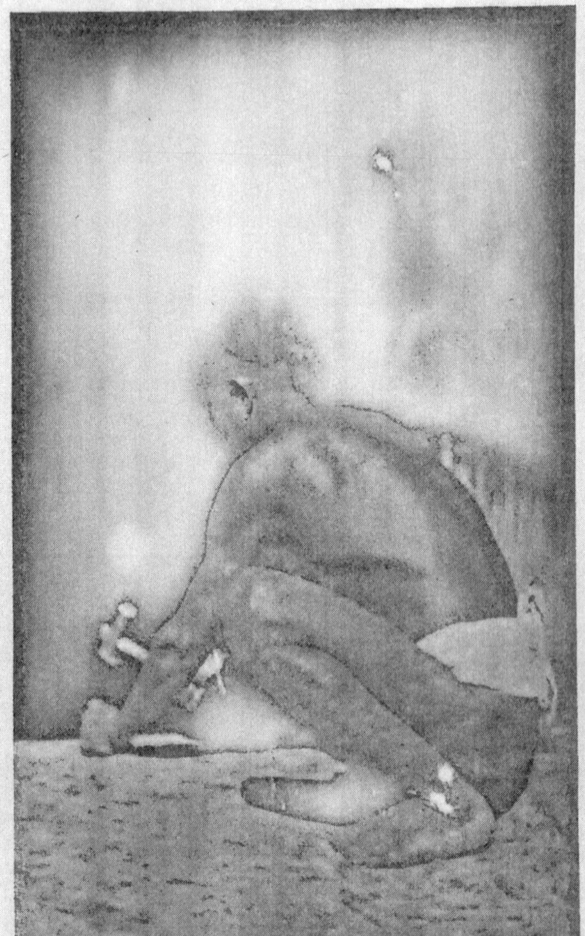

17. Agaria drives a nail of magic iron into the threshold of a house in Bhoira.

while pronouncing a magical incantation'. The people of this area are said to attribute high magical virtues to iron and steel.[1]

V. *Iron in Marriage*

The Agaria and their neighbours use iron, and especially virgin iron, to protect the bride and bridegroom during the marriage ceremony. The bridegroom must keep with him during the entire proceedings an iron betel-cutter. He sometimes wears an iron torc round his neck and an iron bracelet. Elaborate iron-lamps for the wedding-booth are very popular when obtainable. The *chulmundri* wedding-ring is a combination of brass, bell-metal and virgin iron, a potent demon-scarer. At her first entry into her husband's house, the bride steps over a piece of iron. A full account of the use of iron in marriages in western India has been given by Abbott.[2]

VI. *Iron at Death*

At times of death and mourning, the evil spirits are also specially active, and iron must be used for protection against them. When a child is still-born in Burma, the people place a bit of iron near the little body saying, 'Never more return into thy mother's womb till this metal becomes as soft as down'.[3] The Bison-horn Maria, before burying the victims of small-pox or women dying in pregnancy or child-birth, get the local magician to drive nails into the knees and elbows.[4] This custom is common throughout India.

Iron is often buried with the dead. An old Irishman, buried at Kirton-in-Lindsay, is said to have given his wife a key to put in his grave to open the door to heaven. So too the key of Bishop's Norton Church in England is said to have been found under the head of Matthew Lidgett, parish clerk, who died in 1742.[5]

[1] N. E. Himes, *Medical History of Contraception* (London, 1936), p. 38.

[2] Abbott, op. cit., pp. 224ff. [3] Penzer, op. cit., Vol. III, p. 167.

[4] Grigson, op. cit., p. 283.

[5] *Folk-Lore*, Vol. XXV, p. 381 and Vol. XXXVIII, p. 399.

In parts of the Highlands of Scotland, when a grave has been dug, a spade is laid across the mouth to keep evil away till the coffin is put in. Sometimes a Bible, keys and a piece of iron are laid on top of the coffin. Coffin-keys in Scotland are regarded as 'heavy with dread'. Immediately after a death in peasant Scotland, a bit of iron, say a nail, is stuck into the meal, butter, cheese, meat and whisky 'to prevent death from entering them'. Otherwise the food corrupts and the whisky turns white as milk.[1]

VII. *Iron Nails*

A common way of applying the magic virtues of iron is in the form of nails. This is how the Agaria usually bring the comfort of their Virgin Iron to an anxious household; it is thus that the Baiga save the world from the terrors of earthquake.[2] Toothache is cured in the Panjab by driving a nail into a tree. Or a charm is written on a piece of paper and an iron nail twisted in the form of the Arabic letter Jain is driven through it.[3] In Persia there is a common custom of driving nails into the holy trees by the side of a shrine. In China, where silk-cotton trees are supposed to be haunted by a dangerous female demon, she is exorcized by driving long nails into the tree: should a nail go into her head the demon immediately becomes a human being again.[4] In Bastar the malignant ghost of a woman dying in child-birth is sometimes exorcized by driving nails through her hands, knees and feet. When the new *rath* (chariot) is constructed for the Dashara ceremony at Jagdalpur (Bastar) a Savara ceremonially drives an iron nail into the main beam as a protection against evil.

The Romans are said to have driven long nails into the walls of cottages to avert plague. Pliny says that if nails that have been extracted from a tomb are driven into a door, they

[1] W. Gregor, *Folk-lore of the North-East of Scotland*, p. 206.
[2] *The Baiga*, p. 307.
[3] C. S. Burne, *Folk-Lore*, Vol. LXXI, p. 332.
[4] M. J. Walhouse in *The Indian Antiquary*, Vol. X (1881), p. 365.

will protect the household from nightmare. The *Geoponica* recommends that an iron nail should be put in the litter for hens to lay on, for this 'iron is thought to be a protection against all manner of evil'.[1]

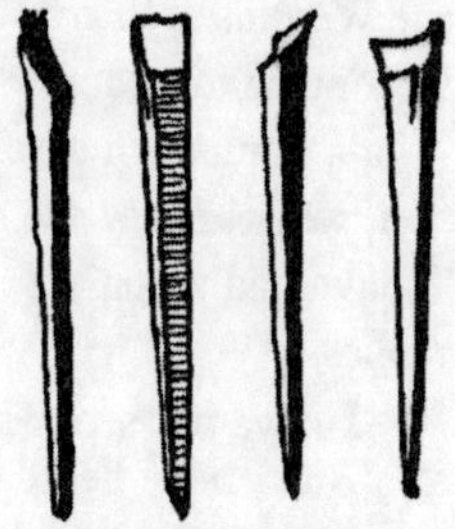

FIG. 8. Nails of Magic Iron
Actual size

All over the world trees may be found covered with nails driven into their branches. For example, near the Holy Well on the Island of Saint Mhaolrubh, many rags were hung from an old tree and the tree itself was studded with nails.[2] And Dr A. H. Sayce records that 'Mr. G. D. Hornblower has informed me that he found an acacia in a village near the Pyramids full of iron nails, and was told that they were driven into it in order to propitiate the *sukkan es-sont*, "the *inhabitants of* the acacia"'.[3]

Nails are commonly used in Japanese charms intended to cause injury to an enemy. They are aften driven into trees with the idea that this will irritate the tree-spirit and incite it to vengeance. A needle may be driven into a drooping willow in order to annoy the spirit and cause it to cure a tooth-ache.[4] In China also, should a 'woman be troubled by the pangs of pregnancy, the first thing necessary is to remove nails which have inadvertently been driven into a wall, door, etc., as they may be harassing some earth-spirit'.[5]

Among Christian people the reverence and fear attaching to nails has probably been reinforced by the medieval devotion to the nails that held Christ to the Cross. In the course of

[1] H. J. Rose, *Folk-Lore*, Vol. XLIV, p. 76.

[2] *Folk-Lore*, Vol. XLI, p. 228.

[3] A. H. Sayce, 'Cairene and Upper Egyptian Folk-lore', *Folk-Lore*, Vol. XXXI, p. 202.

[4] W. L. Hildburgh, 'Notes on some Japanese Magical Methods for Injuring Persons', *Man*, Vol. XV (1915), p. 119, and 'Seven Japanese Variants of a Toothache-charm, including a Driven Nail', *Man*, Vol. XIII (1913), pp. 147ff.

[5] J. J. M. de Groot, *The Religious System of China*, Vol. VI, Bk. II, p. 1257.

centuries many tender and beautiful ideas have gathered about the Wounds of Christ, and these would naturally tend to appear in popular folk-lore in a cruder form.

In a Rumanian carol[1] about the Lady Mary's search for her Son, we hear how she meets a famous smith and weeps saying, 'I have had an only Son and this One I have lost'. The smith replies,

> I have not seen Him,
> But I have heard of Him,
> For I was called to make the nails,
> And well did they pay me.
> They asked me to make big and heavy nails,
> But I made them thin and light.

And she answers,

> Master smith, master smith,
> Blessed shalt thou be.
> Strike with thy hammer,
> And get at once thy pay.

Blacksmiths in England generally refuse to work on Good Friday. Mr R. M. Heanley[2] describes how he was once driving to Skegness on that day and his horse cast a shoe. The smith refused to help him, saying that 'owd skraat' would have him if he touched hammer or nails on Good Friday. In the Isle of Man 'no iron of any kind must be put into the fire on that day, and even the tongs are laid aside, lest any person should unfortunately forget this custom and stir the fire with them . . . To avoid also the necessity of hanging the griddle over the fire, lest the iron of it should come in contact with a spark or flame, a large bannock or *soddag* is made, with three corners, and baked on the hearth.' Ironing clothes or heating an iron on Good Friday was also considered wrong.[3]

VIII. *Iron Rings*

Rings are a simple and obvious way of carrying the protective armour of iron about the person. The Agaria make

[1] *Folk-Lore*, Vol. XXXIV, p. 74.

[2] R. M. Heanley, *The Vikings: Their Folk-lore in Marshland.*

[3] *Folk-Lore*, Vol. XI, p. 92.

8. Agaria drives a magic nail into a cot to protect the sleeper from bad dreams.

19. (*a*) Gourd magic with bow and arrow to protect the smithy (Mandla District).

(*b*) Magic monkey to protect the smithy from hostile magic (Mandla District).

iron rings, anklets and bracelets as charms against all kinds of evil: an anklet is worn by a *lamu* child to protect it against lightning. In Annam, parents are said to sell their children occasionally to the smith who puts an iron anklet on its foot, usually with a small iron chain. After the child has grown and the danger from spirits is over, the anklet is broken.[1]

FIG. 9. Iron ring
Actual size

On the Slave Coast of Africa, when a child is found to be wasting away, the mother lures the demon from its body by a sacrifice of food, and then hastily attaches iron rings with small bells to the ankles and iron chains round the neck to prevent the demon returning.[2] Among the *fellahin* of Lower and Upper Egypt,

FIG. 10. Bracelets
1/2 actual size

the death of a child is often attributed to the influence of the mother's invisible 'companion' or double. Iron anklets

[1] Penzer, op. cit., Vol. III, p. 166.
[2] Frazer, *The Golden Bough: Taboo*, p. 235.

are worn by the mother and surviving children to avert this danger.[1]

In Ireland an iron ring on the fourth finger is believed to cure rheumatism,[2] and in Spain and Portugal steel finger-rings are regarded as protective against 'bad currents of air' which produce paralysis.[3]

I have not noticed in India the idea, common in classical antiquity and in English poetry (Vaughan, for example) that the circle or ring symbolizes eternity or permanence. The Romans often gave the Pronubium, an iron wedding-ring which perhaps had the additional symbolism of modesty and economy. At the end of a bargain, the Romans often exchanged rings.[4]

IX. *The Horseshoe*

In Europe, the iron horseshoe is one of the commonest of lucky talismans. It is a lunar symbol; it is made of iron; it belongs to the horse which has always been a sacred animal in England, where there are famous White Horses cut in the side of the hills at Bratton in Wiltshire and at Uffington in Berkshire. Nailed on a door with its point upwards, it protects the house or stable from evil. Nelson is said to have had a horseshoe nailed to the mast of the *Victory*.[5] Even modern taxi-drivers prefer registration numbers which include the letter U because it looks like a horse-shoe, and two U's are specially lucky.[6]

The small pack-ponies that toil wearily over the Maikal Hills are not shod, and the Agaria there have thus no part in what is perhaps the best-known function of the European blacksmith. Even officials in this Agaria area have to send their horses long distances down to headquarters when they need attention.

[1] C. G. Seligman in *Essays Presented to W. Ridgeway* (London, 1914), p. 450.

[2] Crooke, op. cit., Vol. II, p. 13.

[3] *Folk-Lore*, Vol. XIX, p. 221.

[4] W. Jones, *Finger Ring Lore* (London, 1877), p. 303.

[5] Hole, op. cit., p. 83.

[6] H. Hodge, *Cab, Sir?* (London, 1939), p. 72.

X. *Iron and the Weather*

Iron has an important effect on material objects, which are, of course, generally believed to be possessed by spiritual beings. Its effect on houses is probably due to a belief in sympathetic magic; the undecaying iron will keep the house from decay. In parts of India, while a house is being built an iron pot or a pot painted black is kept on the spot, and when the house is ready the young daughter of the owner ties to the lintel a charm of which the principal ingredient is an iron ring.[1] The Rengma Naga bury rice, iron and a whetstone in the foundations of a house—rice for plenty, iron for durability and the stone for a long life.[2]

Although in some places iron is supposed to have a bad effect upon the crops, in others it is used to stimulate them. In Porto Rico, nails are driven into trees to make them fruitful.[3] In Illinois, if a fruit tree will not bear, the farmers tie pieces of iron to the branches.[4] Sometimes they bury an old iron bucket at the root of a peach tree.[5]

Iron has considerable influence on the weather. The Indians of Canada used to put out their swords in a storm to frighten off the demon of thunder. 'The common belief is that the evil spirit is such a fool that he runs against the sharp edge of the weapon and allows himself to be wounded.'[6] In Upper India, says Crooke again, in order to bring rain, the people sometimes seize the blacksmith's anvil and pitch it into a well or tank.[7] 'The anvil is probably used for this purpose because it is regarded as a sort of fetish and the blacksmith himself is considered as invested with supernatural powers.' Elsewhere in India, the villagers drive away hail by taking out an iron griddle plate and beating it with a bit of bamboo. This should be done, if possible, by a virgin. Sometimes it is enough if an

[1] Crooke, op. cit., Vol. II, p. 13.
[2] Mills, op. cit., p. 57.
[3] *Folk-Lore*, Vol. XXXVIII, p. 62.
[4] H. M. Hyatt, *Folk-lore from Adams County Illinois* (New York, 1935), p. 48.
[5] ibid., p. 50.
[6] Crooke, op. cit., Vol. II, p. 13.
[7] ibid., Vol. I, p. 74.

unmarried girl goes out with an iron plate in her hand.[1]

Iron is a valuable protection against thunder and lightning. Pliny advised farmers to put a piece of iron in the nest of a sitting hen to save the eggs from thunder. The same idea is reported from Illinois, where the farmers are said to put iron round a nest of goose-eggs to save them from thunder.[2] In England (Surrey), among other amulets nodules of iron pyrites are used to protect against lightning and other ills.[3] Readers of Dickens will remember that Mrs Nickleby's eccentric admirer, the old gentleman, proposed to stow away the crystal globules of her tears in 'the fourteen binn, with a bar of iron on the top to keep the thunder off'.

The Spanish Basques, during a thunderstorm 'set a metal axe, cutting edge upward, beside the doorway, in order to protect a house from being struck by lightning . . . In some districts it is considered that similar protection may be obtained from a pair of scissors, or a sickle, or a scythe—all objects which, it should be observed, are sharp-edged implements made of iron—in the place of an axe.'[4] The theory behind this is probably not an idea that the sharp edge will split the thunderbolt, but may be connected with the widespread use of weapons against the supernatural beings who cause the storms, as well as with the very ancient associations between lightning and iron.

'Iron', says Dr Hildburgh, 'may well long have been regarded as containing something very like lightning, for sparks may be struck from it; and meteoric iron, when seen to fall with a flash accompanied by a noise resembling thunder, probably helped to substantiate beliefs of the kind. Thus it may be that iron came, because of these associations, to be employed homoeopathically—just as prehistoric stone implements were employed homoeopathically—as a protection against lightning.'[5]

[1] Crooke, op. cit., Vol. II, p. 13.
[2] Hyatt, op. cit., p. 81.
[3] *Folk-Lore*, Vol. XIX, p. 297.
[4] W. L. Hildburgh, *Man*, Vol. XLI, p. 17.
[5] *ibid.*, p. 18.

XI. *Iron in Medicine*

The medical properties of iron are now universally recognized and the metal is widely used. But long before this, its magic virtues were potent against disease. I will give a few examples from many different parts of the world.

Friend [1] has some interesting remarks about the medicinal use of iron in antiquity. He quotes Pliny (Bk. XXXIV, ch. 44) as recommending a slight puncture with an iron weapon to relieve pains in the chest, cauterization with hot iron as a remedy for the bite of a mad dog, and water, in which iron has been plunged at a white heat as a potion to cure dysentery. The rust of iron serves to relieve no fewer than fourteen ailments. 'It has the effect of uniting wounds, and is possessed of certain desiccative and astringent properties . . . Diluted in wine, and kneaded with myrrh, it is applied to recent wounds, and, with vinegar, to condylomatous swellings. Employed in the form of a liniment, it alleviates gout.'

Iron is the symbol of Mars and perhaps for this reason is regarded as an admirable tonic. It promotes child-birth, and Friend refers to the legend of King Iphiclus of Phylacea who, desiring to have children, was successfully treated by Melampus with iron rust in wine. In comparatively modern times there was a tradition in Frankfurt by which burghers' wives were prohibited from visiting the chalybeate springs at Schwalbach more than twice, lest they should prove too fruitful.

In Africa, the Congo medicine-man rubs two pieces of iron down the legs and arms of his patient three times as a cure for loss of nervous energy.[2] In Morocco, a knife or dagger is often put under the pillow of a sick man to keep off the demons that may make him worse.[3] A knife is likewise effective for warding off attacks of epilepsy among the Rumanian-speaking people of Duboka.[4] In Galicia, where there is danger of

[1] Friend, *Iron in Antiquity* (London, 1926), pp. 95ff.

[2] *Folk-Lore*, Vol. XXI, p. 466.

[3] A. Leared, *Morocco and the Moors* (London, 1876), p. 273.

[4] *Folk-Lore*, Vol. XLIII, p. 235.

rabies, 'the person who has been bitten is taken to the house of the villager who holds the "Keys of Sant Entelo", blessed keys that can open the doors of the parish church. Then both persons go to the smithy, and one of the keys is laid on the forge and heated to a white heat. At once it is quickly applied to the afflicted and a cross made. It is to be noted that it is not placed on the wound itself.'[1]

In South Indiana, a method of curing toothache was to ask the sufferer's name and then drive a nail into some secret place.[2] In the Isle of Skye, a charm for toothache was to take a nail from a coffin in the churchyard and hold it to the aching tooth. We have already seen a similar remedy used in India.[3]

A cure for shingles in Gloucestershire was to place some wheat on the anvil in a smithy and apply it to the diseased part.[4] The *Geoponica* prescribes for spleen a red-hot iron dipped in water which is then mixed with wine and vinegar.[5] A similar cure with water in which hot iron has been dipped comes from County Clare. Near Corofin, it is said, a patient suffering from 'internal trouble' is taken to the smithy and laid across the anvil, when the smith pretends to hammer him. He then makes the sick man drink some water in which hot iron has been dipped.[6] In Illinois, iron put in the water of chickens will save them from white diarrhoea.[7]

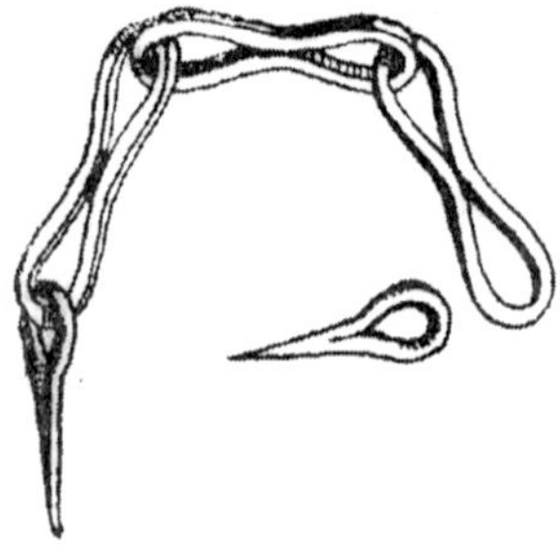

FIG. 11. Iron chains for fastening doors
1/4 actual size

In the Solomon Islands a strained muscle may be cured by mixing the pulped roots of a plant with a quantity of *oin* (a red powder, a variety

[1] *Folk-Lore*, Vol. XL, p. 61.
[2] ibid., Vol. XLVII, p. 364.
[3] ibid., Vol. XXXIV, p. 90.
[4] ibid., Vol. XXII, p. 238.
[5] ibid., Vol. XLIV, p. 89.
[6] ibid., Vol. XXXIII, p. 392.
[7] Hyatt, op. cit., p. 75.

of iron oxide much used for magical purposes).[1] In England, at Alcombe, the smith used to possess a charm by which he could draw out nails from a horse's frog, and heal the wound. This charm, says Miss Hole, could only be told to one person at a time: in 1939 the daughter of the late smith was using it.[2]

In Illinois again, a tub of old iron placed under the bed saves the patient from bed-sores.[3] In Ceylon, a bit of iron placed on a sore keeps off the demons that might exacerbate it. A sick man should not go out of the house without keys or a knife for fear the demons attack him in his weak state.[4]

In India, during cholera people carry axes or sickles to keep the disease away. In Salsette, knives were kept under the pillow as a charm against the nightmare. In a case of jaundice the left arm of the sufferer was branded with a red-hot iron and a hatchet was waved over the patient's body.[5] Among the Lhota Naga, a cure for rheumatism is a piece of iron put into the trunk of a tree that has been struck by lightning.[6] The Kamar regard iron as the emblem of the goddess of small-pox and worship it at Hareli and Dasahra.[7] In Sind, if an insect bite inflames the eye, the sore place is touched with a bit of iron and the patient says, 'Let the iron swell and let not the innocent eye'. So also generally for sore eyes in western India an iron plate is passed over them or the iron filings of a saw mixed with lemon juice is applied. Abbott reports—a cure for jaundice—a piece of iron is heated, dipped in a mixture of curds and turmeric and applied to the soles of the feet and palms of the hands.[8]

The art of 'blood-charming' is also connected with the blacksmith in England. There is a smith now living in West Cornwall mentioned by Hamilton Jenkin. Some time ago a workman cut his head, and with blood flowing from the wound was being taken to a doctor. But as they passed the smithy,

[1] *Folk-Lore*, Vol. XLVI, p. 149.
[2] Hole, op. cit., p. 41.
[3] Hyatt, op. cit., p. 227.
[4] Frazer, op. cit., p. 234.
[5] D'Penha, op. cit., p. 114.
[6] Mills, op. cit., p. 166.
[7] Russell and Hiralal, op. cit., Vol. III, p. 328.
[8] Abbott, op.cit., p. 221.

the blacksmith stopped them. He made some passes over the wound and the bleeding stopped. It is said that without any other treatment, the wound healed perfectly.[1]

It may be of interest to add some account, which will not be altogether out of place in a chapter on folk-lore, of the use to which iron has been put in traditional Indian medicine. U. C. Dutt has treated the matter very fully in his *The Materia Medica of the Hindus*[2] and I will quote him in some detail.

> Three varieties of iron, are used in Hindu medicine, namely *kanta lauha* or cast iron, *mandura* or rust, and *lauhasara* or salts of iron, produced by iron being kept in contact with vegetable acids. The form of cast iron used in manufacture of pans for boiling milk is considered superior to all others for medicinal use. The small particles of iron which are scattered around when hot iron is beaten on the anvil, are called *mandura*. They are allowed to remain in contact with the earth till they become very rusty and brittle, when they are considered fit for use. The properties of *mandura* are said to be analogous to those of cast iron.
>
> Cast iron is purified by beating it into thin plates, heating the plates in the fire, and sprinkling them with cow's urine, sour *congi* oil, and a decoction of the pulse *Dolichos biflorus* (*kulhatta*) seven times in succession. The plates are reduced to powder by pounding them in an iron mortar, rubbing them with cow's urine and roasting the mixture in a covered crucible repeatedly till it is reduced to a fine impalpable powder that will float on water and will not irritate the eyes when applied to them. It is usual to rub the iron with cow's urine and roast it about a hundred times in succession. In some cases it is recommended that iron should be thus roasted separately for a thousand times. *Mandura* is purified and prepared for use in the same way. Prepared iron is a fine impalpable powder of a reddish-grey or brick-dust colour.

This preparation of iron oxides was believed by the practitioners of Sanskrit medicine to increase strength, vigour and longevity—that endless quest of Indian magic and religion—to cure every disease and to be the finest of tonics. 'When gold

[1] A. Hamilton Jenkin, *Cornwall and the Cornish.*

[2] U. C. Dutt, *The Materia Medica of the Hindus*, pp. 46–54.

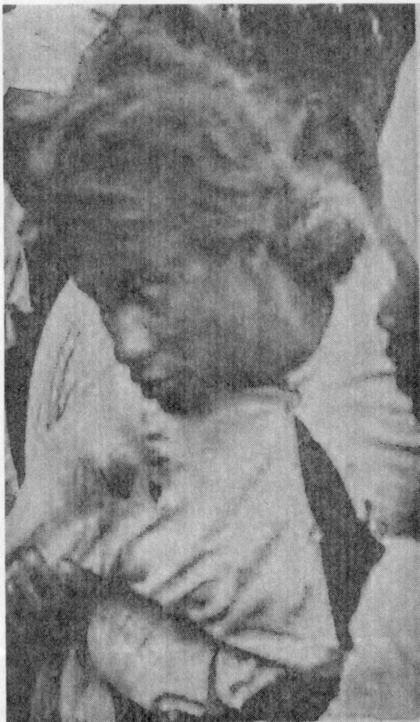

20. (*a*) Agaria of Mandla in trance during a wedding.

(*b*) Agaria possessed by Baghesur Pat during a wedding at Umaria (Mandla District).

21. Party of Agaria from Bhoira, Mandla District, returning from the jungle with ore and charcoal.

and silver are not available,' so Dutt continues, 'iron is substituted for them. It is used in painful dyspepsia, chronic fever, phthisis, anasarca, piles, enlarged spleen and liver, anaemia, obesity, urinary disorders, diseases of the nervous system, skin diseases, etc. When iron is administered the following articles of diet should be avoided, namely *kushmanda* (fruit of *Benincasa cerifera Sari*), sesamum oil, *kulhatta* pulse, mustard, wines and acids.'

I cannot quote the whole of Dutt's exhaustive account. I will content myself with one more paragraph. 'Iron pyrites', he says, 'has been used in medicine from a very remote period... It is purified by being boiled in lemon juice with one third its weight of rock salt in an iron vessel, till the pot becomes red-hot. It is reduced to powder by being rubbed with oil or goat's urine, and then roasted in a closed crucible... It is considered tonic, alterative, and useful in anaemia, urinary diseases, ascites, anasarca, prurigo, eye-diseases, etc.'[1]

XII. *The Agaria's Theory of Magic Iron*

Once only she is virgin: next time she is an old woman.
She is neither human nor animal. What is she?

—Agaria riddle.

We may now turn to consider the special contribution which the Agaria has to make to this great body of folk-lore. It is a by no means negligible contribution for, as far as I know, the Agaria theory of vestal iron and its use in magic is unparalleled elsewhere. Here is an interesting combination of two orders of belief—in the power of iron and in the power of chastity.[2] This is the more remarkable, because the Gond and Baiga neighbours of the Agaria do not generally attach much

[1] Dutt, op. cit., p. 56.

[2] The Bakhlata of Bechuanaland forbade married men to visit their smithies for fear they would bewitch the iron. Livingstone, who records this, was only admitted on his assertion that he was unmarried.—Blaikie, *David Livingstone* (London, 1913), p. 43.

importance to chastity in magic. Most of the beliefs that we have examined in this chapter find their counterpart among the Agaria—but with the condition that the iron used must be the special Virgin Iron.

To the Agaria, not all iron has equal magic power. It is always, of course, dangerous to treat iron with disrespect—for example, a man's feet will burn if he deliberately kicks a bit of iron, and almost any sword or axe or sickle will suffice to frighten away an ordinary ghost. But it is the *kuāri lohā*, the Virgin Iron that is extracted from a new furnace used for the first time, that is most potent for magic and for medicine. Indeed the best *kuāri lohā* of all is made when a group of Agaria move to a new village and there is not only a virgin furnace, but a virgin smithy and a virgin home.

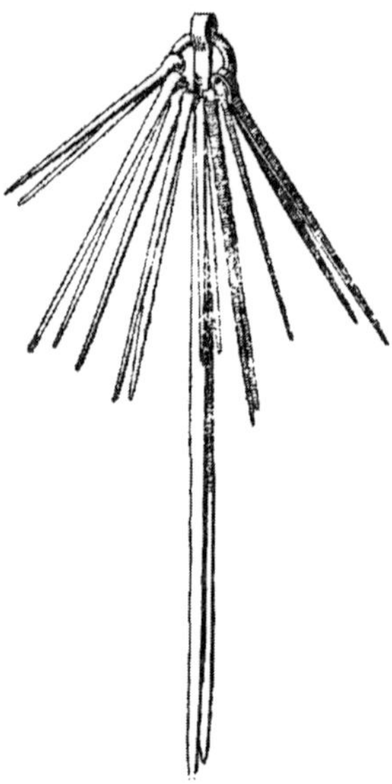

FIG. 12. Ghost scarer
Length, 1' 5"

We have already described the elaborate precautions that protect the erection of a new smithy, the observance of chastity, the rule of silence, the segregation of menstruous women, the clay prepared with *kodon* chaff ground in a virgin grindstone, the coals kindled with virgin fire. The Chokh Agaria of Korba Zamindari have even more elaborate rules. The charcoal must be specially prepared: a green tree is cut and it is offered fire and incense in the jungle. The iron must be dug from a virgin pit. Before starting to dig, the spiritual surroundings of the pit must be sterilized: Lohasur must be placated with a black virgin goat or pig, the *raksa* (ghost of an unmarried man) living in the hillside must be given a bottle of liquor, a *dhitori*-basket and an axe; a black hen must be offered to Dharti

Mata (Mother Earth); and the mischievous Mua must be quieted by a sacrifice of *konda roti*, wheat cakes cooked between two leaves which are heated with fire above and below, and not turned over.

After these offerings have been made, a virgin, or unmarried boy digs in the pit. When the ore has been brought back to the smithy a virgin girl breaks it up into small pieces, and she herself must pour the first lot of ore from the winnowing-fan into the furnace and must work the bellows.

Although a menstruating woman may go into the smithy and work there, provided she avoids the heavy hammer and the anvil, she must on no account enter the smithy when Virgin Iron is being extracted or the furnace will burst.

There are not many actual ceremonies connected with the work on a new furnace. The Chokh Agaria do not put turmeric, but take some flour in a dish with water, place the open hand in the dish, and then put the mark of the hand five times on the kiln. This ceremony is called *hāth dēna*. In Raipur, the God-dhuka colour rice with turmeric and put a *ṭika*-mark on the kiln; after the iron is made they tie a small piece of it round the kiln. The Chokh and Agaria of Udaipur stress the need of finishing the work before dawn and without seeing the face of anyone.

Virgin Iron is not only made from a new furnace. In Matin Zamindari, if a man and his wife go naked on a Sunday or Wednesday to the furnace, and light the fire with flint and steel and *semur* cotton holding their breath as they do so, and if they finish their work before dawn, then the iron they produce is regarded as *kuāri lohā*. It is interesting that the same tradition, which does not seem to exist in Mandla, connects the Asur Agaria of Matin with the Birjhia Asur of Neterhat, for at Jam Tola we were told that there also Virgin Iron was the iron extracted by a man and woman working naked before dawn.

Chokh and Agaria of Udaipur State sometimes make a temporary furnace in the courtyard during an eclipse and extract a little iron from it. Chamru Chokh of Gidkalo is thus reported by Mr M. B. Bhaduri: 'I made my first furnace long ago. It was opened before sunrise, before any man's face was seen. My unmarried daughter worked the bellows. I made a knife with the iron. I have not sold it, I still have it. But I have had to give bits of it away. I have made *kuāri lohā* during eclipses by hurriedly building a furnace in my courtyard and smelting some iron. It is by the power of *Asur Bhut* that we produce iron from stones.'

FIG. 13
Kalāri-rake
Length, 4' 6"

Another kind of Virgin Iron, perhaps not quite so virginal, is made in Mandla at Divali when the Agaria 'wake up' (*jagāna*) the furnace so that they will get more business and make better iron. They offer Lohasur a black chick, and make new charcoal. At midnight they begin work and keep the iron they make then, which they call *jagai huē lohā*, to mix with their other iron.

The Virgin Iron is also preserved very carefully. The Chokh Agaria sometimes keep it in the form of a *kalāri*-rake, off which they cut small pieces from time to time. Otherwise they make a large number of tiny nails, $^1/_2$ to $^3/_4$ inches long. A black chick is sacrificed and appropriate *mantra* are recited. If possible this should be done at the time of the Hareli festival. The virtue of the virgin kiln and iron, the sacrifice, the *mantra*, resides in the iron: it becomes a 'Reserved Sacrament' for these simple people, and is as carefully preserved.

I remember, for example, at Bhoira when at Divali (which they celebrated a month too soon) the Agaria used these nails, they did so without any ceremony. No offerings were made, no *mantra* were repeated. 'It was done long ago,' they told me. The leading Agaria simply made a *tīka*-mark of turmeric on each of the four sides of the kiln, and then took a handful of nails and a hammer and set out on his round of the village. He first drove a nail into the kiln itself, into the main pillar of the smithy, and into the bellows. Then in each of the living-houses, he drove nails into the framework of the doors, into the grain-bins, the hearths, the rice-pounders, the grain-measures, into cots, *măchi*-seats, earthen grindstones, the pillars and doors of the cattle-sheds. He went out to the nearest cross-roads and drove a nail into the ground. Had there been any danger from tigers or wild animals, the nails would also have been driven into trees or stones on the village boundary. This may be done by the Agaria, but as the tribe is not very expert in magic (it produces few Dewar or Panda), this is more often the duty of the Baiga whose special business it is to keep the boundaries of all villages intact.[1]

These nails are the Agaria's insurance against trouble. The nails keep ghosts and bad dreams from the sleeper on the cot, they drive away rats from the grain, they keep the milk from burning on the hearth, and disease from attacking the cattle. Witches will not overlook the smithy, nor will the house be struck by lightning.

The Hindu Lohar of Sarangarh State also make iron nails at Hareli and drive them into the door-posts of the houses. They use iron scraps called *lohā-churna* for medicine. They told me, 'We have been turned into Hindus, but our hearts are in the jungle'. In Jashpur State, the Mahali Lohar use in magic the iron bored out of the hole of a hammer.

Virgin Iron is specially valuable against cosmic dangers, against what the primitive literally supposes to be 'Acts of God'. At the Creation, it was used to make the nails that still hold the world in place, and to this day an earthquake can be stopped by a Baiga driving a nail into the ground. A *Lamu* child is notorious for attracting lightning, but can be insulated by a torc of Virgin Iron round the neck, a ring round the ankles and a small ring on the finger. A hail-storm may be stopped if a man holds his breath and throws an axe or sickle

[1] In Bastar, I have watched the Muria of Antagarh Tahsil perform very similar ceremonies, but they did not use nails but little bits of slag collected round the smithy. The Bastar iron-smelters do not make Virgin Iron.

(in which a little of the magic iron has been mixed) out of the house. In a heavy thunderstorm, the house may be protected by throwing a bit of the Virgin Iron out into the courtyard.

This iron may also, of course, be used in sickness. A *sutia*-torc round the neck will keep away the spirits who cause vomiting and dysentery. The water in which a scrap of Virgin Iron has been washed is used as a cure for syphilis. An anklet of Virgin Iron is a remedy for rheumatism. Hot water in which a piece of red-hot iron has been dipped may cure a cold. To drive away small-pox, a seven-pronged iron stick is made and carried out to the boundary of the village. A pig or a goat is sacrificed, and a nail is driven into the ground to prevent the disease returning.

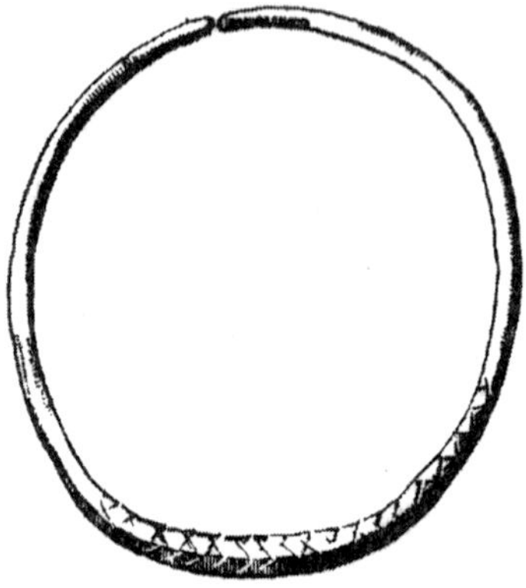

FIG. 14. Iron neck-band
1/3 actual size

If a man gets a bubo on the groin, he should sit on the right-hand side of the threshold of his house. A friend should bring an axe which contains Virgin Iron and should 'cut' the bubo seven times by touching first the ground and then the skin seven times. After this he spits on the axe and takes it away.

At a marriage the ring called *chulmundri* is made of Virgin Iron and is intended to keep away the jealous spirits and witches who infest these ceremonies. In case of an abortion, a drink of the water in which the iron has been washed is useful, and a similar drink, made by washing Virgin Iron five or six years old, is useful in a case of difficult labour. A ring of Virgin Iron may also avert the dangers of lactation.

All weapons are improved by the Virgin Iron, the arrow flies with surer aim, the axe and the spear strike with greater force. A Gond of Matin made a *gothiār phānda* (a 'sounding trap'), putting some twenty rings of Virgin Iron to tinkle in the wind, and it is said that many hares were irresistibly attracted by the sweet-sounding magic.

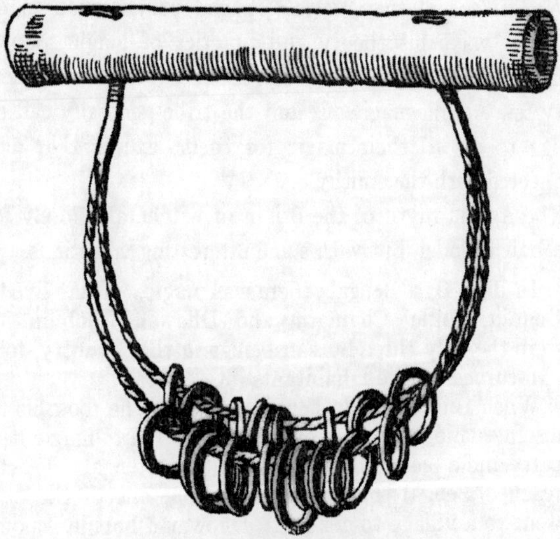

FIG. 15. *Gothiār phānda* trap
1/2 actual size

Virgin Iron should not be sold for money. The first visitor to the smithy after the iron has been reduced from a new furnace should bring a bottle of wine and a little cloth, a gift known as *jadāwar*. In return he will receive a share of the iron. But although the Chokh Agaria sometimes sell the small nails for a few annas, any kind of trade in Virgin Iron is regarded in Mandla as a sin, and not only a sin, but a dangerous sin, Ten years ago an Agaria of Indri near Mawai sold some of the Virgin Iron for money. The next day, the furnace failed. flames leapt up above it and the smithy was destroyed.

The *Vagina Dentata* legend is less common among the Agaria than among the Baiga, but it is only the iron-workers who have discovered a really satisfactory way of dealing with this menace. In an Asur Agaria story of Matin, the hero is faced with the necessity of spending a night with a girl who has already dismissed a score of mutilated suitors. But he is an Asur; he makes a hollow iron sheath of Virgin Iron and uses it both to protect himself and to break the teeth in the vagina of the siren.[1]

XIII. *Other Aspects of Agaria Magic*

Kuāri lohā is the Agaria's special contribution to magic; in other ways his theory and practice of magic follows the Baiga pattern. This was only to be expected, for there are very few Agaria magicians and the tribe generally call on the Baiga to do all their magic for them, except that actually connected with the smithy.

The Agaria myth of the origin of witchcraft closely follows the Baiga model, but with some interesting variations.

> In Bara-Bati-Bengala there was magic. There lived Kani Gondin, Sukhi Chamarin and Dhowan Dhobnin. These were the only three human beings in that country, for they had turned all the inhabitants into cats.
>
> When Guru Daugun heard about this, he took his twelve disciples and gave each of them a pot full of magic herbs to carry and a piece of iron and set out for Bengal. When they reached Bengal they felt hungry and one of the disciples went to a village to get fire. Dhowan Dhobnin was in that village, and she picked up the fire in her hands and offered it to him. But the boy was frightened and ran away. Then the Guru himself went and brought the fire in his dhoti.
>
> There was a pond. They tried to take their cooking-pots there, but there was so much grass they could not get through. While they were struggling with the grass, the Dhobnin turned the twelve boys into stone and the Guru himself into a cat. She kept the cat with her in her house.
>
> At home, Murra-kawar the Guru's son was playing in the courtyard. By accident he broke an old woman's fire-pot. She lost her temper and cried, 'Your father is so clever that

[1] The literature of this curious and little known symbolization of the neurotic dread of sexual intercourse is scanty, but brief references to the subject may be found in Lincoln, *The Dream in Primitive Cultures* (London, 1935), p. 108; Seligman, 'Anthropological Perspective and Psychological Theory', *J.R.A.I.*, Vol. LXII, p. 219; Elwin, *The Baiga*, pp. 423ff.; Pilsudski, *Material for the Study of Ainu Languages and Folk-lore* (Cracow, 1912), pp. 85ff.; Goddard, 'Jicarilla Apache Texts', *Anthropological Papers, American Museum Nat. Hist.*, 1911, p. 202; and Roheim, *Animism, Magic and the Divine King* (London, 1930), p. 53.

he is Guru of the whole world, but he is not so clever that he can escape being turned into a cat in Bengal'.

The boy was frightened and ran to tell Guru Danantar. This Guru went at once to Bengal. He turned himself into a fly and flew into the Dhobnin's house. There was no one there, but a nice cat was guarding the hearth. Danantar by his magic turned the cat back into a man. Then he went to the pond and threw black and yellow rice at the stone figures of the disciples, and they became alive again. So all the human beings in Bengal were changed back from cats into their own shape.

Presently the Dhobnin came home, and now when Daugun Guru asked her for food, the rice she gave turned into scraps of iron. He and his disciples ate the iron and thus they conquered the three witches and got them into their power.

The story now follows the usual course, as outlined in my book *The Baiga*, pp. 340ff. Bhagavan tricks Daugun Guru to his death and his sons cook the body, but are dissuaded from eating the flesh. The witches get hold of it instead and greatly augment their power.

Except for two casual references to iron, there is no reason why the above story should not be part of the Baiga myth which it so closely resembles. Daugun and Danantar are Baiga heroes, and the three witches are Baiga villains. But, as I have said, so far as magic is concerned, the Agaria, at least in the hills, largely depend on the Baiga.

I will add one or two details which are specifically Agaria in character. At Divali, which the Agaria generally keep on the wrong date, about a month too soon, all the women come to the smithy with their babies. Here the position is reversed, and Baiga come to the Agaria for help.[1] A mat is spread on

[1] A somewhat similar ceremony is described by Frazer, following A. C. Kruijt, for the Toradja blacksmiths of Central Celebes. Once a year people assemble in the smithy when, among other rites, the master of ceremonies strikes the palm of the hand of everyone present with a doit, a chopping-knife and a bunch of leaves. Then the sick go to the anvil, and the smith sprinkles them with pig's blood and herbs, then heats the chopping-knife in the furnace, lays it on the anvil, strikes it seven times with his hammer, cools it in water—and the cure is complete. *The Golden Bough : The Magic Art* (London, 1911), Vol. I, p. 159.

the ground near the forge, and a sickle is put into the fire. A small boy is laid on the mat, two men hold his arms and legs, and an old Agaria woman removes the red-hot sickle from the fire and lightly touches the boy's stomach a dozen or so times. The child screams and struggles to the great amusement of the onlookers. But some children lie down laughing. The old woman feels carefully for an enlarged spleen and pays it special attention. After the older children, babies at the breast are put on the mat. Women cut up a *tuma*-gourd into thin slices; a slice is laid on the baby's stomach and the hot sickle is applied to the slice of gourd, not directly to the child's skin. The slice is carefully preserved and taken home. It is hung up in the roof above the place where the child sleeps, with the idea that as the gourd dries so will the burn on the child's body heal.

After the children, men and women come and are treated for stomach-ache, rheumatism, or headache, being carefully burnt in the appropriate places.

The cautery is a purely formal one: it is a magical rather than a medical rite. The iron applied to the body drives away the evil that is attacking it. The Bida ceremony is performed at the same time, this however by a Baiga, its aim being to drive out of the village all dangerous and hostile spirits. It is interesting to note that the Agaria ceremony is performed by a woman.

Anything of a black colour is, of course, potent in magic. The Hindus also use *surma*,[1] which may consist of powdered iron-ore, antimony or galena, or *kājal*, which is simply lamp-black, in marriages, funerals and other important occasions. The Agaria tie a charred and blackened log to an old broom and stick it in the ground in the middle of a tobacco-patch. Then as the log is black, so any magic approaching it will turn black and so disappear. A broken earthen pot is also useful to protect fruit or creepers on the roof. Sometimes lines of white mud and red dots are drawn

[1] To make *surma* out of crude ore, it has to be pounded in a stone mortar.

on it, so that the evil spirit will play with the pattern and forget to do any harm.

There is a method of transferring magical dangers from oneself to someone else. For example, suppose your axe or sickle breaks while you are working it in the forge. Prepare an axe of mud and blacken it with coal. Take it to the bazaar and say to the first fellow-Agaria you meet, 'I give you this. You too make one and give it to me'. If he refuses to take it, catch a chicken and force down its throat some of the ash from the smithy and tell the chicken, 'Go to the house of the man who refused me and trouble him'. Then your axes will be strong and good, and it is his that will break.

I have recorded only two cases of what may appropriately be called 'black magic'. This does not mean that it is rare, but it is always very difficult to persuade people to talk about it. Once in Lalpur (Mawai) a witch made magic of *urad* pulse, a black chick and *chirona* clay and plastered it on top of the furnace. As a result all the iron in that furnace turned into slag, and no iron was reduced until the owner of it went to a Baiga magician and discovered what had happened.

Another way to ruin an enemy's iron is to find the branch of a tree that has been struck by lightning. Strip yourself naked and make a small mud image of your enemy out of your excreta. Go thrice round it and lay the branch at the feet of the image. Cry 'Jai Bir Bhairasin' and kill a black chicken. Take the branch to your enemy's smithy and holding your breath push it well into the roof. Then his furnace will crack and his implements be imperfect.

The 'ordeal' by iron is not unknown in India. According to the *Yajnavalkya-smriti*, the law book of the Mithila school, an accused had to walk across seven circles carrying a piece of red-hot iron without injury to his hands. Brihaspati and Pitamaha add the licking of a red-hot ploughshare.[1]

Iron is also used by the Agaria for certain ordeals. Where a number of people are suspected of a crime, the Agaria comes

[1] See Keith, 'Ordeal (Hindu)', *Hastings Encl. Rel. Eth.*, Vol. IX, p. 524.

with iron *chamīta*-tongs and touches each in turn. It is believed that the tongs will stick to the guilty person.[1]

Another method is to take a number of hemp seeds, one for each suspect, to the Agaria's smithy and throw them into the fire. A goat must be offered to Lohasur. Then the Agaria is asked to kindle the fire and, as he works his bellows and the blast consumes the seeds, the belly of the guilty is believed to swell.

[1] In the Lower Congo, there was an ordeal by passing a hot knife three times over the skin of the leg. If the victim was unburnt, he was declared innocent.—*Folk-Lore*, Vol. XX, p. 18. It is said that the Vikings made an accused man hold red-hot iron in his hand and according to the rapidity or otherwise with which the burn was healed, so was the innocence or guilt of the suspect determined.—Friend, op. cit., p. 112.

CHAPTER VII

CRAFT

I. *Introductory*

An Asur girl and her lover are walking gaily through the wild and lonely forest of Matin. As they go the boy sings with the full vigour of his lungs the first verse of a Dadaria.

> Come to the forest and cut a green tree;
> Come to my furnace and blow the bellows for me, friend.

She at once picks up the tune and answers,

> Press the bellows in the forge, the slag comes flowing.
> Make me sleep with you; I will live in your Asur house, friend.

He replies,

> Come to the bazaar and I'll buy a goat.
> This Asur girl does not know how to work at the furnace, friend.

She again retorts,

> He can cut down trees and collect a little honey,
> But this Asur boy doesn't know how to beat the iron, friend.

But he cannot allow this.

> In his hand there's a pot, and a necklace round his throat.
> First he makes a hammer, and then a pair of tongs, friend.

At last she is conquered.

> The Moharia have come playing on their drums,
> And I—I do not know the bellows-dance, O friend.

In such songs we get a glimpse of the work of the Agaria in their little smithies. There is a still better picture in the following Chokh Agaria song from Lapha.

> She presses down the bellows with the strength of her heels.
> He wields the heavy hammer with all his might.

From the ground he gets stones,
From wood he makes charcoal.
The fire burns fiercely as the bellows blow.
The bellows sound *sair sir*,
The little hammer clatters *tining tanang*,
A shower of sparks flies into her breast.

He puts it in black,
He pulls it out red.
Standing he beats it,
Squatting he fashions it.
The Chokh girl blows the bellows at the forge,
Like a drum it sounds *datur thunda*.
How happy I feel!
The Chokh boy beats with the hammer,
The hammer whistles as he swings it round.
And I feel very happy!

A Karma of Mawai also describes the work of the smithy.

Hai re hai! Without two men and a girl the Agaria's work cannot be done.
He cuts wood, he hollows out the bellows, he stretches skin above them.
The girl dances on the bellows, with both her feet she dances.

The girl dances before the furnace. They pour the iron-stones down the slide.
The furnace is full of charcoal. The ore is on the slide.
In front, they extract the iron; behind, excretes the slag.

The girl dances before the forge, to heat the iron again.
One brings the iron with his pincers, the other beats it with the hammer.
They make the pincers, they make the hammer; to plough the earth they fashion iron, to kill the sambhar they make the arrow.

A few more Agaria songs about work in the smithy may be added here. The first is a Sua dance song of the Mahali Asur.

Who makes the bangles? Who makes the spade?
O the parrot O! Who makes the sword?

The Agaria makes the bangles, the Agaria makes the spade.
O the parrot O! The Asur makes the sword.

How shall we sell the bangles and the spade?
O the parrot O! How shall we sell the sword?

For five rupees we will sell the bangles and the spade.
O the parrot O! For ten rupees the sword.

From Mawai comes a highly technical Karma dance song.

Hai re hai! What earth is used to make the kiln?
What earth is used to strengthen the iron?
What wood is used for the charcoal
Which turns the stones to water?

Hai re hai! The kiln is made with *murminjni* earth.
The iron is strengthened with *chapra* earth.
The charcoal is made with *sarai* wood
And turns the stones to water. Hai re hai!

Here are three short Chokh Karma songs from Bilaspur District.

O brother, the ringing of my hammering!
Tining tining, tining tining!
By my hammering the house is filled with rice!
Tining tining tining tining!

The sparks fly out, O brother,
The showers of sparks fly out.
O the swinging of the hammer!
Who blows the bellows? Who swings the hammers?
Who shapes the iron, slowly O slowly, with the little hammer?
Little brother hammers with the *ghāna*.
Big brother works with the *hataudi*, slowly O slowly!

Why were you born an Agaria?
Can you eat the iron you make?
Sansi, *hataudi* and *ghāna* are hard to use.
Can you eat the iron you make?

The work of the furnace is described in a Karma from Mawai.

The twelve Mukhi brothers make the blast in the furnace.
O iron our enemy, you are like fire itself, you will not cool.

Make the furnace of *chirona* clay; pour in the iron-stones from above.
The Agaria girl blows the bellows. Inside the iron falls on the chaff.
From that iron are made the tongs; from that iron a light hammer.
O the workman's skill will make that iron into a heavy hammer.
The twelve Mukhi brothers make the blast in the furnace.

With these songs we may compare the following sung by the Mahali Lohar of Jashpur State.

Hammer sounds *rana rana*; bellows work with help of heels.
Tongs catch and hammers beat.
Blessed be Ganges, created on earth.

The smith was created on earth to build a furnace out of mud.
He has an adze in his hand, but how will he shape the wooden pan?
There is no knife without its price; how will we cut the hide?
Below is coal, above is sand, yet the iron remains.
Blessed be Ganges, created on earth.

Where there are Lohar, there is an iron-mine.
All over the world the iron is used.
The clay is brought by earth-worms on the bank of Jamuna.
Bellows are made of old goat-hide.
But alas! for the false Malar who do not get even broken bronze.
Alas! for the Malar, who beats his forehead.

It is cold everywhere, and the worn-out ploughshare is not heated.
Alas! for the Lohar who beats his forehead.

Do not waste time at home. There is charcoal burning in the forest.
The smith cuts the wood in the forest,
He burns it and quenches it with dust.

There is a twyer below and the furnace above.
The iron water does not leak out.
The iron goes through the world.

The work of the tongs is stopped,
The hammer is still.
The smith needs a pair of skins,
Then only can he work
Hammer sounds *rana rana*; bellows work with help of heels.
Tongs catch and hammers beat.
Blessed be Ganges, created on earth.

II. *The Iron Mine*

How do the Agaria discover the best places to dig for iron? There are three chief ways. Sometimes Lohasur sends them a dream—in the old days he used to come as a little child—and indicates the place just as he shows them where to build a new smithy. They then go to find the place, and in the old days someone used to shoot a red arrow through the air.[1] Where it fell, they used to dig. I have never actually seen this done, and I am not sure whether the red arrow is still used today.

The Agaria can also recognize by the colour of the soil a good digging site; very often too ore is found on the surface. They sometimes put it very vividly. 'The iron is sending its children for a walk in the open air.' 'Just as rats live in their holes and come to the surface sometimes, so Lohasur lives deep in the earth and comes burrowing his way to the surface, and we find the pit near the iron-holes.' 'The iron comes up to graze. Lohasur comes too as an Ahir comes with cattle, and when the Agaria go to find a pit and call on Lohasur, he brings one stone to show them. They don't notice it at first, and then he brings a whole pile and they realize what it is.'[2]

The pits are small, generally not deeper than the height of a man (in Mandla possibly volcanic strata prevent them going

[1] Lingo, a mythical hero of the Gonds, discovered fire by shooting an arrow into the air, and marking where it fell—near the fire of the giant Rikad Gawadi.—Hislop, *Papers Relating to the Aboriginal Tribes of the Central Provinces* (Nagpur, 1866), Part III, pp. 18f.

[2] Muria Lohar of Bastar search for the 'Mother Stone' lying on the surface. Once they have found the 'Mother', they begin to search for the children which 'must be burrowing along to find her'.

deeper), generally situated in almost inpenetrable jungle. It is work for men, though in Mandla women may accompany the party and spend their time sorting and cleaning the stones or gathering what they can from the surface. In Mandla, before starting from the house, a *mantra* is recited: 'Go and see! Lohasur Mata! Go, lead on ahead! Trusting in thee, I follow!' Then the party sets out with *kudari* (mattocks), *dādu* or *tukna* baskets, turmeric and a bottle of liquor, on its long and tedious climb through forest and up the hill to where the pits are.

FIG. 16. Mattock
1/2 actual size

Should the pit be a new one, the party will have observed strict chastity the preceding night. But this is unnecessary on ordinary occasions.

When they reach the pit where they intend to dig, they sit down for a rest and a smoke, and then offer a little *sarai* gum on a bit of smouldering cow-dung, and throw rice and *dāl* into the pit. On the Jandhi-Bija Hill near Mawai, the celebrant threw down a pinch of yellow turmeric. On the Bhoira hill the Agaria put a cloth round his neck in honour of Lohasur. They recite any of the following *mantra*.

Lohasur Baba, we take refuge in thee. O Mother that givest increase we seek refuge in thee. From little may there be much. From shortage may there be double. Twelve dozen times twelve dozen, generation after generation, depend on thee. Lohasur Baba we take refuge in thee. Heed not what others say. We dig the earth, may it bear gold. I take the name of Agar Sai, Sabar Sai, Logundi Raja their son, from whom I spring. Show me thy greatness. Then will I worship thee.

Go and see! Baghesur Pat, Nangbansi Pat, go before and stop the enemy in the way. Loha Sumarni, Lohasur Baba worship where the virgin iron is born. Go and see! Logundi Raja has a bow and a red arrow. Kariya Kuar shoots it;

> where it falls there the iron-pit is found. This is the order of Lohasur Baba.
>
> Go Lohasur Baba! O twelve Agaria brothers! O thirteen Tamesur brothers! O fourteen Kansasur brothers! we come to thee. Koelasur, Dhua Dharni, we come to thee. Thou knowest that every year I give to thee.
>
> Victory to Lohasur! We honour the ancestors of our family. Give us help. Victory to Suraj Deo!
>
> Accept this, Dharti Mata, Lohasur Bhawani! Help us, Dharti Mata, Banaspati Maharaj. If we get good ore, I will give in the third year a *chandua* pig [that is, one whose mother has a white mark on her forehead] and a black chick.

After these preliminaries, one of the Agaria gets into the pit and begins to dig with his mattock (fig. 16). A basket is handed down to him and he fills it with earth and stones and heaves it up to the others. They empty it and sort the contents. For a time nothing may be found, then the ore

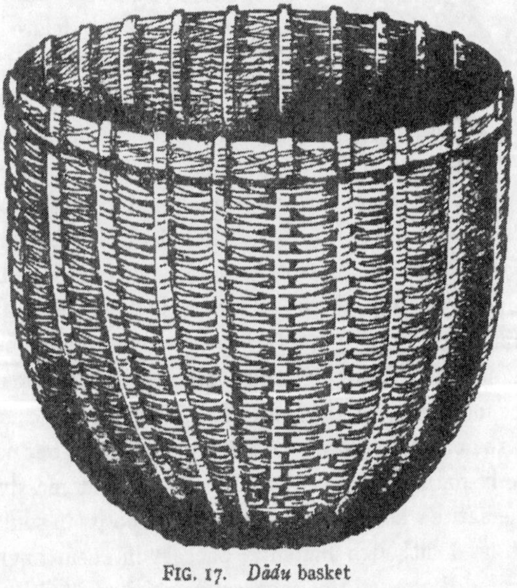

FIG. 17. *Dādu* basket
Height, 1′ 6″

begins, and every basket is of value. The stones are cleaned and sorted on the spot and carefully packed into the *dādu* (fig. 17) and *tukna* (fig. 18) baskets. When they have as much as they can carry the party returns home.

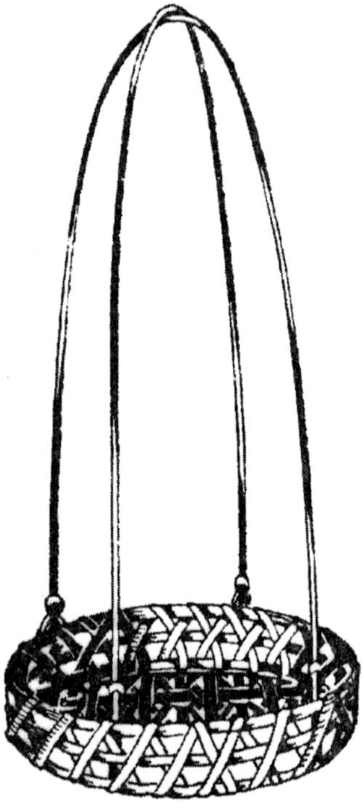

FIG. 18. *Tukna* basket
Height, 3'

There is no private ownership in the pits; there is not even village ownership. Daldal and Bahapur people are equally welcome at the Bhoira pits: in Mawai I saw three different villages come to dig in the same place. Within their clan the Agaria are a friendly, co-operative and closely inter-related people.

The mining efforts of the Agaria, like the technique of their smelting—and indeed the two are related—have been criticized and might well be improved. The small furnaces, using no flux, are unsuited for reducing the unaltered iron carbonates, though clay-ironstone altered more or less into limonite can be used. We have seen how the ore must generally be soft: 'except in very few cases the material used in the Agaria furnaces is some form of hematite or magnetite which occurs in association with lateritic rocks or is to be found in weathered exposure of other rocks. In many cases, the ore is a partially de-hydrated limonite, but not quite a true hematite. It is a remarkable fact that massive steel-grey hematite which occurs in immense deposits in some places is not used although limonitic pockets in them might have been scraped out and this inferior material smelted.'[1] Ferru-

[1] Private communication from Dr C. S. Fox, Director of the Geological Survey of India, 12-8-40.

ginous material of this quality 'would not even be glanced at by an iron-smelter in Europe', for it requires far too much picking and breaking. Were the Agaria furnaces to be improved, they might be able to extend the range of ores that they could use.

III. *The Smithy*

Let us first take a general view of the little hut in which the crude ore from the mine will be transformed into useful and necessary tools.

In Mandla the Agaria smithy is a rough rectangular hut, roofed with a grass thatch and unwalled, varying in size but always small. 'The earnings of the smithy are as small as the hut.' Though there are no walls, it becomes in time almost completely enclosed by the mounds of waste slag and coal that are constantly thrown out. Though there is a lot of rubbish all around, the hut itself is generally kept very clean and tidy.

In Raipur and Bilaspur, the smithy is often out-of-doors and the smelting is done at night. In Jhilmili (Phuljhar Zamindari) I found the smithy in the shade of a great tree outside the village, the tools being kept in the blacksmith's house which was some distance away. But where there is some kind of building, it usually stands in the compound of the Agaria's own house, though this itself may be outside the village.

Let us visit some characteristic smithies of different types. We will first go to the Patharia Agaria village of Bhoira in the Karanjia Range. Here there are six Agaria houses, grouped round a rectangular 'street' in precisely Baiga fashion. At one end of the street a small path leads behind the houses to the main smithy. Here there are two furnaces at one end of a long hut. Baskets of charcoal, piles of iron-ore, little heaps of clay and chaff are scattered about. At the other end of the hut is the forge, a small mud wall with a clay pipe leading to the small fire in which tools are sharpened and iron refined. A large stone serves as anvil. There is a wooden trough for water. Bellows are standing against the pillars of the hut. The tools, hammers, pincers and chisels are stuck into the roof or concealed beneath a heap of dry leaves.

This is the normal arrangement for all roofed smithies. I have seen similar huts in Raipur (Kursipahar, for example), in Bilaspur (at Dumarkachhar, Thanakar and elsewhere) and in Bastar.

But we see a very different picture at, for example, the Khuntia Chokh village of Nunera. Here there are sixteen Agaria houses, in a hamlet of their own apart from the rest of the village, which is a good half-mile away. Near the Agaria hamlet are three clumps of great shady *mahua* trees, and near or under these are grouped no fewer than nine furnaces and a dozen forges. In one place there is a small hut covering a furnace, but the rest are all in the open air, but well shaded. Most of the tools are kept in the houses, but in one tree I found a hole neatly cut in the trunk making a convenient cupboard for storing implements. Round the furnaces I noticed dozens of large charcoal baskets, piles of iron-ore, and a number of cart-wheels waiting to be repaired. The scene was one of great activity, and when several furnaces were working together by night the varied lights were most picturesque.

In some of the Mahali Asur villages, the furnaces are placed in the shade of trees, and some distance away is the forge in a small hut. The forge at Singia, for example, was the poorest and simplest I have seen. Inside the hut there was simply a pair of bellows, a clay pipe to concentrate the blast on the little fire, and the fire itself. There was no wall separating the bellows from the fire, and the stone anvil was outside.

On the Neterhat plateau, I saw three entirely distinct types of smithy. At Doka, a village of Christianized Bir Asur, the smithy was some two hundred yards outside the village across fields, in a sheltered glade overlooking a charming wooded valley. Here was the upright circular furnace typical of the Asur covered with thorn bushes for its protection, and all the implements had to be brought over from the village. Iron-ore was left near the furnace, but charcoal was brought from the houses.

In Bijapath, however, there was a lean-to shed, and a branch roof shading two furnaces and two forges quite in the Mandla pattern, except that the furnaces were of a different shape.

The third type of Asur smithy was in the Birjhia Asur village of Kerakhair, perhaps the most beautifully situated of any I have seen, on a hillside beneath a great tamarind tree, with distant views and the broad swelling belly of a hill above. Three circular furnaces were built into the hillside, and near by were small forges. The houses, where all the implements were kept, were about a hundred yards away. The clearing under the tree was cow-dunged and scrupulously clean. There was no building or roof, but sufficient shade was given by the tree.

FIG. 19. Scourge *Length, 2'*

The choice of a site for a new smithy, and the building of the hut, is a serious matter. When the Agaria decide to move to a new village (which is not seldom) they seek guidance both from dreams and divination. 'Lohasur himself gives us a dream,' so I have been told in Karanjia and Mawai. 'He says that in such-and-such a place he will help us, and that we must make our shop there. In the old days he used to come himself in the form of an old man and would call a child aside and say, " Tell your father that the iron will be good in such a place ". But now he doesn't come himself. He sends a dream.' This sounds like the official, or induced, dream of other cultures. But, however it is gained, it is authoritative.

On the eve of the day they have chosen for their operations, the men sleep apart from their wives—sexual intercourse for that night is taboo. They get up before dawn, 'when you cannot see your shadow or the hairs on your own body', and go without speaking to the place selected. They take a pot of water and seven seeds of *urad dāl*. In Angai they said that they took a bath, but this is rare. When they reach the place, the leading Agaria present puts down the pot on the ground and retreats three or four yards. Then taking Lohasur's name, he throws the seeds one by one into the pot. If at least four find their mark, it means the omens are good. This seems to me a very exacting test in the early morning and I should not be surprised if it were often omitted. Other tests are less severe. One is to measure out the plan of the smithy with string. If they find they have made a perfect square, which they discover by measuring the lines joining the two opposite corners, they consider the site well-omened and remain there. Another test is to go to the place overnight and stick an axe in the ground. If it remains upright all night, they know the site is good. After this they pour out the water from the pot in the name of Lohasur.

The smithy, in which the precious and potent Virgin Iron is made, is the target of every kind of hostile magic. Among the charms which are used for its protection, I have recorded the following:—

I

Lohasur Bhawani! Koelasur Bhawani! Agyasur Bhawani! In my forge let not the iron be spoilt. Let not the eye of any witch fall upon my smithy. Let my iron sell with profit. Whatever enemy or wrong-doer puts his evil eye upon me, seize his body. If the iron does not fail, then every year at Holi, I will offer you a black hen and a coconut.

II

Let the earth quake. I will bind the water. I bind Jalhalli. I bind the lakh-and-a-quarter sacred jungle herbs. I bind the wind. Who binds? Guru Nindhan binds, and I his disciple. I bind the spirit of the boundary line. I bind Khair Bhawani. I bind Thakur Deo of the three worlds. I bind the twelve hundred fetchers of water. I bind the nine lakhs of witches. I bind the familiar of the witches' eyes. I bind Massan. I bind *raksa*. I bind *bhut*. I bind *pret.* Who binds? Guru Nindhan binds. Guru Danantar binds. Guru Daugun binds. Guru Mahadeo binds. I their disciple bind. Let the dry cow-dung sink and the stones float; but let not my words pass away.

IV. *The Furnace*

The first object that will engage our attention on entering the smithy will be the furnace.

The furnace is a cylindrical clay kiln, called *kothi* or *bhatti*, $2^1/_2$ feet high, with a circumference of eight feet at the base and five feet at the top. In Mandla it does not stand upright, but is tilted backwards on a large stone. At the top there is a mouth 6″ by 6″ to receive the charcoal and ore, and at the base there is another mouth 10 inches high and 9 inches broad, to take the blast and to allow the iron to be removed. On the right-hand side towards the back is a flue for the slag called appropriately the *hagān* or—in Bilaspur—*lohā hagōra* (aperture for excretion). From the top of the tilted kiln there runs backward a bamboo platform $2^1/_2$ to 4 feet long and $1^1/_4$ to $1^1/_2$ feet broad, inclining upwards, supported on light poles. This is the *machān*, the slide down which ore and charcoal are poured into the furnace. It is plastered with mud, and provided with little walls 3 inches high.

This is the Mandla model, used by the Patharia Agaria. In Bilaspur, the Khuntia Chokh do not tilt the cylinder, but allow it to stand upright. The *hagān* is larger and has a deep hole in front of it. The *machān* has no walls to guide the charcoal to its goal. The Mahali Asur of Bilaspur make a plain circular furnace without a *machān* at all. The ore and charcoal is shaken directly into the mouth of the furnace from a winnowing-fan.

This is the pattern used by the Bir, Birjhia and Agaria Asur of Palamau and Ranchi. In Kerakhair, the Birjhia Asur had built their furnaces into the hillside. They were circular, upright, supported at the back by a stake driven into the ground and attached to the kiln by bark tied round and round the top. There was no *hagān*, but from the mouth in front there ran two moulds in opposite directions, one for the iron, one for the slag.

At Doka, a Bir Asur village, the furnace was 3 feet high, and had a diameter of $2^1/_2$ feet. It was upright, circular, without *machān*, but with a *hagān* on the right-hand side.

Reuben describes an Asur custom of putting four hard balls of mud on the upper edge of the furnace, near the feed-hole, opposite each other. One by one they are dropped carefully down the shaft. At the bottom they should lie close to one another and each in the opposite corner to its original position, 'otherwise the iron does not clump'. This may be to test the uprightness of the working-shaft.[1]

V. *The Bellows*

The bellows used by all branches of the Agaria tribe, including the God-dhuka Lohar and the Asur of Neterhat, are the same and are distinctive. They differ entirely, for example, from the piston-bellows of Assam and Africa and the hand-bellows of the Lohar.

The Agaria bellows,[2] which are frequently illustrated in this volume, are made out of sections of the trunk of the *Trewia nudiflora* (Linn.), a little over a foot in diameter and about $3^1/_2$ inches thick. The wood is chopped out with an axe or sometimes burnt with a red-hot iron. A hole is made on one side to take the bamboo twyer which will carry the blast to the fire. Pieces of cow-hide or buffalo-hide (in Mandla) or of sambhar-skin (generally in Bilaspur and Raipur), sometimes of goat-skin, are stretched across the top and tied down 'like the paper tops of English jam-jars'.[3]

There is a hole in the middle of each cover and a cord (known as the *kutidor*) is passed through this and held in place by a small twig. The other end is attached to a springe stick (generally of bamboo) called *dāng*, or in Raipur *āda-dāng*,

[1] Reuben, op. cit., p. 13.

[2] Bellows are *katauti* in Mandla, *jettar* in Raipur, *dhantar* in Phuljhar.

[3] The phrase is Mr Grigson's.

2. Agaria urning charoal.

23. Smithy at Jobhipath.

which is fixed in the ground behind the usual place for the bellows.

The pair of bellows lie side by side before the furnace or forge. Two hollow bamboo poles called *tonda* or *behngul*, two to three feet long, lead to an earthen twyer (*nari*) that concentrates the blast upon the fire.

The bellows are, in Agaria folk-talk, 'two black sisters that fart turn by turn', 'two co-wives with but one throat between them', 'two snakes that whisper in a single hole', 'two heads that speak with one voice saying *phusur phusur*'.[1] Work on the bellows is often described as dancing.

> The bellows are made of wood, their covering is of skin.
> The girl is dancing before the furnace.

The work of the bellows is also described in this Karma from Mawai.

> Hai re hai! I have seen the Agaria smithy.
> What wood do they use for the bellows?
> What skin is stretched upon them?
> What are the feed-poles made of?
> Who blows the bellows? I will go and see.
> The bellows are made of *khamar* wood
> The skin is made of cow-hide.
> The feed-poles are of bamboo.
> The Agaria girl blows the bellows.

Before the bellows are used, they are soaked in water; when the skin cover is sufficiently pliable, the Agaria's wife or daughter, or son—but rarely the Agaria himself—stands with one foot on each of the bellows and depresses them in turn. The holes in the centre act as valves, and as his foot descends his heel serves as a stopper to the valve and forces the air through the bamboo pipe into the furnace or fire; when he releases the bellows, the bamboo stick behind springs up, lifting the cover and refilling the bellows with air. The

[1] In Uraon riddles, the bellows are described as 'a dead cow breathing' and 'a beautiful woman blowing from time to time'.—Archer, *The Blue Grove*, pp. 181 and 185. Grierson recorded a proverb about the bellows. 'O Tulsi! God cannot withstand the sigh of a poor man: the blowing of dead leather reduces iron to ashes.'—Grierson, *Bihar Peasant Life*, p. 87.

bellows-blower holds a *kalāri* (in Raipur a *kona-dāng*) stick [1] in her hand, partly for support, partly to rake down the ore and charcoal from the slide into the furnace.

The spirits living in the bellows are Dhukan Mata, the Blowing Mother, and Pawan Kuari, the Virgin Wind. Small offerings are made to them and a *mantra* is recited in order to ensure a proper blast of air.

> Go and see the wooden bellows! There is Basin Kaniya [the Bamboo Maiden] where the string is tied. There is Dhukan Mata where the two poles are fixed. I go to see. O Pawan Kuari [Wind Maiden] this is for you. To you will I give Virgin Iron. So may the bellows blow and cherish the flame.

We have already noticed the division of the Agaria according as they keep their bellows in place with a heavy stone or with pegs. The Patharia Agaria of Mandla, the God-dhuka of Raipur, the Mahali Chokh of Bilaspur and the Bir and Birjhia Asur of Bihar use stones laid across the bamboo poles just in front of the bellows. The Khuntia Chokh, however, fix the bellows in place with two bamboo pegs attached to each by a cord made of *mohlain* creeper tied tightly round the frames. The pegs remain attached to the bellows even when not in use, and are driven into the ground with a hammer when the bellows are to be used. The Khuntia Chokh almost invariably make the coverings of their bellows with sambhar-skin, and regard cow-hide as taboo.

So important is this distinction that there can be no inter-marriage between those who use a peg and those who use a stone, no inter-dining, and they will not share one another's pipes.

There is a persistent tradition both in Mandla and in Bilaspur that leaf-bellows were in use until comparatively recent times, though I have been unable to find anyone who has actually used them. They figure frequently in the myths. Sabar Sai used leaf-bellows to make the first nails of Virgin Iron, so did Rikki Muni and Aginjhar. Jwala Mukhi first of all tried to

[1] In Korba Zamindari this stick was called *jāra-kanchnaha*.

make fire by blowing down a hollow tube. When this failed he made bellows of mud and a covering of lotus leaves or, as some say, broad *mohlain* leaves stitched together as if for leaf-plates. These bellows burst as a result of the curse of Mahadeo, possibly a symbolic way of saying that they disappeared before the spread of civilization. The Agaria are adept in leaf-work; they make leaf-crowns for weddings, leaf-plates and leaf-cups, and large leaf-baskets for carrying charcoal. There seems no reason to doubt their own tradition that they made leaf-bellows also.

Such bellows are made, for example, by the Dafla of Assam and by the Kharia of Bihar. The latter use 'a pair of rude bellows made up of a pair of conical caps about a cubit and a half in height, made of leaves stitched together with grass and firmly planted upon hollows in the ground. The blast produced by the alternate and sudden swelling and sinking of the caps is conveyed through a pair of bamboo tubes to a heap of ignited charcoal.' These bellows are, or were, used, says S. C. Roy,[1] by the Hill Kharia of Barabhum in Manbhum and Dhalbhum in Singhbhum who live away from villages occupied by Lohar or Kamar blacksmiths. He implies that the leaf-bellows are now used only 'in rare instances'.[2]

FIG. 20. Razor
1/2 actual size

[1] S. C. Roy, *The Kharias* (Ranchi, 1937), p. 82.

[2] With the kettledrum bellows of the Agaria we may compare the pump or piston bellows used by the Naga of Assam (Hutton, *Angami Nagas*, p. 63; *Sema Nagas*, p. 52; Mills, *Rengma Nagas*, p. 70) which are thus described by Hutton. 'The bellows are made of two sections of a large bamboo, or more often in the Angami country of hollowed sections of a tree placed upright together on the ground. From a hole in the bottom of each of these a short bamboo tube is led... The air is pumped to the fire by means of two pistons, the ends of which are usually covered with the skin of the flying squirrel or with chicken feathers. These are worked alternately by a man standing behind the bamboos and holding a piston-rod in each hand. The soft fur, or feathers, with which the end of the rod is bound fits closely in the bamboo and acts as an efficient pump.'—*Angami Nagas*, p. 63. Similar bellows are used in Polynesia and Madagascar. But these hand-bellows are not used in furnaces for extracting ore.

VI. *The Twyer*

The *nari* or *nari-thondi* is a clay cylindrical twyer, splayed open at one end, tapering slightly at the other, which is set in the luting of the furnace or the forge to collect and concentrate the blast upon the fire. The size varies from 7 to 10 inches; one of those in my possession measures $9^1/_2$ inches in length, and is 2 inches wide at the broader end and 1 inch at the narrower. Another measures $1 \times 3 \times 1^1/_2$ inches.

On a reversed bellows, the wooden bottom of which makes a smooth and convenient platform, a woman works up the clay (*nari-māti*). She beats it with a special rounded stick called the *thondi-beth* and then makes it into a ball. In the middle of this she shapes a hole, inserts the stick, rolls out the clay along it with her hands, presses it out and smoothes it by rolling it on the platform, gradually splays out one end, removes the stick, and carefully shapes and finishes the cylinder with her hands, finally placing it to dry standing on its broad end in the sun. Half-a-dozen are made at a time.

VII. *At Work at the Furnace*

We are now in a position to see the Agaria actually at work: we must first, of course, watch them at their principal task of iron-smelting.

During the day, men and women (in Bilaspur men only) have been out in the jungle collecting the ore and making charcoal. In the evening a little procession returns home, with bamboo or leaf baskets filled with the day's spoils.

As the sun sinks to its setting, the women of the house go to prepare the smithy for the morrow's work. They sweep and tidy it, throwing the refuse on the long barrow of slag round the hut. They remove the lumps of ore from the baskets and break them up into small pieces and clean them of earth. Then they roast them in an ordinary fire of wood and bark. Some say that the reason why they do not wear glass bangles is that these would break when they were preparing the ore.

Then a girl brings a basketful of *kodon* chaff and empties it on the left of the furnace, makes a pile of *nari* clay near it,

24. Women making nari twyer.

5. (a) Khuntia Chokh bellows fastened to the ground by pegs.

(b) Bellows of Hindu Lohar in Sarangarh State.

and to the right of the furnace makes piles of sand, earth and the red dust from the broken ore. A basket of white *chirona* clay is placed near the forge, and a pile of cow-dung ash is kept handy. The iron tools are put in place, the hollow wooden *kotna* trough is filled with water, and one or two water-pots, each with its gourd ladle, are put ready. There are already piles of charcoal near the furnace and the forge: if these are not sufficient, more charcoal is tipped out of the *ghandri* baskets that have been brought in that afternoon. Everything is prepared with great exactness: the smithy is swept clean and tidied; when the heavy workers arrive in the morning, they will find everything at hand.

Then water is poured over the skin covers of the bellows, and they are placed before the furnace, one face downwards on top of the other.

Now a woman, generally an older and experienced woman, squats down in front of the furnace and proceeds to repair the 'mouth' with *nari* clay. She also plasters the top and the waste-flue. After this, she takes the *kodon* chaff (which had been burnt the last time the furnace was worked, and is now black and dirty) and cleans it by shaking it up and down in a winnowing-fan, thus removing all the rough fragments, just as if it were rice for dinner. This chaff she pushes into the mouth of the furnace, filling the depression in the ground inside, and presses it down firmly with a useful little stick known as the *tokna-lāthi*.[1] She smoothes the chaff till it presents a smooth surface that may serve as the seat or throne of Lohasur and the bloom of the half-molten iron. It is also called the *āsan* or *pendi* for the 'buttocks of the iron', or the iron's *bistara*, its 'bedding'. Some of the chaff is now slipping out through the *hagān* flue, and she stops this up with earth.

Now the woman mixes the sand with water, and makes a wall about an inch high across the front of the 'mouth'. When this is ready she puts in more chaff up to the level of the wall, again patting and smoothing it carefully with the sharp edge of

[1] In Raipur this was called *dhangi lāthi*.

the stick. If there is not enough *kodon*, she may use charcoal-dust but this must be put at the very bottom. The strong emphasis on the *kodon* chaff has already been noticed in the myths.

On the little wall, the woman places the twyer in position, so that its wider mouth appears at the edge of the wall. She plasters more wet sand all round it. Then she beats some charcoal with her stick, puts the broken bits into a winnowing-fan and pours it into the furnace by way of the slide, filling it right up to the top. Some of the charcoal spills out of the 'mouth', but she pushes this back and quickly plasters the whole 'mouth', pressing the wet sand back against the mass of charcoal, pressing it in hard with both her fists. In front of the twyer, she makes a little platform of sand, and on this she lays the *tokna-lāthi* which thus provides a shelf for the hollow bamboos that will carry the blast from the bellows.

Finally, she washes her hands in the *kotna*-trough, attends again to the bellows, pouring water on the skin-covers, and sees that all is in order. She places the *kalāri*-rake in readiness beside the furnace and goes away to supper and an early bed.

At any time between midnight and dawn the women get up; sometimes a man comes to help them, but he need not.[1] But a man has to come if the iron has not been good and they want the proper *mantra* recited. It is very difficult indeed to get Agaria *mantra*—I think they still have a belief in a secret tradition—and I have only been able to record two, both probably incomplete.

A *mantra* for working the furnace so that good iron will come.

Go and see! O Agyasur! O Dhua Dharni! I take refuge in you! When Logundi Raja and his twelve brothers blew their bellows they did not honour you, but I honour

[1] This division of labour is illustrated by a proverbial dialogue. A woman is gossiping in the smithy: her husband tells her to get on with her work. 'It doesn't matter what I do,' she retorts, 'so long as I do my *bak-bak* and you do your *tak-tak*', thus contrasting the noises made by the bellows and the hammer.

you. Go and see. O Lohasur Baba I take refuge in you! Out of a little bring double, and then I'll worship you.

A *mantra* to increase the iron.

Victory to Lohasur Baba! My ancestors, I rely on you! Agyasur, I rely on you! Koelasur, I rely on you! Our babies and our children are yours! Out of little may there come much! Then will I praise and remember you.

The woman who is to work the bellows places them in position, bends down the *dāng*-springes and ties the *kutidor*-cord, twisting it round twice and knotting it. The bamboo pipes are placed so that they converge at the mouth of the twyer, and a heavy stone is laid on them to keep them in position. The woman mounts the bellows and another woman puts some fire—in ordinary times it can be 'fire-leavings', coals from an old fire—in the mouth of the clay twyer and the first woman, holding her rake in one hand and sometimes a stick in the other, or occasionally supporting herself by holding on to a cord suspended from the roof, begins to work the bellows. The blast quickly forces the fire into the furnace and soon smoke pours out of the top.

The second woman shakes a charge of ore out of a winnowing-fan on to the *machān*-stage, and this gradually slips down into the feed-hole[1] and mixes with the charcoal. Five or ten minutes later, she lights the smoke with a blazing stick: 'otherwise we would get drunk with it': and afterwards red and blue flames play fantastically above the kiln. After about half an hour, the second woman opens the flue with a stick and begins to pull out the *gu* or iron-excreta with the tongs.

And now there is no sound but the rhythmic tread of the bellows and the roar of the blast. The hut is lit with the weird flames above the furnace and the red glow from the flue. Members of the family drop in one by one; they make little fires and crouch silently above them, roasting maize. There is no singing and little talk. As the charcoal and ore

[1] The feed-hole is called *ghongha* by the Chokh of Bilaspur.

slips down into the furnace, someone pours more charcoal (from the left) and ore (from the right) on to the stage.

The work continues from two to five hours. 'We know it's ready when the furnace says *bangor bangor*, or when the ore has been put in ten times.' In Nunera I timed a girl and her young husband: they worked from 5.30 P.M. to 10.15 P.M. In Mandla I have seen it done more expeditiously, from 3.30 A.M. to 5.15 A.M. and from 6 A.M. to 8.45 A.M. Of course, a lot depends on the kind of ore used, and the amount of iron that is required.

When they judge the iron to be ready, a man comes forward—hitherto everything has been done, or could have been done, by women—and the bellows are removed. With a stick he breaks down the sand luting of the hearth and removes the twyer. The blazing coals pour out in a red cascade. Shielding his face the Agaria adroitly rakes the sand into a heap on his right-hand side (where it will be ready for use again) and the coals to the left. A woman stands by with a gourd ladle full of water which she throws on to the coals. Then the man with *sansi*-tongs lifts out the rough spongy bloom of glowing semi-molten iron and slag, and carries it to the anvil. Here it is hammered, rather gently, with the heavy hammer, and most of the included slag, which is still in a state of fusion, is removed.

Immediately, one of the women empties a basket of fresh *kodon* chaff into the mouth of the furnace. It begins to burn, and the Agaria brings back the still glowing ball of iron and drops it into the chaff which burns therefore all the quicker.

I have witnessed this process again and again in every part of the Agaria country, but it hardly ever varies. The domestic ritual is meticulously observed.

I noticed one slight variation in Nunera. The Chokh Agaria there did not use the *tokna-lāthi* to smooth the chaff (which incidently was rice chaff, since *kodon* was not grown in the neighbourhood) and when the hearth was fully plastered a little cup-like platform was made in front of the *duāri*, as the mouth of the furnace was called. On this the hollow bamboos rested.

When the bloom is large and strong and comparatively little slag falls from it when it is hammered, there is great jubilation. On the other hand, the failure of the iron causes bitter disappointment, fear also of the witch who must have charmed the furnace or of the god who must be displeased.

I remember poor thin Gautam of Daldal—how miserable he was when a great ball of red-hot stuff gradually fell to pieces beneath the hammer. After two hours' work only a small lump, hardly fit for one axe-head, remained.

VIII. *A New Furnace*

The building of a new furnace is an important matter, not only that a good supply of iron may be assured, but because the Virgin Iron is to be extracted, and there must be no mistakes in the ritual. In October 1939, I watched the building of a new kiln and the extraction of the *kuāri lohā* at Bahapur (Dindori Tahsil). This is the normal time, for during the rains many of the kilns through storm and neglect collapse, and it is in October when the rains cease that new furnaces are made.

The mud cone is first prepared. A red clay, called in Bilaspur *lāl-pila* earth, is mixed with water and the chaff of *kuāri kodon*, or *kodon* ground in a new mill. This is plastered by the women on a grass frame which is afterwards burnt. The Chokh of Bilaspur build up the cone without a frame, doing about a foot every second day: when the first layer is dry and hardened they add another story. When it is ready, the cone is left to dry and often remains for months before being used. At Pungaon, Pandulal had kept his kiln unstarted for a long time while he settled his many complicated matrimonial affairs. At Umaria, they did not want to start a new furnace till a wedding was over, but they got it ready and put it aside. In Bahapur, the old furnace was cracked and broken, flames were coming through the cracks, but it was being used to the end.

I shall not easily forget that visit to Bahapur. All the paths had been washed away or overgrown during the rains, and after struggling through tall grasses for some hours I reached Bahapur, and the little Agaria hut that had been set aside for me, in a state of high fever. After a few wretched hours of wakefulness, I was roused by the roar of the bellows, and wrapping myself in a blanket I went still shivering with ague to the smithy. It was long before dawn, and fire had been kindled in the old furnace for the last time. As the bloom was removed the first light crept coldly into the hut, competing vainly with the glorious orange-red of the blazing iron. The *machān* broke at the first touch of the day.

The new cone was standing outside. Two of the men turned it over on its side, and one of them enlarged the 'mouth' with his axe. Then when the old furnace had cooled a little, they put a stout pole down its throat and broke it in half. Men and women busied themselves removing the debris, picking up hot lumps of solid earth, clearing the dust with the *tokna-lāthi*, sweeping away charcoal and chaff with bamboo brooms.

Then a woman scooped out all the refuse from the hole in the ground below where the old furnace had been, sprinkled water liberally over it, threw in fresh earth, and filled up this hole and all other depressions in the ground, treading it down till the floor was smooth and clean. Then the men pushed and heaved the new cone into place. This took a lot of time, for it had to be adjusted exactly above the old hole and under the middle of the roof. Stones were put under it to make it slope forward.

Although Badwa my host was the owner of the smithy, his old mother was clearly in command, and when the cone was at last in place she cleared a space round it with her iron-spud, and then with the same implement drove a hole through the mud for the flue, and again enlarged the 'mouth'.

Meanwhile the men dug holes in the ground for the wooden poles that would support the slide. The old woman plastered the inside with ordinary wet mud and scooped out the hole in the ground to a depth of five or six inches.

Now the men placed the poles, which had niches cut in the tops, and fixed cross-bars in position. They laid strips of bamboo loosely across them and tied them in place with very thin bark-rope.

The old woman put wood-shavings, scraps, refuse, bits of chewed maize into the furnace and lit them in order to dry the earth she had plastered. As the little fire blazed up, she continued lightly plastering all round the working shaft, and then attacked the slide, plastering it and building up a three-inch wall round it, grumbling the while at the amount of work she had to do.

A boy came in with two baskets of *chirona māti*, clay from the river. The women began to mix it at once, with water and bits of straw, making it very smooth and fine. When this was ready, a very special old woman with itch, Badwa's grandmother, who had not appeared before, came to improve the flue and scoop out a little channel along which the iron-excreta would flow. Then they plastered the whole kiln with the new clay, making it smooth and white, and it was ready.

When it was fairly dry, it was prepared in the usual way, which I have already described. Oil and *haldi* was smeared on it, and as the Virgin Fire was lit a *mantra* was recited by Badwa:—

> Go and see! Logundi Raja, Udhdaraj Raja, Kariya Kuar, Lohasur Mata, Koelasur Mata, Mother Jwala Mukhi, Agyasur Mother, I remember you all. I have made the furnace hollow within, and there sit Lohasur and Koelasur. O Mother Agyasur, care for the flame. When the Virgin Iron is born, I will fall at the feet of all the godlings.

Another, simpler, *mantra* is sometimes used:—

> Lohasur Bhawani! I apply the sign of turmeric and cow-dung. Help us. Let the iron come well; let it not fail; and in the third year I will give you a black pig.

IX. *Technical Defects in the Agaria Furnace*

The Agaria furnace suffers from several serious technical defects: if these could be remedied there would be a saving of labour, an increase in production and a general improvement of prosperity. The first and most obvious defect in the smelting process is that no flux is used.' It is hard to see the reason for this. Limestone is the commonest surface rock all over the plains of Chhattisgarh: it is available in Mandla. In Drug, P. N. Bose wrote that 'the Raipur (Lower Vindhyan) limestone is usually not far off from the iron-ore localities. As regards Dhalli, the nearest outcrop of it is at a distance of twenty miles.'[1] The absence of flux means longer and harder work and a lot of waste. The slag is highly ferruginous, the silicon in the iron being oxidized and forming with a portion of the iron a fusible ferrous silicate. 'Not only therefore is a portion of the metal wasted in the slag, but it also seems certain that the removal of the silica cannot be so complete as it would be with the adoption of a suitable flux, and so extra labour is required to refine the resulting iron from the impurities still contained in it.' During this refining from 20 to 30 per cent of slag separates out from the iron. An experiment made with the *kheri* iron obtained from the manganiferous ore of Dhanwahi, showed that the rough iron lost as much as 38 per cent of slag in the refining, while a later experiment with the Partabpur ore gave a loss of only 24 per cent.[2]

Another defect is the absence of any means of cooling the twyer. The two bamboo poles that lead air from the bellows terminate about an inch from the mouth of the twyer, with the result that there is an obvious loss of blast and the fire does not achieve anything like the heat that might be possible.

The result is that in proportion to the result the expenditure of charcoal is very great. Ball estimates 14 tons of charcoal to 1 ton of finished iron. Hole, more optimistically, estimated that 180 seers of ore and 180 seers of charcoal produced 30 to 35 seers of iron. In any case the method is wasteful, and —as we have seen—much metal remains in the slag. It is said that in the Salem District, magnetite containing 72 per cent of metal yields only 15 per cent of its weight of bar iron. The iron is very good, but the smelter cannot charge more for it.

[1] *R.G.S.I.*, Vol. XX, Part IV, p. 169.

[2] *The Agricultural Ledger*, op. cit., p. 19, note by R. S. Hole.

Another disadvantage of the Agaria smithy is that it is so constructed that it cannot be used during the rains and thus four months' work is lost every year. A proper building, with some method of storing ore and charcoal would increase the out-turn of the furnace by one-third.

X. *At Work in the Forge*

The Agaria of the Central Provinces, unlike their brethren in Mirzapur, do not confine themselves to smelting iron: they go on to work it up into tools. We must now watch this process.

The smithy is, in fact, in many ways a happy and cosy place; especially in the cold weather, there is company and a fire, and it is always pleasant to watch other people working.

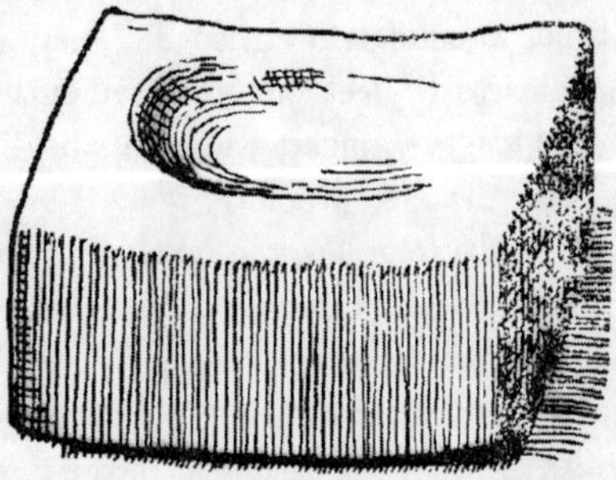

FIG. 21. Anvil
Length 3½", height 2¼"

We are then to imagine, in a typical roofed smithy of Mandla, that the Agaria have been up from before dawn and have reduced a fine ball of iron. The furnace is left to cool, and the workers turn their attention to the little forge, or *dukān* (shop). 'The woman gives birth and the man cares for it'; that is to say, the iron that was born in the furnace must now be refined in the forge. The bellows are shifted to the other end of the hut, and placed so that the bamboo poles converge on a small clay nozzle fixed by mud in the ground and pointing slightly downwards towards a small hole filled with charcoal. On the right-hand side and at right angles to the line of this nozzle there is a small earthen wall about two feet high and three feet long (but often considerably smaller than this) which is pierced by a hole leading to a still deeper depression in the ground. This acts as a flue and an escape for any slag that is still further forced from the iron on its refining.

Near by is a large stone which serves as an anvil for the heavier and rougher work; there are probably a couple of welding hammers or *ghāna* lying near it. The *ghāna*, the 'rice pounder which any man can wield', may be found in two types: one (generally used in Dindori) is a solid block of rounded iron, with a hole through the centre to hold the wooden shaft; both ends are the same, blunt and round. It measures five inches in length, has a diameter of three inches and weighs, without its shaft, 2 seers 14 chattaks.

The other type of *ghāna*, which is commoner in the east of the Province, in Bilaspur and Raipur, is a long piece of iron with its haft at one-third of its length, blunt at one end and pointed at the other. A typical hammer of this kind from Lapha Zamindari, weighed $4^1/_2$ seers (without handle). The handle was $2^1/_2$ feet long, the head of the hammer being exactly a foot long, $1^3/_4$ inches wide at its broad end and $^3/_4$ of an inch wide at the narrow point.

Near the forge lies the *sansi* or tongs, again of two types—straight-lip tongs, with straight pointed ends, and gad tongs (called *kokti-sansi*) with the ends bent over to ensure a firmer grip. A normal length is 1 foot 8 inches and the weight is $^1/_2$ to $^3/_4$ seer. They are described in the riddles as the 'mother and sister who have one waistband between them' or 'the bride and bridegroom with a single navel'. We shall also find the *hataudi* or light hammer, clearly illustrated in fig. 1, and weighing from 11 chattaks to 1 seer. The hammer is compared with the *ghāna* in the saying, 'Big brother says *tanā nāna*: little brother says *tining niti*'.

There are also a number of small, but very necessary, tools which the Agaria keeps hidden under leaves, pushed away in the thatch of the hut, or—where the smithy is out-of-doors—in his house or in a hollow tree. First among these is the iron *matorna* (fig. 21), a small anvil flat on one side and slightly hollowed on the reverse to make a sort of swage-block when turned upside down, $3^1/_2$ inches long and $2^1/_4$ inches broad. The

26. (a) Open-air forge at Koteya, Neterhat.

(b) Open-air forge at Jam Tola, near Neterhat.

From U. Ball's *Jungle Life in India.*

27. Iron-smelters of Palamau.

tussa (fig. 22), a punch of iron 2 inches long, is used to cut the iron or to make deep indentations. It has a sharp edge at one end for this purpose. The *suja pawāri* (fig. 23) is a round iron bar $3^1/_2$ inches long, and is used to cut holes in the iron; handles also are hammered round it, as we shall see presently. The *paslor* (fig. 24) is very similar, but it is thicker, the exact size for an axe-handle, and the iron hafts of the axes are hammered round it.

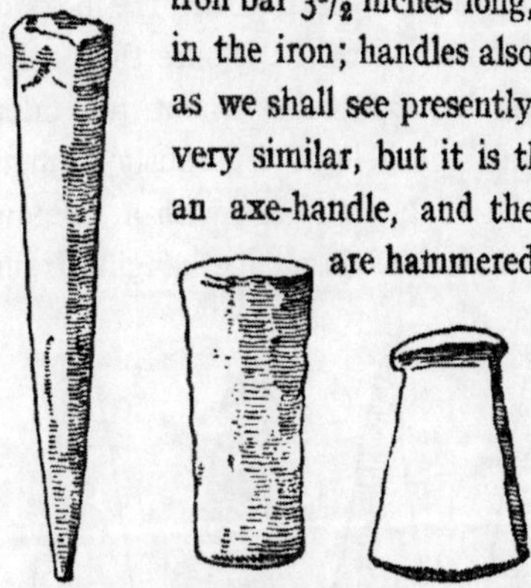

FIG. 22. *Tussa*. FIG. 23. *Suja pawāri*. FIG. 24. *Paslor*. *Longest is 3½"*

Now a woman brings a bit of coal from the kitchen and places it in the twyer of the forge. She ignites the charcoal with a few short sharp blasts of the bellows and then settles down to the regular rhythm of the 'bellows-dance'. The first business is to deal with the ball of iron that has just been extracted from the kiln. At present, with the slag and charcoal that was adhering to it hammered off on the stone anvil,[1] it is known as *dhidha*. Sometimes it is cut in half with an axe, and the two pieces are put in the refining fire of the forge and left there while other work proceeds. After two hours or so, it will become *pajar* iron and fit for the most exacting and important work.

Presently an old Gond arrives with a dozen sickles tied together on a pole across his shoulder. These have suffered during a heavy season and need a new edge and sometimes a new curve. With him is a Baiga demanding a fresh arrowhead. The Agaria, leaving the *dhidha* iron in the fire, immediately starts work on the damaged sickles.

Gripping the wooden handle of the sickle, he places the beak in the fire, brings it out, hammers the edge, puts it back,

[1] Grierson has a Bihari proverb about the anvil. 'If the anvil has nothing on it, the bellow falls on its head.'—op. cit., p. 86.

hammers out a sharp point, improves the curve which has been lost through constant work, dips it in water for a moment—putting the point in first and immersing it with a slow circular motion and pulling it out with a sharp jerk. He looks down the edge and goes on hammering till he is sure the beak is in perfect order again. Each sickle takes about ten minutes. Meanwhile, the girl works the bellows vigorously, sometimes shielding herself from the heat of the fire with a winnowing-fan, sometimes supporting herself on a rope hanging from the roof.

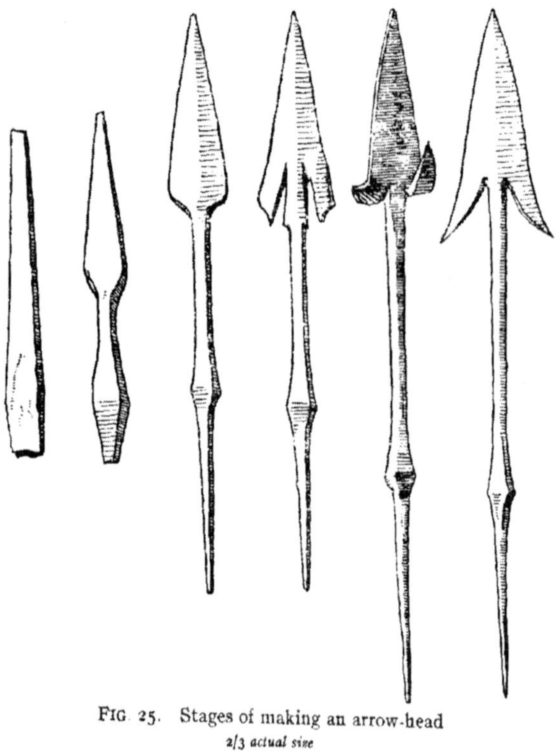

FIG. 25. Stages of making an arrow-head
2/3 actual size

After half an hour's work on the sickles, the Agaria decides to make the arrow-head. From the roof where it has been concealed, he produces a small strip of iron, and puts it in the fire. When it is ready, he hammers out the tip of the iron-strip into a blade. Then with the sharp end of a chisel (*cheni*) he makes indentations in the blade about an inch from the tip. After heating the iron twice, he is able to cut it right through. He bends the two wings over and hammers out the shaft of the arrow till it is long and thin. He cuts off from the rest of the strip a sufficient length, and hammers this out till it is round and straight. Then he devotes himself to the two wings, hammers them back and pushes them out a little till they form the two wings of the arrow in the familiar form. He makes the point very sharp, and twirls it round on the anvil to see if it is true. He hands it to the Baiga, who finds it so hot that he drops it. The whole process has taken three-quarters of an hour.

Other visitors arrive in the smithy. A Gond *panda* magician comes with four dogs frisking round him. He is heavily armoured with protective iron, for he has four different kinds of iron bangles on his arms, two iron torcs round his neck, an iron chain, an iron trident and an iron spoon. All these, of course, are of Virgin Iron and very powerful. But no one pays very much attention to him: more notice is taken of an Ahir (cowherd) who brings a winnowing-fan full of rice to pay for the repair of three iron ploughshares and a spade.

The Agaria now takes the tongs and pulls out of the fire the ball of *dhidha* iron that he had put there an hour ago. He holds it on the anvil with his left hand while with his right he hammers it with the welding hammer. His son is already on his feet and he grasps the second hammer raises it above his head and brings it down heavily on the iron. For several minutes they hammer in perfect unison, the father swinging the hammer round his shoulder, the son high above his head. When they have thus removed some more of the slag they put the ball back into the fire. This is the Mandla custom. But in Bilaspur and Raipur and—so far as I had the time to observe—in Bihar, where the hammer is heavier, two men do not hammer together, but only one uses the hammer while an assistant holds the iron with the tongs.

The Ahir wants a *khurpa* (knife) which he will use for removing the skin of animals and for cutting meat (fig. 26). The Agaria brings another long strip of iron from the roof, heats it, beats it to a point at either end, bends it round into a rough horseshoe, sharpens the long cutting edge, and finally brings the two ends together and beats them into a single spike. The Ahir has brought a small bit of bamboo to serve as handle, and when the spike of the *khurpa* has been made red-hot it is pressed firmly into this and the knife is ready.

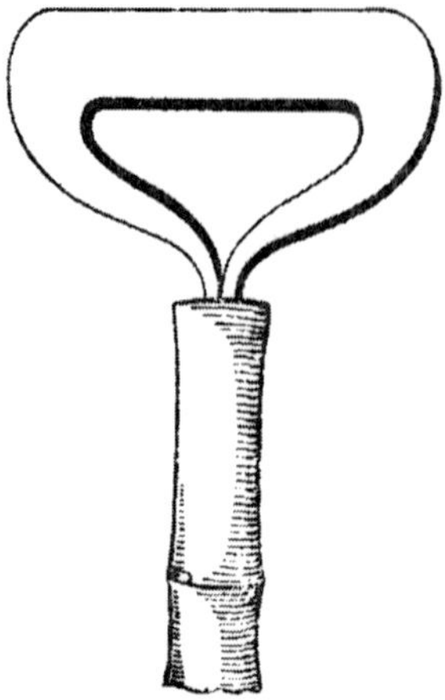

FIG. 26. *Khurpa* knife
Breadth 6"

The ball of iron is again removed from the fire and beaten. It is now ready, real *pajar* iron. The Agaria decides to make a *tabla* axe with it. With heavy hammers father and son beat it into a rough square and return it to the fire. The Agaria then dips it in a pile of cow-dung ashes 'to stop it peeling too much' and again beats it out with the heavy hammer till it is flatter and longer. He takes some lumps of *nari māti* and crumbles them, and now whenever the iron is in the fire he throws pinches of the dust on to it. Gradually he beats the block of iron into shape, making a broad head and a long narrow tail; he constantly has to dip the tongs into the *kotna*-trough to cool them. Then he hammers out the two ends of the tail, puts it on the anvil and beats the tail over and back to make a handle. The *paslor*-pin is now inserted and the handle beaten on to it, and gradually the two side wings are also beaten into the handle. Now he makes with the *tussa*-punch some deep indentations in the 'waist' of the axe between the handle and the blade. He stands the axe blade downwards, and gently taps it until the blade becomes broader. This one process took half an hour. An anvil is made for this by driving the welding hammer point downwards into the ground and beating on the broad end. At last the axe is tempered by being put very slowly into water. It took just two hours to make.

By now the visitors begin to drift away, for it is nearly time for the morning meal. The Agaria too decide to stop the work of the forge. They have been hard at it for six hours without refreshment. The woman unties the bellows, and puts them away face to face in a corner. The man packs up his small tools in a little box, and pokes the larger implements into the thatch of the roof.

I will now describe the processing of a few other common articles.

Nails. The Agaria beats a small lump of *kuāri lohā* into a thin strip, concentrating on one end. When the end is thin enough and has a good point, he places it across the *malorna*-anvil and, bending the end to the length of $^3/_4$ inch over the edge, breaks it off.

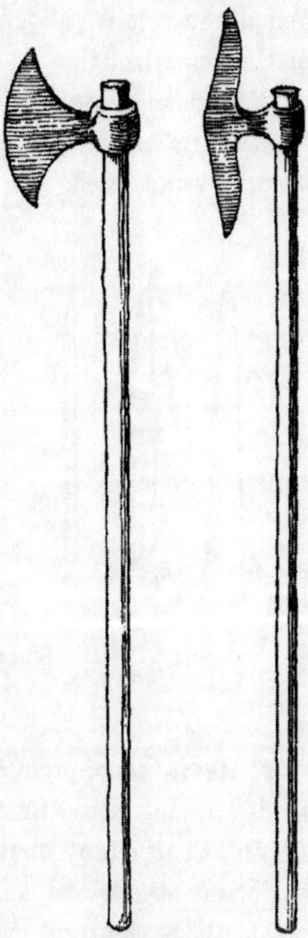

FIG. 27. Axes
Blade length 7"

A ring. Gotam Agaria made an *aitwār mundri* for me at Daldal in this way. He took a small lump of iron and beat it out into a thin strip. He caught one end with the gad tongs, and with the straight-lip tongs twisted it round and round. Then he bent it into a ring round the handle of the rake (which was thinner than his *paslor*), carefully hammered the two ends together, and dipped it for a moment in water.

To temper and strengthen the iron, little pinches of *chirona māti* are thrown at it while it is in the fire. Sometimes it is dipped into a pile of cow-dung ash. Lemon and salt is used by the Chokh: if the iron is not amenable to working, the lemon and salt is rubbed on it and is also put in the water of the *kotna*-trough. A clay called *mitti kā sohāga* is also used 'to make the iron soft and help the bits to stick together'. Implements are always dipped in the *kotna* after they have been fully processed.

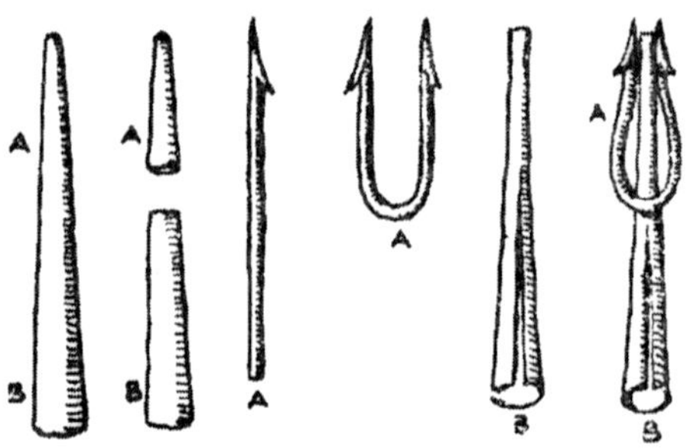

Fig. 28. Stages of making a *sāndi*
Iron 7¼" length

A *sāndi,* three-pronged fork used by cow-herds, useful also for catching snakes. In Bhoira, Chaitu beat out a ball of iron into a bar broad at one end and tapering almost to a point, about eighteen inches long and half an inch thick. Then he broke off six inches of the thinner end and put it aside near the fire, He placed the broad end in the hollow of the swage-block and hammered a slight indentation in the middle, laid the *suja pawāri* across it and beat it over, so that now there was a handle capable of taking a stick. Now, squatting the while on an old inverted bellows-frame, he hammered out a thin bit of iron to a point, bent it over so that it made a small hook, but then hammered the hook into the original rod, did the same for the other end, placed it in the hollow of the swage block and bent it over into a horseshoe, and then hammered the two points of the horseshoe close together. Now he placed this over the handle and very carefully placing them together put them in the fire and then hammered them so that there was now a prong with three points. He straightened the middle point with the tongs and pushed the two side points out a little with the file; and the *sāndi* was ready.

When separate pieces of iron have to be welded together as in the manufacture of a *sāndi*, this *mantra* may be used to ensure success.

> Go and see! Bai Agyasur, Logundi Raja, Dhukan Dhahu! Then we did not acknowledge you! When Baba Lohasur's name was taken, the two were joined together, strong as an iron pillar. Victory to Lohasur Baba.

A razor. Out of a strip of thin iron, not more than an eighth of an inch thick, the Agaria broke off a small piece four inches long, and hammered it to a very fine edge. He cold-worked this for a long while, then heated it, dipped it for a moment into the tempering water, and then pushed the red-hot spike into a small handle of *katai* wood.

XI. *The Products of the Agaria's Skill*

Of the articles made by the Agaria some of the most interesting are those with a religious or magical purpose. Iron ornaments nearly always have a magical significance. Three kinds of rings are made—

Aitwār mundri (fig. 9) is a ring of twisted iron, usually made of *kuāri lohā*, and worn by a *Lamu* child as a protection against lightning.

Surāhi mundri is an ordinary ring of plain iron. It has no special purpose, but would serve as guard against the ordinary pains of rheumatism and other diseases.

Chulmundri is used in weddings by Gond and Baiga as well as Agaria. At a dramatic moment the bridegroom chases and captures his bride and forces this ring on her finger. It is supposed to be the combined work of the Lohasur, Tamesur and Kansasur brothers, and has copper mixed with the iron.

Chhura is an anklet of plain or twisted iron, generally of *kuāri lohā*, worn by a *Lamu* child on the left leg. *Chhuri* are bracelets worn by men or women as a protection against magic.

The magicians who are in constant conflict with the unseen powers sometimes wear an entire armoury of defensive iron ornaments, all made of *kuāri lohā*. Round the neck is the torc, the *sutia* (fig. 14), usually worn by women. It may be reinforced by the *sakri*, a chain in which the wearer's special deity or guardian angel may reside. Sometimes the magician also wears iron *bahunta* round his arms above the elbow. With iron bracelets and anklets, and an iron *trisul* (trident) or *chamīta*-tongs (fig. 12), a very efficient 'ghost scarer' in his hand, he feels fairly secure against his supernatural enemies.

Much of the power of the Gond and Baiga magicians is due to their ability to fall into a state of ecstatic excitement. While in this condition they are expected to prove themselves by scourging, sitting on spikes or swinging violently on a spiked swing. Iron is the only substance strong enough to beat a man who is thus possessed by supernatural power. The objects used at this time are these :—

Pīdha. A wooden board about 19 by 15 inches and covered with nails projecting half an inch from the wood: the specimen in my collection has 161 nails. The magician sits on this seat and 'prophesies', throwing his head to and fro and contorting his body. It is sometimes placed on a swing.

Kharaut (fig. 29). These are wooden clogs also covered with nails, worn by mediums.

28. Birjhia Asur furnaces at Kerakhair.

29. Bir Asur furnace at Doka.

Gurud is an iron scourge, two feet long, with which the magician flagellates himself. Its knobs and spikes make it a formidable weapon.

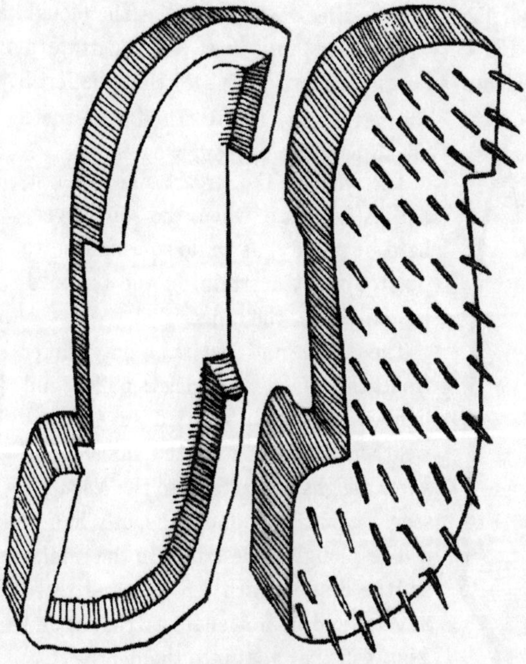

FIG. 29. Spiked *kharaut* shoes
1/4 actual size

Barāhi or *Katāhi* is also a scourge, but made of the hair from a cow's tail, and fitted with iron tips and spikes.

Hiranoti is a very elaborate lampstand used in marriages and for worship before some special shrine. Only a few Agaria know how to make it, and it is considered a very great honour to be presented with one, requiring a gift of at least a small bullock in return. As will be seen from fig. 7 its most striking feature are two beautifully made deer, which with the thrust forward of their heads give a real impression of movement. On the other side are four cobras with hoods erect, and on top a man facing some kind of bird. The larger of the two specimens in my possession stands 3 feet 5 inches high and weighs $4^1/_2$ seers.

But, of course, incomparably the most important things made by the Agaria are the 'implements of husbandry' as Major Vans Agnew called them in 1820. The plough, he says, is 'of a very rude kind' and does not penetrate more than six inches 'as in this country it is said that the fertility of the soil lies on the top'.[1] In Mandla there are three kinds of ploughshares:—

The *olaha* is the largest and heaviest, and is not used when the soil is very hard or muddy, as to do so would be to put too great a strain on the bullocks, but only after the rains.

The *kurra* and *bataraha* only differ from the *olaha* in being smaller and lighter. The first is used in the hot weather, the latter in the rains. The *kurra* weighs 9 chattaks to the *olaha*'s 1 seer, 1 chattak, or almost exactly half.

The plough is described in the riddles as 'the cripple with ten feet and three navels' and its iron share as 'the roasted *bāmi* fish that goes into the depths'.

The share is fixed into its trough in the sole of the plough by a clamp, the *jaru*.

FIG. 30. Ploughshare *Length 1′ 2″ to 1′ 6″*

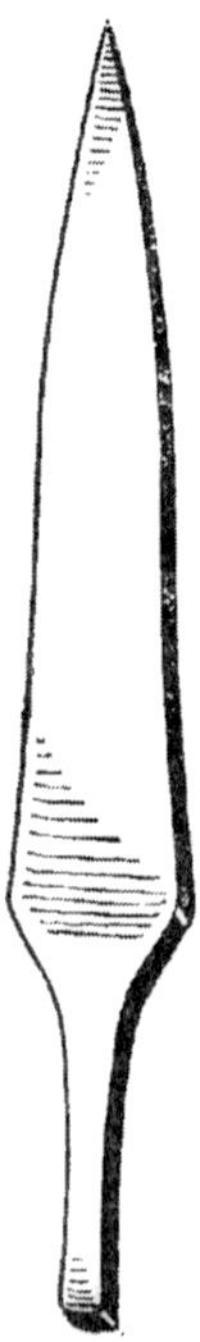

FIG. 31. Ploughshare *Length 1′ 2″ to 1′ 6″*

Also used in ploughing is the *painări* which has an iron point called *kaluha* fixed in place by a small nail (*arhai*). This is used to drive the bullocks forward, to cut grass and thorn bushes, to break off earth that has stuck to the plough, to dig for rats.

The *bakkhar* is the paring harrow. It is fitted with a share

[1] Vans Agnew, op. cit., p. 33.

(*pans*) (fig. 40). It is used for rooting up stubble and breaking the clods of earth that the plough has turned up.

The *kānta* or spud is used to dig up roots or to make holes in the ground. It is a favourite implement of the Baiga, who use it for making holes in their *bewar*-clearings for sowing pulse.

The *hassia*, or 'rude reaping hook', is the sickle used to reap rice or *kodon*, to cut grass, to weed, to cut meat. It is 'the cow with a crumpled horn that wanders through the jungle'. It is often applied, heated, to the body as a cautery or to drive out an evil spirit, and it is carried by pregnant women as a protection against magical dangers. In Raipur, a much larger toothed-sickle with a span of 14 inches and a serrated edge is used.

The *gaend* is a large iron ring which is fixed round the pole in the centre of the threshing floor, and to which the rope controlling the bullocks is attached.

Several kinds of digging implements are used. The *sābar* is an iron bar, one foot long and weighing 4 seers, slightly pointed at one end. Sometimes it is made with one rounded end and the other squared into a spade. It is then a very useful tool indeed, and is even used for pounding rice. The *kudari* (fig. 16) is a small mattock used for digging ore from the pits, clay from the river, embanking the fields or any other purpose. In Mandla it generally has a sharp point, but in Bilaspur it sometimes has a broad spade-like blade.

The *basula* (fig. 42) is an adze, used for smoothing the wood of a plough or indeed for planing any kind of wood. It is sometimes also used for digging.

For hunting and fishing, the Agaria make a few weapons. There are three kinds of axes:—

The *tangia* is the ordinary and most serviceable axe. It is used for cutting wood. It weighs 1 seer.

The *tangli* is of the same pattern, but lighter (only 5 chattaks) and can be used for cutting bamboo and bark. The *tabli* (weighing $^1/_2$ seer) has a much broader cutting edge, and can do the same work more quickly.

The *pharsa* and *pharsi* (fig. 27) are large and small 'battle-axes' used for killing animals and in defence.

For fishing and killing snakes, the three-pronged *sāndi* (fig. 28) is made, a very effective instrument, with which many snakes have been destroyed in my own house.

The Agaria make a number of arrow-heads of different patterns. These are illustrated in fig. 32.

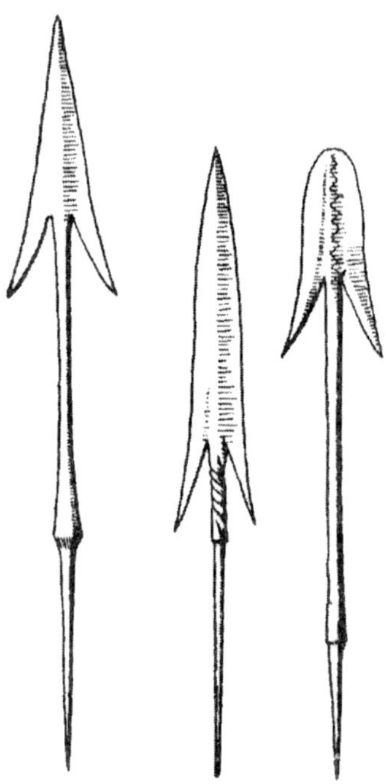

FIG. 32. Arrow-heads
Length, 5¼"

Traps are sometimes fitted with iron. The *gothiār phānda* (fig. 15), or 'talking trap', has little tinkling points of iron attached to it. The *dhimra phānda* is a fishing net weighted all round with bits of iron. It is thrown on to the surface of the water, and sinks down on top of any fish there may be.

There are two kinds of spear, the *sāng* made entirely of iron, and the *barchi* (fig. 43) which has an iron blade and tip fitted to a wooden shaft.

The Agaria make a number of tools and implements for ordinary domestic use. I give a list of them here.

Bindhna, bindhni and *kol bindhni* are chisels of different sizes for making holes in ploughs, doors, beams and so on. The *kol bindhni* is concave-bladed and can make round holes.

Bāki (fig. 5) is a small knife for cutting bamboo to make baskets. *Chhura* (fig. 20) is another knife or razor used for shaving the beard or hair, and sometimes to cut the umbilical cord.

Khurpa (fig. 26) is a cutting instrument for chopping up flesh and removing the skin of animals. It is also used to root up *dub* grass.

Sakri (fig. 11) are chains for fastening doors.

Chalni is an iron sieve (fig. 39) for cleaning rice or sifting flour [1]

Jhāra (fig. 38) is an iron perforated spoon used for removing wheat cakes from the oil in which they are being cooked.

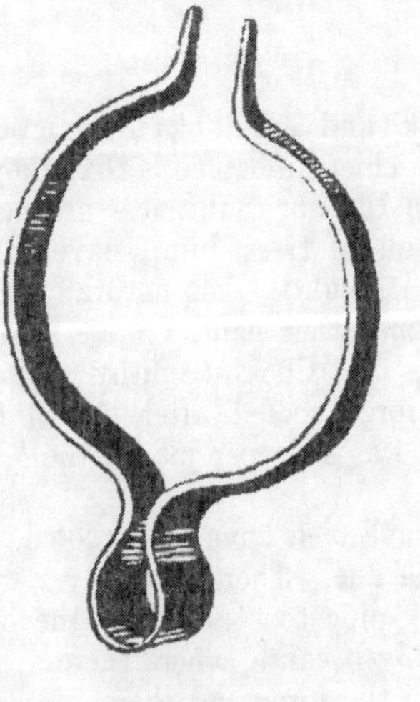

FIG. 33. Hair extractor
Length, 3½"

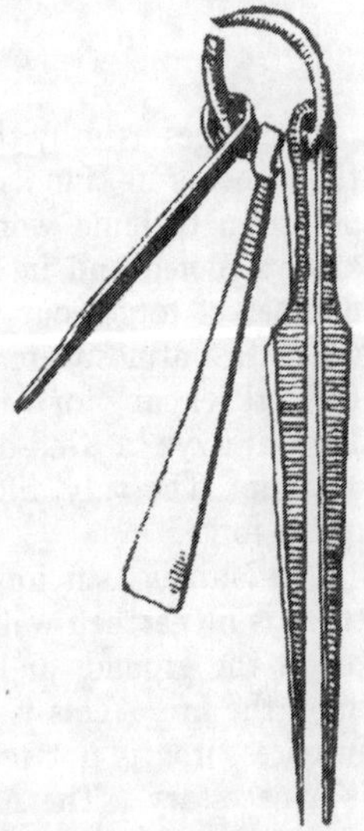

FIG. 34. *Kānta chimti*
Actual size

Chamaj (fig. 38) is used in making sweets.

Rukni or *karauni* is used for extracting pulp from gourds, etc.

Māni is an iron nail for holding the upper and lower grindstones together.

The iron hub of a wheel is often made in Bilaspur.

[1] Grierson has two proverbs about the sieve. Of an extravagant man it is said, 'whose cow have I become? he has brought a sieve into which to milk me'; and a Bihar version of 'the pot calling the kettle black' is 'the sieve which had a thousand holes sneered at the winnowing-basket' —op. cit., p. 117.

Jhumka is an iron cymbal used in dancing. Sometimes it is fixed in a stick.

Nakua chimta (fig. 33) is used for removing body-hair.

Kānta chimti (fig. 34). A combination of tweezers, tooth-pick and a third tool which may be used either as ear-pick or to help the extraction of nails from the feet. This is, in fact, the 'chatelaine', an instrument of ancient pedigree and wide distribution.[1]

Randa. A plane.

NOTE TO CHAPTER VII

I.

The forges used by the Chokh and God-dhuka are practically the same as in Mandla. The chief difference is that they do not seem to mind working in the open: furnaces are nearly always roofed and in the shade of trees, but I have seen a number of forges out in the sunlight. This naturally alters the entire atmosphere. On the other hand I have seen, at Dumarkachhar for example, a Chokh smithy and at Rajasawayya a God-dhuka forge roofed after the Mandla pattern. The only difference was a deeper pit for the *hagān* in the forge.

The Mahali Asur forges I have seen have been roofed, and there is no earthen wall with a flue. There is simply a small pit in the ground, and a clay pipe to concentrate the blast upon the fire. This is probably because, where there are no furnaces, iron is not refined in the forge and therefore a flue is unnecessary. The Asur of Neterhat made similar arrangements, even when there was a furnace.

A Lohar forge is a very different affair. It is often in a properly plastered and even tiled house. As the bellows-blower, who invariably works the bellows with his hands, has to sit much nearer the fire, there is often a mud wall between him and the fire. The Agaria make their mud wall at right angles to the bellows, and the wall is not a protection from fire but serves to make the flue. In Baldidih (Raipur) for example,

[1] See Clarke, 'Modern Survivals of the Sumerian Chatelaine' in *Essays presented to C. G. Seligman* (London, 1934) and M. B. Emeneau, 'A Chatelaine from Coorg' in *Man*, June 1940.

the Lohar had a wall three feet high with a little cup at one end for money or tobacco. In a village on the Sambalpur border of Sarangarh State I saw a very smart Lohar shop in an open shed where the arrangements were as shown in Plate 32.

But it would be wrong to say that there were any rules governing the furniture of a forge: practical and local needs are the real directors of technique.

II.

R. S. Hole gave a description in 1898 of an Agaria furnace and its working in Raipur which shows several small deviations from the Mandla model.

The furnace employed is probably the simplest form of the iron furnace now to be found in the world. It is built entirely of clay and sun-dried bricks. From behind, the furnace appears as a semi-circular erection rising 3 feet above the level of the ground. In front a trench is dug to a depth of 3 feet, 3 feet 6 inches wide at the bottom, 4 feet wide at the top and about 11 feet long. From the bottom of this trench to the front of the hearth of the furnace is 1 foot and the hearth which slopes up towards the back of the furnace is about 2 feet by 1 foot 10 inches. From the front of the hearth (the back of the hearth being 5 feet higher) to the throat of the furnace is 4 feet 10 inches and at the throat the shaft is 10 inches square. The side walls are 10 inches to 12 inches thick and the hind wall 16 inches to 18 inches, these being constructed of sun-dried bricks overlaid with a mixture of two parts of clay and one part *kodon* straw. These slope slightly outwards from the top of the furnace towards the ground.

The front wall is only two inches thick, and in this there are no bricks. The bottom of this front wall is 1 foot 1 inch above the front of the hearth and slopes slightly outwards towards the top of the furnace. This front wall has to bear most of the pressure of the burden, and as it is only supported by its adhesion to the thick side walls it must, at the same time, be kept thin. As a general rule, therefore, it only lasts about eight days and then has to be replaced. The top of the furnace is covered in by a light clay roof about 1½ inches thick, the large hole about 6 inches square being left open.

The man who plies the bellows sits in the trench in front of the furnace and to prevent the smoke and ashes blowing from the charge-hole (which also acts as the chimney) into his face, a thin screen of clay 1 inch to $1^1/_2$ inches thick is erected on the top of the furnace, 3 inches high in front and 2 feet 6 inches at the sides. In front of the furnace a roof of branches and leaves, supported on four posts, is placed as a shade from the sun. The whole furnace takes from ten to twenty days and sometimes longer to prepare, costing about Rs 8. As it is built of clay, it has to be constructed in sections, each of which must be left to get thoroughly dry, to allow the clay to consolidate before the work is continued and so the construction of the furnace is necessarily a matter of some time. The usual arrangement is that nothing is paid for actually making the furnace. A lessee having engaged a *bhatti-walla* for the season at Rs 7 to Rs 8 per month, the latter sets to work to construct the furnace, he and his family devoting three or four hours to the work every three or four days, letting it get dry in the interval. As their usual occupations, therefore, are very slightly interrupted, the smelter gets nothing for this and is only paid after the furnace is finished and in work. On the front of the hearth a *gaderi* is placed which looks like a long, curved brick made of sun-dried clay, about 2 feet long, 2 inches thick and 5 inches broad. In this about 20 holes are bored, the centre upper one not being perforated. In the latter a stick is placed which, resting on the bottom of the trench, supports the *gaderi* in its place. The bottom of the furnace is then filled with a mixture of charcoal and cow-dung, about 7 seers of the former and 5 of the latter, to the level of the top of the *gaderi*. On the top of the *gaderi*, equidistant from the sides of the furnace and from each other, kept pressed against the bottom of the front wall of the furnace by two stones resting on the *gaderi*, are two twyers or *badtais*. These are directed so as to converge at the back of the furnace. They are made of sun-dried clay, about 1 foot 9 inches long, the diameter of the aperture at the large end being 2 inches and at the small end $^3/_4$ inch, the outside diameter being 4 inches and 2 inches respectively. The whole of the front of the furnace from the front of the hearth to the bottom of the front wall is then closed up with clay, leaving the apertures of the two twyers of course uncovered. On the side of the trench opposite the furnace a step is cut, and resting on this and on a pole placed in two forked sticks leaning against the side of the furnace, and two or three flat boards, the end of

30. Interior of smithy at Umaria, Mandla District.

31. Open-air furnace at Dumarkachhar, Bilaspur District.

the boards coming just below the apertures of the twyers so that the blower who sits here can comfortably ply the bellows. The bellows are made of goats' skins, about 1 foot in diameter and from 2 feet to $2^1/_2$ feet high when stretched. They cost about Rs 12 and last a whole season. The whole furnace is then filled with charcoal from the charge-hole, about six large baskets being necessary, or about 42 seers. The furnace is then fired by blowing live charcoal through the twyers and the whole is speedily in blast. When the furnace is thoroughly heated and the charcoal is sufficiently sunk for the purpose, a basket of ore (this is circular, 9 inches in diameter and 6 inches high, holding about 9 seers of ore), and a basket of charcoal (this basket is also circular, 1 foot 6 inches in diameter and 11 inches high, holding about 7 seers of charcoal) are added through the charge-hole. This is then done at regular intervals of 40 minutes, during the 12 to 14 hours that the furnace is in blast, in all 20 baskets of ore and 20 baskets of charcoal being used. Thus altogether, 189 seers of charcoal (4 maunds 29 seers) and 180 seers of ore ($4^1/_2$ maunds) are used. Periodically at intervals of 30 or 40 minutes, a hole in the *gaderi* is opened with an iron poker and the slag allowed to run out, while the iron remains behind as a pasty mass. As the work continues the twyers are gradually burnt away until, at last, only about 3 inches to 4 inches are left.

After continuous working for 12 to 14 hours a porous bloom of iron is obtained weighing 30 to 35 seers, about 1 foot 9 inches by 1 foot 4 inches by 5 inches in size. The *gaderi* is then dug out with a pick, the iron pulled out while hot into the trench and left there during the night to cool until the next morning. If this rough bloom of iron is then sold, as it is, it fetches from Rs 1-2-0 to Rs 2, but it is generally first refined.

The iron is refined as follows:—

The rough bloom having been broken into two pieces, these are taken away to an ordinary blacksmith's forge and heated to a red heat in a small furnace about 1 foot 6 inches high and 10 inches to 12 inches square. It is then beaten by heavy hammers on an anvil and formed into round cakes, in which form it is usually sold at Rs 2-8-0 to Rs 3 per maund.

From 45 to 55 seers of charcoal are used daily in the refining furnace and it is worthy of remark that, whereas any wood is used indiscriminately for the charcoal employed in the smelting furnace, charcoal made from dead bamboos is exclusively used for the refining furnace. The bellows also in this case are smaller, being about $1^1/_2$ feet high when stretched and costing about Rs 5.

Hole gives no description of the bellows, and from the above account it sounds as if they were worked by hand, though this seems to me improbable.

III

The iron-smelters of Chanda are not Agaria, but the work is done by Gond, Teli, Mannewar and others. The furnace used is taller than in Mandla. The expenditure, output and profits also differ very considerably. There is a full account in *The Agricultural Ledger*,[1] which it is worth quoting in detail.

The iron ore, crystalline hematite, was quarried from the following localities, during the year 1897:—(1) Lohara hill, about 6 miles east of Talodi, on the main road from Mul to Brahmapuri, (2) near Gaujewahi, about 2 miles south-east of the village from hill called 'Aswal Dongri', (3) a small hill in the Dewalgaon village lands, about 6 miles of Armori, (4) a hill called Sattighat, about 8 miles east of Wairagarh, (5) hills near Pariswada (Sironcha tahsil).

The ore was for the most part dug out in big lumps and then broken into convenient sized pieces and stacked in heaps. It was then carted by the *Kotkars* or smelters to their furnaces or *kothees*, the cost of carting the ore varying according to the distance of the village from the quarry.

It will not be amiss to here explain the kind of furnace and the method of smelting. No doubt the system employed does not give anything like the outturn that should be obtained from the iron put into the furnaces. There is also a greater waste of fuel than need be. Worked under different principles, the iron industry of the district should be made to pay a good profit instead of being the hand-to-mouth business it now is.

The furnaces, locally called *kothees*, are built up chiefly of clay and small stones 6 feet in height of an irregular conical shape with a projection in front. The flue does not run straight down the centre, but slopes down from the top to the opening for the nozzle of the bellows at the bottom.

[1] *The Agricultural Ledger*, op. cit., p. 16.

The flue of the furnace is from 12 inches to 13 inches across at the top to 6 inches at the bottom. The entire furnace on the outside, with the exception of the firehole, is closed. On the furnace being charged with alternate layers of ore and charcoal and the fire put in, the fire hole is closed with bricks and plastered over with wet earth, leaving only a small passage for the nozzle of the bellows to fit into. As the charcoal and iron ore burn, more layers of ore and charcoal are put in. After four hours a small hole is made at the bottom of the furnace for taking out the slag; the hole is then closed. After another four hours the furnace is opened, and the iron which has by this time formed a lump at the bottom is taken out, and in some cases subjected to a second process of smelting in a smaller furnace, whose height is only about 1½ feet. This furnace, besides having the nozzle hole for the bellows, has a hole in front kept open for any slag remaining to run out. This second smelting was not, however, used by all *Kotkars*, and consequently the prices obtained for one smelting were much lower than if a second smelting had been done.

During the year 1897 there were twenty-three furnaces working. These furnaces were worked from January to the end of May, five months in all. No working was carried out during the rains.

The average amount of ore used in the furnaces monthly was about 182 tons to give a yield of 40 tons of rough iron. This would give the total quantity of iròn ore quarried at about 910 tons in the district and the yield to smelters after one smelting of 200 tons of iron.

For the working of each furnace monthly the *Kotkars* paid a royalty of from Rs3 to Rs5. This royalty enabled the *Kotkars* to remove the ore free, and to cut wood and manufacture charcoal from the Government forests. To smelt one ton of ore about 1-2/5 tons of charcoal were required, which gives the total amount of charcoal consumed at about 734 tons during the year.

For the working of each furnace when home labour was not available, an establishment was maintained of three coolies to blow the bellows and charge the furnace at Rs 4 each monthly, two coolies to burn and supply the charcoal at Rs 5-8 each, and, to break the ore into small pieces fit for the furnace, three women at Rs 1-14 each. This gives a total of Rs 28-10 for establishment per furnace. Besides the above, a charge of Rs 14 per furnace was incurred for digging and collecting the ore into heaps and then carting to the furnace.

Lastly, each furnace requires monthly a new pair of bellows at a cost of about Rs 4.

Thus the total expenditure including royalty for the upkeep of each furnace monthly was during the year from Rs 49-10 to Rs 51-10.

The selling price of the impure iron of one smelting per furnace was 15 seers for the rupee, or Rs 56 for the 840 seers turned out.

The monthly profit was then calculated to be Rs 4-6 on each furnace. This, of course, was the case where no home labour had been employed, but such cases are very exceptional, so that a profit of Rs 15 to Rs 20 may safely be put down for each furnace, and as each furnace has nearly always two men as partners, a safe average of Rs 7-8 per *Kotkar's* house may be taken.

Notwithstanding this fair profit per house the *Kotkars* are exceedingly poor, for like their village brethren, whether in trade or agriculture, they are deeply in the hands of the Sowkar, who at the prevailing high rate of interest, swallows all the profits and barely keeps the *Kotkar's* household going in food.

The entire quantity of iron turned out is bought and consumed locally, little or nothing going out of the district. The iron is used in the manufacture of wheel tyres, plough pins, axes, etc.

IV

The primitive furnace of Bastar, used by the Maria and Muria smelters, is of the same general pattern as in Mandla; but it often has no *hagān* or slag-vent and the slide leading to the feed-hole is often part of a solid block of earth which includes the cone of the furnace. It has been fully described by Grigson in his *Maria Gonds of Bastar*.[1]

V

It may be of interest to add a few notes on the technique of iron-smelting in other parts of India.

In the Waziri Hills, the smelters add limestone as flux. This seems to be the only place in India where this is done.

[1] Grigson. op. cit., pp. 175ff.

The ore, which is brown hematite, is first roasted and then worked either with nummulitic limestone or pieces of the coral reefs, and smelted with charcoal in small furnaces. It is smelted only to a paste. The iron produced is soft and fine-grained, but apt to exfoliate as a result of being half worn-out by its extensive hammering.[1]

After Cracroft

FIG. 35. Smelting in the Khasya Hills

In the very first number of the *Journal of the Asiatic Society of Bengal*,[2] which has now been running for over a hundred years, there is an account of the method of smelting in the

[1] A. M. Verchere, *J.A.S.B.*, Vol. XXXVI, Pt. II, p. 21.

[2] W. Cracroft, 'The Smelting of Iron in the Khasya Hills', *J.A.S.B.*, Vol. I, pp. 150ff.

Khasya Hills. Large grass huts were erected at least 25 feet in height, with the thatch reaching down to the ground on all sides. Two large double bellows were used, their nozzles pointing downwards, on the upper part of which a man would stand with one foot on each, his back supported by two planks. He held a stick in his left hand which was suspended from the roof, and had two sticks attached to it below, connected with the two bellows. These were worked quickly by a wriggling motion of the loins and the strength of the leg.

From the bellows a tube led to the hearth over which was a chimney of pipe-clay braced with iron hoops, two feet in diameter at the bottom and about six feet high. A trough at the top of the chimney was supported by a forked stick which contained damp charcoal; the operator tumbled this down the funnel with a long spoon. When the softened iron had formed on the hearth, it was taken out with tongs and beaten with a heavy wooden mallet on a large stone.

In Kathiawar the furnace was rectangular in section and horizontal instead of vertical.[1]

In Birbhum in 1852 the furnaces are said to have been of unusual capacity and produced pig iron.[2]

In Puppadoung, in Upper Burma, the furnace worked by natural draught only. No bellows were used.[3]

Oldham has described the primitive furnaces of Manipur in the Naga Hills. The furnace is externally a truncated cone, eighteen inches high, the diameter of the base being a few inches more than that of the top. It is perched on the edge of a terrace of earth 4 to 6 feet high. The twyers are inserted at the *back* of the furnace at the level of the terrace on which it stands and point downwards, while opposite to them is a roughly semicircular aperture 9 inches broad and of the same height. Above this hearth the walls are thickened and the central aperture is reduced to 6 inches in diameter. When at work the blast impinges on the hearth and passes out with all the products of combustion through the aperture in front. Fuel and ore are fed through the chimney.

The Manipur furnace would thus seem to show 'one of the first steps in the transition between the original method of reducing the ore in an open fire and its reduction in a scientifically-constructed blast furnace. Doubtless the Indian furnace is the descendant of such a structure; some inventive

[1] Jacob, in *Select Records of the Government of Bombay*, Vol. XXXVII p. 467.
[2] R. D. Oldham, in *Select Records of the Government of Bengal*, Vol. VIII.
[3] W. T. Blandford, *J.A.S.B.*, Vol. XXXI, p. 219.

genius experimentally inclined tried the experiment of closing the aperture opposite the tuyères and forcing the products of combustion to escape upwards through the chimney, and finding his experiment a success, inaugurated a new era in the reduction of iron.'[1]

H. Warth made a report on the iron-smelting of the Chota Baghal District in Kangra seventy years ago—[2]

> I saw the iron-making and the ore deposits of this district in May, 1873. I started from Bir, east of Baijnath, on the

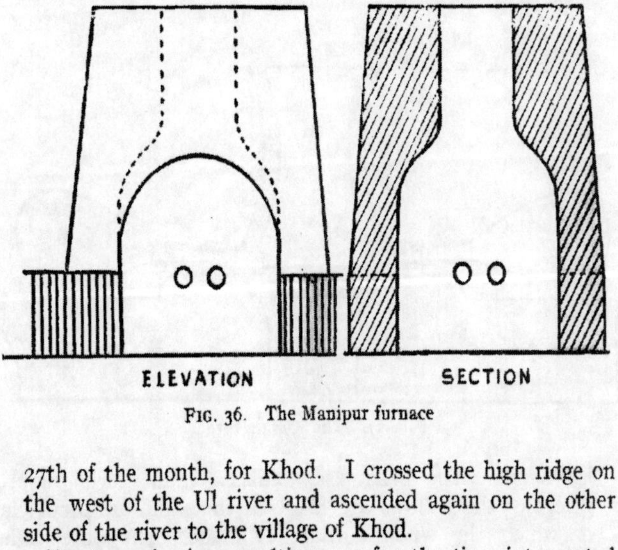

FIG. 36. The Manipur furnace

> 27th of the month, for Khod. I crossed the high ridge on the west of the Ul river and ascended again on the other side of the river to the village of Khod.
>
> The lease for iron-smelting was for the time interrupted and the manufacture of iron at a standstill. A furnace was, however, set going at Khod to show me the method. The material used for smelting was black sand of magnetic oxide of iron, obtained from the ore, as will be hereafter described. The fuel was charcoal from the pine, called here 'toss' (*Abies webbiana*). No flux was used, only the ashes of the charcoal acting as such.
>
> The furnace is an upright cylinder with an oval section measuring 9 inches and 12 inches inside. The walls are made of clay and are 3 inches thick. The natives call the

[1] R. D. Oldham, 'Report on the Geology of parts of Manipur and the Naga Hills', *M.G.S.I.*, Vol. XIX, pp. 24ff.
[2] H. Warth, 'Report on the Iron District of Chota Baghal', *Panjab Gazette*, March, 1873.

furnaces 'gunti'. The tuyères they call 'nal'. The tuyères are 9 inches long, their mouths 1 inch wide. They are fixed with clay in the sides of the furnace opposite each other and near the bottom. The bottom of the furnace, called 'tola', consists of a plate of clay 1 inch thick perforated with holes for the slag to run through. Below the plate is a slag pit (C) 18 inches deep and open in front. The bellows (B) are 4 in number, a pair for each tuyère. They are of leather and have no valves. The man who works a pair of bellows provides for the admission and the confinement of the air by opening and closing slits with

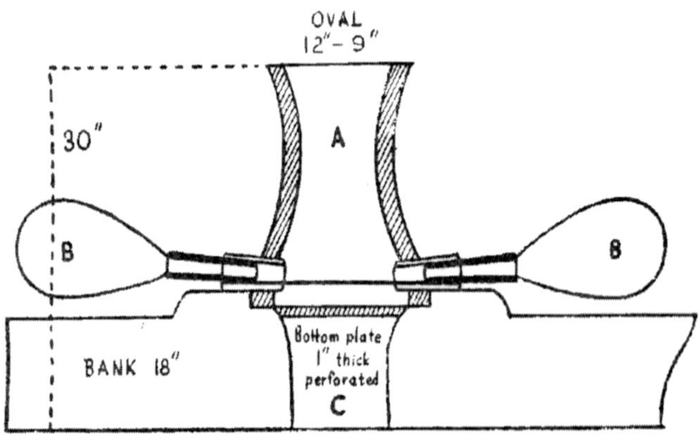

FIG. 37. The Kangra furnace

his hands. The bellows are called 'khull'. The mouthpieces of the bellows are made of the same fire-proof clay of which the whole furnace is made. They are called 'sangothu'. During the operation the four bellows are worked by two men, and a third man is in attendance behind the furnace. His business is to charge charcoal and magnetic sand. A fourth man remains in front of the furnace and looks after the tuyères and lets the slag run through the bottom plate. The men who do this work are called 'Dhaugris' from 'dhau', iron-ore.

To begin with, the bottom of the furnace was first covered with a layer of small charcoal, and then the furnace was filled with full-sized pieces of charcoal. The weight of charcoal required for filling the furnace was 7 seers. Fire was then introduced at the tuyères and the blowing commenced. When the column of charcoal began to settle down fresh charcoal was given up, and with it some magnetic

32. (a) Characteristic Muria furnace near Kondagaon, Bastar State.
(b) Oriya forge in the Sambalpur District.

33. Mirzapur
Agaria at work
in the forge

sand. This was continued until sufficient ore had passed into the furnace. Then no more fuel was given up, and the column permitted to settle down. When only a small quantity of charcoal remained, the blowing ceased. The whole time occupied by the process up to this was six hours. The bottom plate was now broken through, and a small lump of wrought-iron fell out. It was beaten with a wooden hammer upon a boulder of granite which served as anvil. By the beating, projecting portions were united with the main lump.

A small quantity of slag was passed out of the lump by the hammering, but the remaining mass consisted mostly of pure wrought-iron. Forty seers of highly purified, moist, magnetic sand had been used. The sand was moist when the weighment took place. The quantity of charcoal consumed was 56 seers. I also weighed the slag which had resulted during the process. It turned out to be 28 seers. The raw iron lump weighed 12 seers.

At this rate 100 seers of rough iron lumps require 333 seers of washed iron sand and 466 seers of charcoal. Thus far the work is not so very unfavourable, considering that wrought-iron is produced directly. This wrought-iron consists, however, merely of rough lumps, and is therefore, in spite of its good quality, as a rule, less valuable than the imported wrought-iron, which is already in the shape of rods.

CHAPTER VIII

GETTING AND SPENDING

I. *The Income of the Agaria*

For all their labour, the Agaria remain obstinately poor. 'The earnings of the forge are as small as the hut.' 'All day his hammer sounds, but he only earns a handful.' 'The sweat of his privates goes even to his head, yet he cannot get enough.' 'The profit from charcoal scatters like its ashes.' With such proverbs the Agaria half-humorously console themselves. But their poverty is very real. Of them, at least, is true what one witness stated before the Bourne Committee, that the average villager 'got less to eat than the prisoner in jail'.[1] Their little huts are bare of possessions, they keep the scantiest reserves of grain, their women have few silver ornaments, and I have never seen men wearing the gold earrings which is one of the ways in which the Gond bank their savings. They found it difficult to understand questions about partition and inheritance, for there was practically nothing to divide.[2] 'How black are the buttocks of an Agaria, yet he cannot buy enough cloth to hide them.'

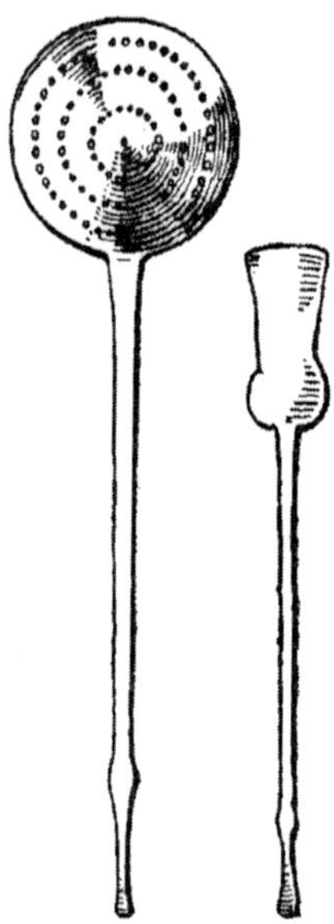

FIG. 38. Iron spoons
Length, 1' 4"

In a bazaar it is often hard to find the Agaria's shops. In Pali I found them hidden away disconsolately under

[1] *Report of the Central Provinces Provincial Banking Enquiry Committee* (Nagpur, 1930), Vol. I, p. 54.

[2] After a father's death, the sons divide the 'practice' equally: if the smithy had been serving fifty ploughs, they take twenty-five each. The eldest son takes the *ghāna*, the younger takes *sansi*, *hataudi*, etc.

carts; in Raipur they actually covered their exiguous wares under bits of cloth, apparently for fear that some jack-in-office would demand them free of charge. The Mahali Asur sing this Karma song:

He makes a spade, he makes a pick.
His girl takes them to the bazaar to sell.
But it is long before anyone comes to buy.

He makes a sickle, he makes an axe.
His girl takes them to the bazaar to sell,
But it is long before anyone comes to buy.

He makes an iron spoon, he makes a sieve.
His girl takes them to the bazaar to sell,
But it is long before anyone comes to buy.

It is notoriously difficult to assess the income of the Indian villager: estimates have varied from the obviously biased Congress figure of Rs 23 to the equally biased official figure of about Rs 200 a year. *The Mandla District Gazetteer* estimated in 1912 that 'by working hard an Agaria can manage two smeltings a day in each furnace, about one seer of refined iron being the outturn of each smelting . . . Smelting ceases during the rains, and the smelters have to supplement their earnings by other means, generally agriculture or ordinary daily labour . . . The net earnings are not more than Rs 30 from each furnace per annum.' Elsewhere the Gazetteer states that 'each furnace consumes 25 seers of charcoal daily, and turns out one-and-a-half seers of cast iron (*sic*). This is further purified and made into wrought iron, the final outturn being about one seer.' [1]

On the other hand, the Divisional Forest Officer, Mandla, when making inquiries about the proposed reduction of *nistar* rates in 1940, estimated that the average earnings of an Agaria were between Rs 100 and Rs 120 a year. 'Enquiries made in the Motinala Range from Agaria show that they are paid in kind at rates varying from 5 to 10 *kuro* of grain (each *kuro* being 5 seers) per plough by the villagers whose agricultural implements they repair. The rates paid depend on the number of

[1] *Mandla District Gazetteer*, p. 179.

ploughs in each village, higher rates being paid where the number of ploughs is small. At this rate I estimate that each Agaria earns between Rs 80 and Rs 90 worth of grain. From the statements of Agaria questioned, each manages to sell

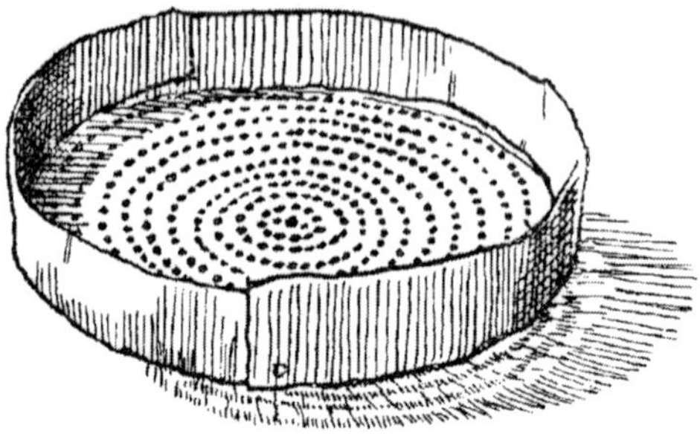

FIG. 39. Iron sieve
1/4 actual size

implements to the value of on an average Rs 2 to Rs 3 per mensem. Thus the average earnings of an Agaria were estimated at between Rs 100 and Rs 120 per annum.'[1]

My own figure, as I will show presently, is between Rs 60 and Rs 80, but even the higher figure of Rs 100–120 is very low, when it is understood that it represents the earnings of *a whole family*. It generally takes two men and their wives and at least one other relative to work the furnace. The Bourne Committee found that the earnings of an average cultivating family of five, after deducting marketing expenses and costs of cultivation, were Rs 217. In Mandla District, the all-round average expenditure of the family, 'having regard to the high value of money and the low prices prevalent, could not exceed Rs 175 per family'. The balance sheet of a family thus worked out something like this:—

	Rs
Net outturn	217
Maintenance	175
Rent	12
Balance	30

'To this we can safely add Rs 50 income from subsidiary sources.'[1]

[1] Private communication from the Divisional Forest Officer.

Even on the highest estimate of the Agaria's income, this is double theirs.

How is the income of the Agaria derived? It depends, of course, on many factors—whether there is a good bazaar in the neighbourhood, on the size of the village, whether there is much competition of alien iron, whether there are two crops or one. Thus the Agaria in parts of Motinala are very much worse off than those in Karanjia who live on the main trade route down to the lowlands—the latter are able to take their wares to the big bazaars of Chhattisgarh. The Chokh in Bilaspur District who live along the main road from Ratanpur to Katghora get a great deal of business from cartmen who need the bosses of their wheels repaired, and where there is regular embanking of rice-fields there is an extra demand for spades and picks. Where there is only one crop there is obviously less work to be done in the way of repairing agricultural implements. There is less work too where the soil is friable and easy to work: the ploughshares, for example, do not blunt so quickly. Where there is an abundant supply of ore and charcoal near at hand the smith can obviously earn more than when he has to waste half his day tramping to a distant hill.

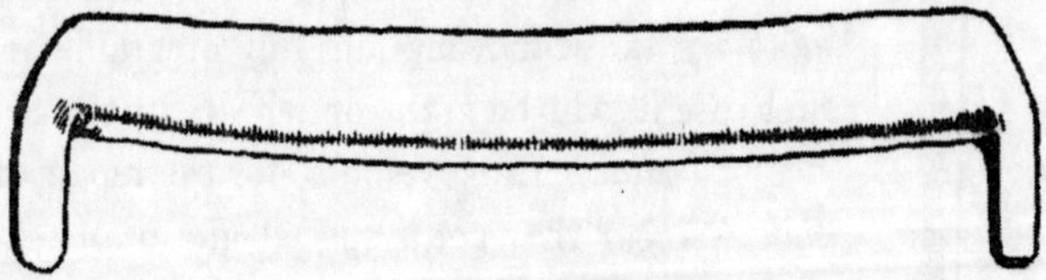

FIG. 40. Harrow
Length, 1' 5"

The first source of income is called *jewar*. For the villagers of his own circle (which may include one or more hamlets) the Agaria performs two duties; he repairs all the iron implements, sickles, ploughshares, axes, etc., and he supplies new

[1] *Banking Enquiry Report*, op. cit., Vol. II, p. 650.

ones when they are needed. For the first duty he receives an annual tribute of grain called *jewar*. The amount of this varies from place to place. In the Karanjia Range, for pointing the ploughshare and sharpening the sickles and axes he is given five *kuro* of grain a year for every plough. If he also repairs the *bakkhar* and all other implements, he gets ten *kuro*.

In the Motiṅala Range, the *jewar* depends on the character of the soil; where there is easy black cotton soil and the implements require attention only three times a year, he gets five *kuro* a plough (and five *kuro* more if he attends to the *bakkhar*, etc.). Where there is rocky, sandy soil and the ploughshares have to be attended to almost every week, the rate is ten *kuro* a plough.

In the Bilaspur Zamindaris, the usual rate is five *kuro* a plough, while for sharpening the iron of the plough or an axe, one pice or two cupped handfuls of grain is charged.

FIG. 41. Iron peg for tethering horses *Length, 1'*

The Agaria also get what is known as *bij-phutti* (that is, two-and-a-half seers of seed) in the month of Asar to use, not for sowing, but as food. At the same time, the Ahir give them one day's supply of milk. Also at the harvesting of both the spring and the autumn crops, they get what is called the *kanhiāri*, a winnowing-fan full of grain—in the first case it will be gram or wheat, in the second rice or *kodon*. In November, for the repair of the *olaha nāngar* they get a special gift of one-and-a-half to two-and-a-half seers of grain.

For the making of new implements, the Agaria make a regular charge, whether they sell their goods in the smithy to their neighbours or take them to the bazaar. The neighbours usually get them slightly cheaper. I will now give a list of the Agaria's tariff as it was in 1939 before the war; I give the money prices, but it must be remembered that very often the price is paid in kind.

Olaha nāngar (ploughshare)	..	As 5
Battar nāngar lohā ..	..	As 3
Bakkhar (barrow) ..	..	Re 1
Small *bakkhar* ..	..	As 12
Sickle	..	As 2
Sickle for cutting *mowa* grass	..	As 3-6
Tangli-axe	..	As 2
Tabli-axe	..	As 4
Kulhārda (axe) ..	..	As 8
Basuli (adze) ..	..	As 4
Basula (adze) ..	..	As 8
Kudari (mattock) ..	..	As 6 to 8
Bissār (arrow-head) ..	..	As 2
Sāng (spear) ..	..	Re 1
Barchi (spear) ..	..	As 12
Bindhni (chisel) ..	..	As 1
Kol-bindhni	..	As 1-6
Pharsa (axe) ..	..	As 8
Sābar (digging tool) ..	..	Re 1-4
Medha (iron ring for pole in threshing-floor)	..	As 4 to 8
Sāndi	..	As 2 to 4
Trisul (trident) ..	..	Rs 3 to As 8 according to size
Barāhi (scourge) ..	..	Re 1
Pīdha (seat)	..	Re 1
Kharaut (clogs)	..	As 8
Gurud (scourge)	..	Re 1
Sakal (chain)	..	As 3

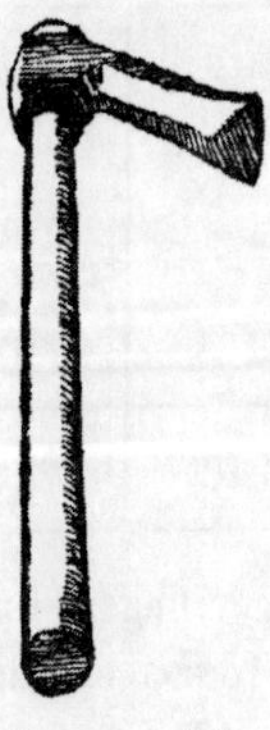

FIG. 42. Adze
¼ actual size

There are a number of other things also made—for example I paid Rs 5 for the elaborate *hiranoti* made for me by Badua of Bahapur—but the above list will serve to show the variety of implements and the sort of price they fetch.

But iron is still used as a medium of exchange. In the Bilaspur Zamindaris, the Agaria pay their taxes in iron bars. Axeheads are still sometimes used as currency and were once common. The

Agaria more often than not sell their goods for grain and purchase them with iron implements.

We are now in a position to estimate the income of a few typical Agaria families in Dindori Tahsil.

Silpuri

Silpuri is the central village of the Baiga Chak in Mandla District. There is an Agaria smithy with one furnace and a forge, manned by two brothers Kubra and Ganga and Kubra's two sons Suna and Bodra. Kubra has three wives, Ganga two and Suna and Bodra one each; Kubra has one daughter and Ganga one small son and two daughters. Thus four men, seven women and four children work in the smithy and are maintained by it. The general earnings of the smithy are shared by the whole family, but each member also has his *pogri*—what he is able to earn by making implements or by special work for the Forest Department.

The Silpuri smithy serves three villages and receives the following payment in kind:—

Village	*No. of ploughs*	*Jewar*		*Kanhiāri*	*Bij-phutti*
		khandi	*kuro*	*kuro*	*kuro*
Chara ..	6	2	..	5	4
Silpuri (Gond and Dhoba)	19	5	..	12	10
Silpuri (Baiga)	12 axes	1	10	..	..
Tanta ..	20	5	..	12	9
TOTAL ..	..	13 *kh.*	10 *ku.*	1 *kh.* 9 *ku.*	1 *kh.* 3 *ku.*

Thus, the total amount of grain paid by the villagers for the repair of their ploughs, sickles and axes comes to sixteen khandi, two kuro which, at the rates in force in 1939 just before the war, is worth Rs 46, reckoning seven kuro of *dhan* to the rupee.

But Kubra's family also has fields, and from these he expects to get annually:—

From rice	6 khandi	2 kuro,	worth	Rs 17-8-0
,, *kutki*	6 ,,	4 ,,	,,	12-6-0
,, *kodon*	2 ,,	9 ,,	,,	6-2-0
,, *ramtilli*	1 ,,	10 ,,	,,	5-0-0

The total earnings of the fields are thus Rs 41.

In addition to this the family estimated that they earned about Rs 20 a year from making and selling iron implements. This is probably an understatement for such a large family, and we shall not be far wrong if we put down Rs 30 under this heading.

As Silpuri is a forest village, there is regular employment on road-making and boundary-cutting at certain times of the year. Kubra estimates that they receive between them some Rs 10 annually for this.

The total income of the family, therefore, is :—

From *jewar*, etc.	Rs 46
,, agriculture	41
,, sale of implements	30
,, labour wages	10
ANNUAL TOTAL ..	Rs 127

This is the income of eleven adults and works out at about Rs 11-8-0 a head. The family paid Rs 10 in taxation for the furnace[1] and Rs 2 for the fields, or 10 per cent of the total income.

Bhoira

Bhoira is another forest village not far from Silpuri. There is a whole colony of Agaria here, and only one family receives *jewar* from the neighbours. The others have to depend on the sale of implements and agriculture for their support. Let us briefly consider Naulu's sources of income. In his family there are two men, four women and two children. He gets no *jewar*. From the sale of implements he makes Rs 4 a month for eight months of the year, but the furnace is closed during the rains. From his fields he gets :—

[1] This figure is now reduced, see pp. 233 and 247.

From rice	6 khandi	worth	Rs 17-0-0
,, *kodon*	5 ,,	,,	12-8-0
,, *ramtilli*	10 kuro	,,	2-8-0

making a total of Rs 32.

For about two months of every year, the men get employment from the Forest Department. The Department allots certain sums of money for the work to be done, and this is divided among the villagers. *The actual amounts received*[1] by Naulu's household—which contributed one man a day for the period of the work—were:—

22 days' work on the roads ..	Rs 3-0-0
7 days' work on a new road ..	1-5-0
17 days' work cutting parasites on trees	2-0-0
16 days' cutting fire-lines ..	2-0-0
7 days' marking boundaries ..	1-5-0
TOTAL, 69 days' work ..	Rs 9-10-0

I went very carefully into this and questioned a number of Bhoira people independently; they all agreed on the number of work-days and the remuneration received. It works out at about 2¼ annas a day.

The total income of Naulu's household is thus:—

From sale of iron implements	Rs 32-0-0
,, agriculture	32-0-0
,, labour	9-10-0
TOTAL ..	Rs 73-10-0

This is the income of six adults and works out at Rs 12-4-0 a head. The family was paying Rs 10 in taxation for the furnace and Rs 2 for the fields, or nearly 17 per cent of the total income.

Titru Agaria of the same village, with three men and three women in his household, and eight children, received in addition Rs 20 as *jewar*—for his household had the right of doing the iron repairs of the village. On the other hand, he only got grain worth Rs 17 from his fields.

[1] Which are not necessarily the same as those sanctioned by the Forest Department!

4. (*a*) Agaria of the Mawai area sharpening a chisel.

Photographs by courtesy of the curator, Lucknow Museum.

(*b*) Mahali Asur with a fish trap.

35. Khuntia Chokh with oil press.

Chuchuhi

Chuchuhi is a *malguzāri* village. The household of Phagnu Agaria contains seven adults and three children. They have a forge but no furnace. They receive the following payment in kind:—

Harvest	*No. of ploughs*	*Jewar*	*Kanhiāri*	*Bij-phutti*
Spring ..	23	2 *kh.* 18 *ku.*	16 *ku.*	8 *ku.*
Autumn..	..	5 *kh.* 15 *ku.*	..	..

The total value of this is about Rs 28-8-0.

From their fields, the family earns Rs 23 worth of rice, *kodon* and *kutki*, Rs 5 worth of *ramtilli* and Rs 5 worth of rye, in all Rs 33. Their income is thus:—

From iron work..	.. ..	Rs 28-8-0
,, agriculture	.. ..	33-0-0
,, casual labour, say	.. ..	5-0-0
	TOTAL ..	Rs 66-8-0

The family paid Rs 6 for its forge and Rs 12 for its fields. The income works out at Rs 9-8-0 a head, and the taxation came to about 27 per cent of the total income. Since the reduction of the tax the family has started a furnace, and is better off.

Summaries

I will add some summary statements of income and taxation for other villages.

Daulu Agaria of Angai Ryotwari

Household of 4 men, 2 women and 2 children.

Income from iron repairs	.. ..	Rs 17
,, ,, sale of implements	..	25
,, ,, agriculture	.. ..	38
,, ,, casual sales and labour	..	5

Total Rs 85, or Rs 14 per head.

Boka Agaria of Umaria Ryotwari

Household of 8 adults and 5 children.

Income from iron repairs ..	..	Rs 57
,, ,, sale of implements	..	30
,, ,, agriculture ..	..	37
,, ,, casual labour	..	5

Total Rs 129, or Rs 16 per head.

Kutru Agaria of Kuteli, a forest village

Household of 1 man, 2 women and 2 boys.

Income from selling implements	..	Rs 20-0-0
,, ,, repairs ..	..	5-0-0
,, ,, agriculture ..	..	17-8-0
,, ,, labour ..	..	7-8-0

Total Rs 50, or Rs 17 per head.

Taxation: for furnace ..	..	Rs 10
,, fields ..	..	Re 1

Total taxation: Rs 11, or 22% of income.

Gautam Agaria of Daldal, a forest village

Household of 3 men, 2 women and 8 children.

Income from sale of implements	..	Rs 24-0-0
,, ,, repairs ..	..	8-0-0
,, ,, agriculture ..	..	5-0-0
,, ,, labour ..	..	7-8-0

Total Rs 44-8-0 or about Rs 9 per head.

Taxation: for furnace ..	..	Rs 10
,, fields ..	..	3

Total taxation: Rs 13 or 28% of income.

From these estimates it will be seen that the Divisional Forest Officer's figure of Rs 120 quoted on page 224 is for a whole family. The annual income per head, excluding children, works out at from Rs 9 to Rs 16, according to the size of the village served and the amount of subsidiary agricultural profit obtained.

The taxation, according to the old rates, was from 7½ per cent to 28 per cent of the total income of the family; but the higher percentages were more common. Now with the reduced rates,[1] taxation consumes a more reasonable proportion of the pitifully insufficient income. In the forest and *ryotwari* villages of Mandla, it has come down approximately.

In Silpuri from 10% to 5½%
In Bhoira from 17% to 10%
In Kuteli from 22% to 12%
In Daldal from 28% to 15½%

II. *The Economics of Yesterday*

It may be of interest to record the earnings obtained from iron work in former years. In P. N. Bose's survey of the Agaria furnaces of Raipur (now mainly Drug) District, written in 1887, he considers that the industry might be a fairly profitable one.

> The ore selected is almost invariably the softest, though not always the best, available. The metal turned out by the furnace is refined in an open hearth, and is made into bars called *chul*, which are sold to blacksmiths at an average rate of five annas per *chul*. The outturn per day from each furnace, supposing eight persons to be employed for preparing and bringing fuel and ore, and for working at the bellows, would be four *chul*, selling at one rupee four annas. Fixing the wages of workpeople at two annas per head, this leaves a margin of four annas for the proprietor. The duty on the furnace has to be paid from this sum, and it may be as low as one rupee, and as high as seven rupees per annum. This, however, is inclusive of all dues on account of trees cut down for charcoal. As the only expensive portion of the apparatus employed is the bellows, which costs from three to four rupees, and as the proprietor's supply of labourers is usually drawn from his own family, he being one of them, iron-smelting is considered a fairly profitable industry where fuel is abundant, and the duty on the furnace not too high.[2]

[1] See p. 247.

[2] *R.G.S.I.*, Vol. XX, Part IV, p. 170.

Ten years later, *The Agricultural Ledger* which we have frequently quoted—for it is, I think, the only authority we have for the state of the iron industry in the C.P. at the end of the last century—gave a lengthy survey of the profits of the furnaces; the figures were collected by the Assistant Conservator of Forests, R. S. Hole, from reports furnished by Deputy Commissioners and Forest Officers.[1] They may or may not be correct, but they are all we have. The report begins with Saugor District, where there were six iron-mines at work in Banda Tahsil.

> These mines are not leased out but are open to all paying annas 8 for each furnace. The total number of persons employed was 1,844, the total earnings Rs 604 and the total wages paid Rs 211. The details of furnaces are given below :—

Name of village	No. of furnaces	Annual duty Rs.	a.	p.
Tigoda	12	6	0	0
Hirapur	15	7	8	0
Baretha	8	4	0	0
	35	17	8	0

Of Mandla it is said that 'the earnings in 1897 are stated by the people themselves to have been from Rs 25 to Rs 30 per furnace'. In Narsinghpur, 'in the two mines which are regularly worked, each person employed for digging ore gets six pies for a basketful of ore dug. In this way each labourer earns three to five annas.' In Balaghat, 'it is said that a family (one man, his wife and two or three children) when employed in smelting iron can earn about Rs 3 to Rs 5 per month'.

Labour conditions in Jubbulpore were examined in greater detail, and though the Agaria furnace has now practically vanished from the District I will quote the report in full for the light it throws on former times.

[1] *The Agricultural Ledger*, op. cit., pp. 1–7, and 16–19.

The number of furnaces at work generally in this district on smelting iron ore is twenty-eight for the current year. In previous years the number was fluctuating.

As a matter of fact the industry is one which is considerably influenced by the European iron which is fashioned to meet all requirements of the market, whereas the native iron produced in the district is sold in lumps as locally prepared, and is very costly to work into shape. The number of persons employed daily from 1st November to 31st May per furnace from the time the furnace is made, to that when the crude iron is turned out, is as follows:—

For cutting wood and converting it into charcoal	7 men
For extracting the iron ore	2 "
To attend to the furnace	2 "
For refining the iron, bellows and hammermen	4 "
Refiner	1 man
For making separate charcoal of dry bamboos for refining purposes ..	5 men
TOTAL ..	21 "

Furnaces are annually worked for about seven months, i.e. from November to May. During the rains no work is done.

(a) *The cost of making and maintaining a furnace is estimated at Rs 261.*

Each furnace when in work consumes daily $3^1/_2$ maunds of iron ore and 4 maunds of charcoal. The outturn at the end of the day's work of crude iron varies from 33 to 50 seers.

The estimated outturn of crude iron, called locally, 'Tickole' or 'Bloom', in the seven months' season would be about 275 maunds, which sells at about Rs 4 per gon = 3 maunds = Rs 366-10-8, leaving a profit of Rs 105-10-8. This bloom is then resmelted into pig iron locally called 'Chaudia'. For this refining purpose 10 men are engaged, these men can refine in one day the crude iron obtained from the furnaces, or about 220 maunds. The cost of the last operation is estimated as follows:—

		Rs
Labour at Rs 14 per mensem and 1 blacksmith at Rs 8 per mensem, converting 275 maunds bloom iron into pig iron for $2^1/_3$ months.		51
Cost of preparing bamboo charcoal	..	35
Forest dues on bamboo charcoal	..	9
TOTAL	..	95
Add cost of making bloom ..	..	261
TOTAL	..	356

The outturn of pig iron from 275 maunds bloom is equal to 220 maunds, which, at the average market rate, viz., Rs 2-8-0 per maund, yields Rs 550, or a profit on the whole operation of Rs 194.

The above details refer to the cost of working one furnace. Multiplying them by the number of furnaces working some idea of the extent of the industry may be formed.

Roughly estimated, it comes to about Rs 16,000, of which 64·73 per cent is spent on labour.

The area required to supply the quantity of charcoal noted above is about 30 acres per furnace, i.e., 840 acres in all.

The pig iron so produced finds its way into all the local markets for all agricultural and domestic requirements, and it is even exported for similar purposes to Mirzapur, Ghazipur, Agra, Cawnpore, Lucknow, Benares, Dinapur, Nagpur, Bhusawal, and Khandwa. The famous Olphert's oxide of iron paint was also manufactured in Murwara Tahsil, being ground in mills worked by water power. It appears they engage about 50 women and children, and the annual outturn is about 1,500 maunds, which is exported all over India, at a cost here of Rs 5-8 per maund of 82 lb.

For Bhandara District, the following calculations were made:—

There were 14 furnaces in operation in Tirora Tahsil for smelting iron from iron ore during the year 1897. They worked during the eight dry months of the year. Six persons were at work at each furnace, of whom four were men and

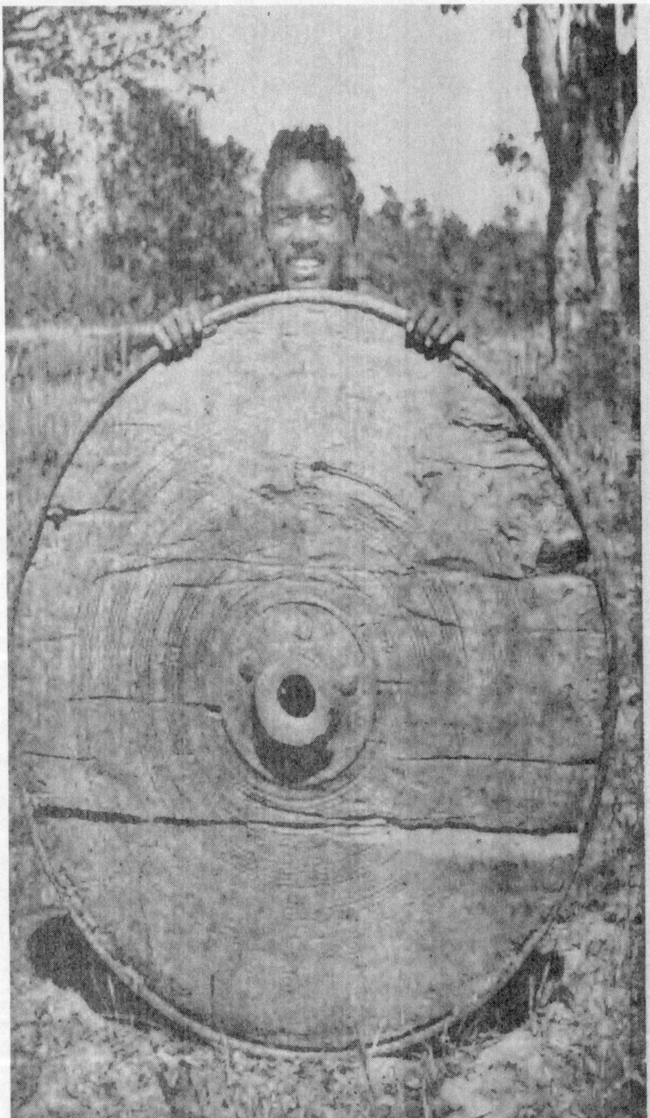

36. Khuntia Chokh of Nunera with cart wheel.

two women. Thus 56 men and 28 women were employed during the year for production of iron. The total output of iron smelted at 14 furnaces was 45,696 seers, each furnace giving about 3,264 seers in eight months. This quantity was worth Rs 2,150 at a price of one rupee for $2^1/_2$ pieces weighing $21^1/_4$ seers. Accordingly the gross earnings of each furnace were Rs 154. The cost of wages paid to labourers employed was Rs 1,792, each male labourer being paid two pieces of iron worth about Re 0-12-9, and each female getting one piece worth Re 0-6-4 per week. In addition to the above amount a sum of Rs 112 at the rate of Rs 14 a month (Re 1 for each furnace) had to be paid to the zamindar within whose local limits iron ore is produced, for coal, fuel and bamboos removed from the forest for use at the furnace. Thus the total expenditure on the business amounted to Rs 1,904 or Rs 136 for each furnace, and the net earnings of the workers were Rs 246 or about Rs 17-9-0 from each furnace.

This account of Raipur District may be compared with Bose's description ten years before.

There are in all 33 furnaces working in the district. The workers pay Rs 11 per furnace as royalty to the zamindar. The cost of quarrying and charcoal used is estimated at Rs 350 per furnace. Thus the total estimated expenditure per furnace is about Rs 361. They use as much iron ore as they can take out from the quarries throughout the year and there are no data to find out exactly what quantity is used in each furnace during a year. The approximate quantity as far as could be ascertained is in round figures $8^4/_7$ tons. Each furnace produces about $2^1/_7$ tons of smelted iron, which is wrought and sold at the rate of four seers per rupee. Thus the gross income from each furnace is nearly Rs 550 per year. The net income after deducting the cost of quarrying, charcoal and royalty is consequently Rs 189 per furnace per year.

We now come to the first decade of the present century, the years when the District Gazetteers were being prepared. In 1906, in Saugor District, it is said that 'each furnace employed six or seven persons in smelting and working up the iron and produced some twenty pounds of iron a day'. The Gazetteer estimates that the earnings of a furnace were not more than a hundred rupees for the eight months that they were worked.[1]

In Balaghat at the same date the Lohar were being paid two-and-a-half *kuro* of grain for each plough, if the cultivator provided the charcoal; otherwise they got five *kuro*. One rupee was paid for the iron parts of a *paili* cart.[2] These Lohar were probably Agaria, for they are described as performing the special rite of the Agaria—the driving of nails into the doors at Divali, Jiwathi and Pola. The Agaria are also described as smelting the ores 'into rough semi-circular shapes called *chulas*, averaging in weight about 10 lb. each. These are sold in the bazaar at 2 to 4 *chulas* for a rupee'.[3]

Mr O'Malley describes the poverty of the Agaria in Palamau in 1907. The *giri*, or ball of iron, that is extracted from one smelting, was often handed over to the Lohar to work up. 'Four annas is a common price paid for an ordinary sized *giri*, and as but two of these can be made in a very hard days' work of five hours duration and a considerable time has also to be spent on the preparation of ore and charcoal, the profits are small. The fact is, that although the actual price which the iron fetches in the market is high, the profits made by the *mahajans* and the immense disproportion between the time and labour expended and the outturn, both combine to leave the unfortunate Agaria in a miserable state of poverty.'[4]

The iron was made into axes, ploughshares, well-buckets and guns, which sold at Re 1 a span according to the length of the barrel.

[1] *Saugor District Gazetteer*, p. 172.
[2] *Balaghat District Gazetteer*, p. 196.
[3] ibid., p. 19.
[4] 'O'Malley, op. cit., p. 138.

CHAPTER IX

DECAY

I. *Of Matter: Collapse of an Industry*

The collapse of the cottage industries of India is one of the most disastrous results of that great country's contact with the industrial world. The death of material culture brings idleness, dullness, immorality and hunger. Compare the ordinary Indian village with the peasant communities of Africa and the South Seas: in the former is dirt, drabness, mediocrity, in the latter, life, colour, movement, variety, the strong excitement of creative work.

In this general decay of simple useful arts which made poor people happy, busy and prosperous, there is none more tragic than the collapse of the village iron-smelting industry. No Mahatma has arisen to revive it. The interests of big business on the one side and sheer ignorance and carelessness on the other have combined to suppress it. It has no political or religious significance. Yet at one time it brought wealth and happiness to thousands.

There are no figures, but there can be no question that 'iron-smelting was at one time a widespread industry in India, and there is hardly a district away from the great alluvial tracts of the Indus, Ganges and Brahmaputra, in which slag-heaps are not found'.[1] Among these we may mention the cinder mounds in the Bellary District, the great mound at Kudatini,[2] and the slag heaps at Wai in the Bombay Province. Let us make a brief and melancholy survey of these monuments of decline.

Let us turn first to South India, industrious and energetic for all its burning heat. In Madura there was once a 'consider-

[1] *R.G.S.I.*, Vol. XLVI, p. 99.

[2] K. N. Dikshit, *The Scope of Pre-history and Anthropological Work in India*, p. 7.

able' iron-industry: it is now extinct. In Trichinopoli, ferruginous nodules from the cretaceous rocks were used extensively: today they lie forgotten. In 1854 there were over a hundred large furnaces working full blast in Malabar; where are they now? In Salem, the outturn was already decreasing at the end of the last century. In North Arcot in 1855 there were smelting operations in 86 villages; but the industry has died in less than a century. In Nellore, it is said, 'iron used to be smelted, but the industry appears to be extinct'. In Mysore, we are told that 'the output of iron has greatly diminished during the last few decades'—and that was in 1898.[1]

FIG. 43. Spear *Spear-head 1', with handle, 6'*

A recent writer mourns the decline of the once prosperous Salahuva Vakkalu, the ancient iron-mining caste of Mysore. 'Some fifty years ago the castemen were very rich. Even now it can be seen, in places where they reside, there are hills or hillocks of iron refuse which testify to their iron-mining industry and extraction as also trade in iron by these men in former times. These hillocks stand as memorable monuments of their iron industry and immense wealth as the result of their occupation at one time. They used to supply iron all over the State by collecting the ore from hills in their neighbourhood . . . The decline of this industry reduced them to comparative poverty.'[2] We may doubt whether anyone got immense wealth by smelting in 'very crude' blast furnaces, but there is no doubt that these iron-workers have come down in the world. Thurston tells the same story of the Telugu Kammara who used to make a living wage—to put it without exaggeration—by manufacturing the huge shallow iron pans used for boiling sugar-cane. The iron was smelted by the Kammara themselves, and carried down on bullocks from

[1] Watts, op. cit., p. 505, and throughout the paragraph.

[2] A. K. Iyer, *The Mysore Tribes and Castes*, Vol. IV, p. 553.

the hill Jambunath Konda, but even thirty years ago 'English iron' had taken its place.[1]

Our mournful pilgrimage takes us next into Bombay. In Dharwar, formerly, when fuel was plentiful much iron was smelted in the Kappatgudd Hills—but the roar of the bellows is now silent. In Belgaum, the industry was extinct by the end of the last century. In Ratnagiri lateritic ore was once largely smelted, as also in Rewa Kantha, to which large heaps of slag still testify. In Kaira and Ahmedabad, there is nothing left of the prosperity of an earlier day but large heaps of slag. In Kathiawar, the industry was moribund by 1840; it is now extinct. In Cutch, it is extinct.[2]

We now go east, to Bengal and Bihar. Even as early as 1880, Ball noticed the collapse of the smelting industry in Birbhum.[3] In Hazaribagh, where furnaces were once numerous, few are in blast today. On the Neterhat Plateau, I myself noticed a remarkable decline. Only a few furnaces were working where once, the people said, there had been many, and even those were going furtively with many a backward glance.

In Assam, there was once iron-smelting in the Khasi-Jaintia Hills,[4] but it has now completely died out. The same is true of the Naga Hills, where formerly nodules of clay-ironstone were smelted; by 1841 the industry was all but extinct. Today the Angami Naga gets his iron from the plains in the form of cheap spades, where formerly it came from the furnaces of Manipur.[5] The Sema Naga re-work imported hoes.[6] The Rengma Naga, some of whom are expert smiths, likewise bring their iron up from the plains.[7]

We return finally to the Central Provinces, where the industry has always flourished and where it has even now held

[1] Thurston, op. cit., Vol. III, p. 140. For the collapse of the iron-kilns of South India, see also G. Slater, *Some South Indian Villages* (London, 1918), p. 102.

[2] Watts, op. cit., p. 506.

[3] Ball, op. cit., p. 225.

[4] Watts, op. cit., p. 507.

[5] Hutton, *The Angami Nagas*, p. 63.

[6] Hutton, *The Sema Nagas* (London, 1921), p. 53.

[7] Mills, op. cit., p. 87.

out more manfully than elsewhere. Yet even here there is a tragic tale to tell. The number of furnaces working in the Province fell from 510 to 136 in thirty years (1909 to 1938). In Balaghat, many of the 50 families who were engaged in iron work, have had to take to other livelihoods. The 160 furnaces of Bhandara have disappeared. The 'abundant and wonderful deposits' of ore in Chanda District are today worked by only four village furnaces. Fifty years ago there were six times as many. The equally remarkable ores of Drug are largely neglected, there being only six furnaces now at work. In Jubbulpore, where in 1891 no fewer than 1,850 persons were engaged in iron work, the industry today is practically extinct. In Mandla the number of furnaces decreased from 65 to 19 in three decades. In Raipur, where there were 230 furnaces in 1909, there are now only 50. In Saugor, where there was once a flourishing industry, it is now almost extinct. In 1855 there were 70 to 80 furnaces in Narsinghpur: by 1898 there were only 25; today the industry is extinct.[1]

What are the reasons for this disaster? In a discussion on the disappearance of such useful arts as canoe-building, pottery and the bow-and-arrow in Oceania, Rivers suggests that 'the causes of the disappearance are not simple, but that social and magico-religious, as well as material and utilitarian, factors must be taken into account'.[2] One obvious cause is the

[1] See Chapter III for all references. Mr Grigson, however, considers that in all these areas a few Agaria are probably still working their furnaces. 'I cannot help feeling,' he writes, 'that more enquiry would have found that there were still some Agaria working in various places where the Tahsildars have said that the industry has disappeared. Many zamindari settlement assessment papers show that at the last settlement a small sum was still being levied by way of commutation dues on blacksmiths' smelting forges. You say that the 160 furnaces of Bhandara had disappeared. I have just turned up a note that I made at Chhote Dongar in Bastar on 15th February, 1930, according to which the local Muria Lohar there consider themselves superior to Maria Lohar, but were despised by some Gond Agaria wheelwrights who had just settled there. The Muria Lohar did not know how to make the tyres for a cart wheel; I think I must have used the word "wheelwright" of the Agaria only because they were able to make and fit iron tyres on to cart wheels.'

[2] Rivers, *Psychology and Ethnology* (London, 1926), p. 190.

absence of raw materials. There may also be social causes: in Oceania the manufacture of things is confined to special groups, and if one of these limited groups dies out, the industry dies with it. It was this that in the Torres Islands led to the disappearance of the canoe; and the dying out of skilled craftsmen caused the disappearance of the art of making stone adzes in Woodlark Island.[1]

In the same way, the collapse of the smelting industry in India is due to complex and diverse forces. First and foremost, of course, we must put the competition of foreign and 'factory' iron. A few examples will be sufficient. 'In recent times,' says A. K. Iyer, 'with the import of foreign iron procurable at cheaper cost, the professional income of the Salahuva Vakkalu has become considerably lessened and so many of them have taken to cultivation in its stead'.[2] Similarly the *Chanda District Gazetteer* gives foreign competition, famine and heavy charges for fuel as the factors which reduced the number of furnaces in the District from 52 in 1900 to only 9 in 1906, the production of iron dropping from 125 to 18 tons in six years.[3] Jubbulpore and Saugor were naturally—in view of their accessibility—particularly sensitive to this competition. Between 1895 and 1898, the 'English' iron imported into the Jubbulpore Municipal area increased from 5,178 to 7,599 maunds while the village iron decreased from 5,806 to 3,237.[4] The process then begun has naturally progressed considerably since that date. It was probably this that caused the number of furnaces in Saugor (where the royalty was only eight annas a furnace) to fall

FIG. 44. Ox-goad *Length, 5' 6"*

[1] Rivers, op. cit., p. 200. [2] A. K. Iyer, op. cit., p. 553.

[3] *Chanda District Gazetteer*, op. cit., p. 129. Among the Zulus, the competition of European iron has practically destroyed the primitive industry.—Krige, op. cit., p. 209. [4] *The Agricultural Ledger*, Vol. VII, p. 149.

from 78 to 31 in four years (1899–1903) and in Jubbulpore from 71 to 47 in a single year (1906-7). In Mirzapur also, in the first decade of the century 'the trade suffered disastrously from the competition of Belgian iron'.[1]

How far the great famines at the end of the last century destroyed the industry is a matter of some dispute. The Agaria of Seoni gave up their furnaces then and never took to them again. Ball attributed a decline in the number of Kamar iron-smelters in a Ho village west of Chaibasa to the famine of 1866-7.[2] Famine is said to have had 'a prejudicial effect upon the industry in Mandla as several iron smelters abandoned their special occupation and took employment as common labourers'.[3] In Narsinghpur, 'some of the men died and some left their work during the famine (of 1896) which diminished the demand for iron'.[4]

On the other hand, there was 'an unusually large demand for Indian iron for tools for relief works, etc.',[5] during the famine of 1896, and advances were made by Government to enable the poorer smiths to make tools from their accumulated stock of iron to use in relief works. Rs.2,188 were thus advanced and over 13,000 tools were made and sold, to the relief of some 290 persons (mainly Agaria) every month.[6] The famine probably worked in two different ways: in the remoter districts it undoubtedly discouraged the iron industry: but in more accessible places where Government relief was available, it may even have encouraged it.

In some places official interference has undoubtedly led to the closing down of furnaces. Many of the Kondar iron-smelters, who in 1891 numbered 479 in Saugor District and

[1] *Mirzapur Gazetteer*, op. cit., p. 24. [2] Ball, op. cit., p. 479.
[3] *The Agricultural Ledger*, op. cit., p. 3. [4] ibid., p. 11.
[5] ibid., p. 23. [6] *The Agricultural Ledger*, op. cit., p. 23. During August 1900, 181 Agaria were relieved in the official kitchens. This came to 11·28 per cent, a fairly normal proportion of the total population of the tribe. Only 8·70 of Baiga, 10·21 of Gond, 2·24 of Brahmin and 10·71 of Lohar were so relieved. But 49·54 of Bhil, 29·24 of Korku and an average of 23·58 of 'untouchables', including 17·91 of Panka, got relief. *Census of India*, 1901, Vol. XIII, Pt. I, p. 209.

1,274 altogether, were said 'to be leaving the district on account of the stringency of the forest laws making it difficult for them to obtain the supplies of charcoal they required'.[1] In the Dondi Lohara Zamindari of Drug District where 'the villages of Dhalli and Kondekassa once possessed a very large number of furnaces, these had been given up'—even as early as 1880—'owing, I heard, to the zamindar of Lohara having raised the duty levied on iron furnaces'.[2] About the same date, Ball visited Deocha, in the Santal Parganas, where he noticed some large furnaces, 'the sole surviving remains of an industry now well-nigh extinct in this part of the country, owing to the restrictions placed upon it by the Birbhum (Iron) Company which bought up the sole right to manufacture, and owing also to the royalty subsequently (after the works were closed) inflicted by the native landlord'.[3]

In Salem, the outturn decreased 'partly from the growing scarcity of charcoal and partly from an influx of English iron'. In a number of Zamindaris and States, the villagers are forbidden to make charcoal, and in one State which is very anxious to preserve its forests and thus the game, a royalty of As 8 a basket is charged for it. No iron work can live under these conditions.

Taxation[4] has varied greatly from place to place. In Saugor it used to be only As 8 a furnace. In Drug it was, in 1907, Rs 2 or 3 for fuel. In Damoh the Malguzar (?) is said to have levied a duty of Rs 16 per kiln in lieu of the fuel obtained from *malguzari* forest. In Jubbulpore the forest dues were Rs 9, in Chanda Rs 3 to 5, in Bhandara Rs 12, in Raipur Rs 11. The higher charges seem usually to have been

[1] *Census of India*, 1891, Vol. XI, p. 206.

[2] *R.G.S.I.*, Vol. XX, Pt. IV, p. 169.

[3] Ball, op. cit., p. 225.

[4] It is worth noting that in the zamindaris the taxes are often paid in kind. At Dumarkachhar, for example, they were paying the zamindar of Korba 12 iron bars (for use in ploughs) every year for each furnace, and six bars for each forge. Iron tools are often bartered in the bazaars, but this is the only example I know of the Agaria using iron as currency, a custom once common among the Nagas. See Hutton, *Angami Nagas*, p. 71.

made where the furnaces were being worked on contract by some middleman.

In modern times, the taxation has generally been more moderate. In the Bilaspur Zamindaris, the tax ranges from Rs 2 to 7. In Matin it is Re 1 for a forge, in Lapha Rs 2 for a forge, in Chhuri Rs 1-8 for the forge and Rs 3 if a furnace is also worked. In Korba the forge costs Rs 3 and furnace with forge Rs 6. In the *malguzari* areas of Katghora, a furnace and forge is taxed at Rs 7. In the Drug Zamindaris the tax on the furnace is Rs 6.

In Raipur, I was told that the tax was Rs 3 and Rs 6, while in Rewa State it is Rs 1-8 for a forge and the same charge for a furnace—but there they are not allowed to cut *sarai*.

In Bastar State, the taxation is far lower. Each family of blacksmiths pays As 8 commutation dues (which cover charcoal-burning), nothing for the extraction of ore, and As 4 to Re 1 *thotha patti* for his house-site. There is a royalty on all ore exported (6 ps. per head-load, 4 as. a Muria cart, etc.) but as no ore is exported, this does not affect the blacksmiths. In 1940 there was a proposal to tax imported ploughshares, axe-heads, etc., in order to protect the local industry.

It was mainly, however, in Mandla District that the tax pressed most heavily upon the Agaria, and undoubtedly led to a decline of the industry.

The *Mandla District Gazetteer* states on p. 179 that 'the net earnings' of the Agaria 'are not more than Rs 30 from each furnace per annum'. On the very same page, without apology and without any apparent sense of incongruity, it gives the fees that are levied 'in cases where the Agaria have to obtain their material from Reserved Forests', or in effect practically everywhere.

For one furnace ..	.. Rs 8 per annum
For two furnaces ..	.. Rs 12 per annum
For three furnaces ..	.. Rs 15 per annum

That is to say, the Government of the time took it for granted that it was a right and proper thing to take from the aboriginal craftsmen about 27 per cent of their income, that income being assessed not by political agitators but by themselves.

This was in 1912. Before that, when, for example Colonel Ward made his first Settlement Report, he found that the Agaria 'used formerly to pay a royalty of four annas for the right of digging and smelting iron'.[1]

That was a fairly reasonable rate for people living on the borderline of starvation. But in 1923, the commutation rates for the Agaria (which include the royalty on the iron and the price of the fuel used for smelting) were raised to Rs 10 for one furnace and Rs 16 and Rs 20 for two and three. The reason given was the development of the District by improvement in communications (in 1930, the Bourne Committee reported that the Mandla communications were the worst in the Province) and the need for checking the destruction of the forests.

The result of this was that the iron-smelting industry of Mandla, the only peculiar industry of the Province as it had been called, began to die out. The number of furnaces dropped from 65 in 1912 to 19 in 1939. The people sank into ever deeper poverty. Many Agaria did not build furnaces but were content to maintain small forges, for which the tax was Rs 6 a year, at which they could repair the villagers' tools. The creative urge was checked, and all the romance, mythology and religion that centred round Lohasur and his temple the furnace was in danger of disappearing.

In 1939 I brought these facts to the attention of the local Government, and immediately Mr V. K. Maitland, Conservator of Forests in the Eastern Range, took the matter up. After full inquiries, it was decided to reduce the *nistar* commutation rates (as the tax was known officially) to a flat rate for both forge and furnace of Rs 5 a year. Two furnaces would be

[1] Ward, op. cit., p. 87. I have in my possession an official memorandum which on one and the same page estimates the local standard of living at Rs 2-8 a month or Rs 30 a year for *a whole family* and states that in Mandla special efforts were made to encourage the Agaria industry by charging royalty on the 'absurdly small scale' of Rs 8 per furnace or 27 per cent of the income.

allowed for Rs 8 and three for Rs 10. At the same time, the Revenue Department was moved to extend this concession to *ryotwari* villages in Mandla District, and this was done by the end of the year. Similar concessions were allowed in the Balaghat District.

The prompt and ready sympathy which Government showed on this occasion was very striking, and I have little doubt that the reduction of the tax will lead to a revival of the ancient industry.[1]

At one time it was believed, especially in Jubbulpore where there was every reason for the opinion, that the middleman was the real curse of the industry. The difficulty of persuading the iron-worker to act in his own interest, however, has been well put by R. S. Hole.[2]

> In 1885, when the first effort was made in Jubbulpore to revive the industry, it was believed that the baneful influence of the middleman was the principal cause of the miserable state of the smelters, and in consequence, it was decided (in the words used at the time by the Commissioner) 'to let native iron smelters take out a license from Government direct at a fair rate, while licenses should be renewable annually at the same rate for a period of say 10 years or longer if thought necessary'. This would give these men the security which, at present, it is said, they have not and would encourage them, if anything is likely to, to improve their furnaces and plant. At the same time the high octroi duty and excessive taxation to which they had been subjected were reduced. Whether these measures resulted in the construction and working of a larger number of furnaces is not evident, but certainly no improvements were made in the furnaces or plant. In a report made by Mr Bose (of the Geological Survey of India) on the subject in 1888, the following remark occurs: 'These men are too

[1] In sixteenth-century England there was a flourishing village smelting industry. But in 1558 an Act forbade the felling of timber for charcoal and the opening of new works anywhere save in Surrey, Kent and Sussex. In 1585 these counties were also included. Foreign iron began to be imported, and from 1665–1740 the number of native furnaces fell from 300 to 59. In the middle of the eighteenth century, the iron works were moved from the woods to the coal-fields, and the modern iron industry began.

[2] *The Agricultural Ledger*, op. cit., pp. 12ff.

ignorant to properly understand their own interests,' and he gives as an example of their stupidity that when one year Mr Olpherts gave a large order for all the refined iron smelted in the furnaces on the Lora Range, they were very pleased at having cheated his agent by giving him the rough bloomery iron with about 30 per cent of slag instead of the refined iron. At the same time, the smelters complained of the trouble necessary to get a license direct from Government, and said they preferred getting it from a lessee, who, three years before, had been cited by the Deputy Commissioner as the greatest curse of the industry, inasmuch as he was able by refusing a license 'to throw out of employment the resident smelters or to compel them to betake themselves to other localities'.

In 1894 the industry had apparently once more sunk to its own level, and from 1894 to 1896 efforts were again made to revive it. This time the course of action was to hand over all the more important mines to the Forest Department to prevent the smelters 'being crushed by the heavy royalties imposed by middlemen', and a royalty of Rs.50 for wood and Rs.10 for ore for one furnace, for a whole season, was fixed for all the furnaces which obtained their wood from Government forests. For the first year only Rs.50 was charged, the royalty on the ore being remitted. Arrangements were also made that coupés should always be open within easy distance of the furnaces.

At first the number of furnaces rapidly increased, and in 1895 there were probably more than 60 furnaces in work. Then came the famine, and the demand for the articles usually made from the Indian iron decreased, the iron could not be sold and the smelters had to stop work. Then help came in the shape of money advances from Government, and a number of smelters again started work with the result that a considerable quantity of iron was manufactured which could not be sold. A certain amount of it was eventually disposed of by manufacturing tools for the relief works, but a great deal was still left on the market. Consequently, the number of furnaces is now again decreasing, and the industry returning to its normal state of stagnation. It is true that the advances were generally given to the lessee or middleman (notably to the Malguzar of Sunawal who had 15 furnaces under him), but it is very probable that, if the money had been given direct to the smelters, such as they now are, the final results would have been much the same. As a relief work, the money advances no doubt did a great deal of good in keeping the smelters at their customary congenial occupation, instead of allowing them to burden the Government works, but, as far as improving or reviving the industry went, this policy was absolutely useless. To deal primarily with the middleman who naturally puts his own interest in the foreground and on whom the smelters are more or less dependent is an obvious mistake, and to increase the outturn of iron, without reducing the labour or improving the methods by which it is produced and so reducing its market price, can only end in drugging the market and in throwing the smelters eventually out of work.[1]

But perhaps more potent than anything else in discouraging the industry is the heavy and profitless nature of the toil involved. All observers have been impressed by the poverty of the Indian iron-worker. For the Agaria of Mandla I have assessed this in some detail in another chapter. The Agaria of Mirzapur, says Crooke, have 'a particularly gaunt appearance and worn expression of countenance, which is undoubtedly the result of the severe occupation which they follow'.[2] And the Gazetteer adds that 'the work, as now carried on, is very exhausting and laborious, particularly in the hot weather. All the profits go to the middleman Bania, and the Agaria, with wife and family, does not obtain on an average more than 3 or 4 annas a day'.

Watts quotes Ball as saying that 'the iron-smelters in many regions are the hardest worked, but poorest, amongst the population. The iron is sold at a high price, but the bulk of the profit goes to the traders through whose hands the metal passes. The amount of iron produced bears but a miserable proportion to the labour, time and materials expended'.[3]

This is partly due to the technical faults which I have noticed elsewhere. The addition of a flux, some arrangement

[1] See also A. E. Nelson, *Jubbulpore District Gazetteer*, pp. 220ff., for another full description and a long quotation from L. F. Begbie on the decline of the industry.

[2] Crooke, op. cit., Vol. I, p. 2.

[3] Watts, op. cit., p. 502.

for cooling the twyers, and provision for continuing the work during the rains would make a great deal of difference to the progress of the industry. Drake-Brockman thought that 'the only likelihood of its resuscitation lay in the utilization of coal fuel and the invention of some simple form of furnace adapted to its use and capable of being worked by hand'.[1]

A final cause of collapse is the social reproach that the iron-worker has to face. We have already examined this at length in another chapter. Here we may notice that, as Risley says, 'iron-smelting is supposed to be a much less respectable form of industry than working up iron which other people have smelted'.[2] As a result of this a number of Agaria have given up their furnaces and restricted themselves to the more select labours of the forge in a forlorn hope of raising their social status. This process has been at work mainly in Raipur.

It is evident, therefore, that a considerable variety of factors has operated to cause the decay of the iron-smelting industry in India. In the more open and accessible districts, like Jubbulpore, Saugor and Drug, the competition of foreign and factory iron has been most powerful in driving the village smelter out of existence. In Raipur, the chief influence has been a social one, the desire to abandon an activity that caused the workman to be despised. In the remoter parts of such Districts as Seoni and Balaghat the great famines struck the death-blow to an already weakened industry. In Mandla, where there is little foreign competition owing to its remoteness and poor communications, and the Agaria are less despised than elsewhere owing to the strong local belief in their virgin and magic iron, the chief cause of the decline in the number of its furnaces from 65 to 19 in three decades has undoubtedly been over-taxation. Everywhere a poor technique, heavy work and miserable returns have tended to depress and crush the Agaria.

[1] *Mirzapur Gazetteer*, op. cit., p. 25.

[2] Risley, op. cit., Vol. II, p. 23. In Jubbulpore 'those Lohars who were not clever enough to make their living as smiths became *bhatti-wallas*', i.e. iron-smelters.—*The Agricultural Ledger*, op. cit., Vol. XVII, p. 9.

We have seen the effect of this general atmosphere of collapse and degeneration upon the economic life of the Agaria: how has it affected their mind and spirit?

It is obvious that we cannot assess the psychology of a whole tribe. There are well-to-do Agaria; there are happy, courageous, friendly Agaria: to these the remarks in this chapter will not apply. But the majority of Agaria known to me live in the pitiful condition of frustration and poverty that I have described, and in many cases this has led to a morbid condition of anxiety which takes the form of continuous apprehension, exaggerating even the most ordinary events and transforming the most harmless persons into figures of fear and terror.

II. *Of Spirit: A Tribal Neurosis*

The Agaria lives in a dangerous and hostile world, and his mind is full of fears. He is indeed, even among Indian aboriginals, exceptional for his timidity. The myths indicate the extent to which the tribesman from the beginning of time has been at the mercy of his enemies. Bhagavan himself, crafty and deceitful, the fiery and destructive Sun, the triumphant forces of the Hindus, destroyed his kingdom. That was long ago, but even today the Agaria feels that every man's hand is against him. He is socially despised. Like every village craftsman he is the prey of the minor official who prefers his iron, like his food, as cheap as possible.

But this is not all. The very nature of the Agaria's occupation renders him peculiarly susceptible to supernatural interference. The forces of evil gather round the smithy where the all-powerful Virgin Iron is prepared and do their best to destroy it. The witch, the menstruous woman, the malignant dead, a host of hostile or offended godlings—no one knows how the blow may fall—may set fire to the smithy, break the furnace or turn the ore to slag.

Wherever I have been among the Agaria I have found this nervousness. In the Zamindaris of Bilaspur, the people trembled and sweated as I talked to them, and even Sunderlal (who was no stranger to them) found them unusually timid. In Mawai, where the other villagers would come crowding out to welcome us, the Agaria kept in hiding. The Asur of Chota Nagpur were, I thought, less forthcoming and friendly than the Uraon and Ho.

I have noticed a great difference in this respect between the Agaria and the Baiga, possibly because the Baiga—being magicians—are better able to fight against their fears. Rivers, dealing with the psycho-neuroses of the World War, found that so long as a man was able to meet danger with some form of intelligent and often complicated activity—Rivers called it 'manipulative activity'—there was no great fear or collapse. 'In the presence of danger Man, in the vast majority of cases, neither flees nor adopts an attitude of aggression, but responds by the special kind of activity, often of a highly complex kind, whereby the danger may be avoided or overcome.' For the Baiga, this is usually magic, a 'manipulative activity' requiring skill and attention including the use of the hands. The Baiga is subject to exactly the same fears as his neighbours, but he can do something about it, and so he is not subject to collapse. The absence of effect, however, is probably due to suppression, for when these experiences are reproduced later by the Baiga in their dreams, intense fear is sometimes present.

The Agaria reaction to danger resembles Rivers' 'immobility', 'the complete cessation of movement'. The instinct which leads to this, says Rivers, 'seems to go very far back in the animal kingdom. It is often associated with purely physiological modes of reaction, such as changes in the distribution of pigment, which increase the chances of safety of the animal by making it indistinguishable from its background.'[1] This exactly describes the impression I have received from the appearance and manner of frightened Agaria.

Let us now consider in detail the fears which trouble the Agaria, for otherwise we shall not understand the psychological motives underlying many of their customs and habits.

[1] Rivers, *Instinct and the Unconscious* (Cambridge, 1920), pp. 54ff.

We will first examine *the menace of the godlings.* In Agaria mythology as in Baiga mythology, we find not only the tribal godlings but even the mighty and adorable Hindu gods represented as crafty, hostile and destructive. Bhagavan destroys Logundi Raja by deceit in alliance with a witch; he tricks the sons of Daugun Guru and robs them of their father's magic. Mahadeo, however, is a craftsman who teaches the Agaria much of their art and skill.

The Agaria do not normally worship Bara Deo, and revere Thakur Deo only when the rest of the village do so. As we have seen, their special godlings are Lohasur, Koelasur, Agyasur, Pawan Deo and Dhua Dharni. All these are very dangerous, and very touchy. The slightest mistake, the least neglect, annoys them and rouses them to fearful vengeance. In the myths Lohasur appears as a rapacious demon: he wants to devour Jwala Mukhi in one story, the son of Kariya Kuar in another. He manifests himself sometimes as a burning babe, red as molten iron, sometimes in a cloud of flame and smoke. He must be satisfied with the flesh of cows and bullocks or he may destroy the smithy.

The first appearance of Koelasur was equally alarming. Out of the smoke rising from the charcoal pyre appeared a black and terrible form with long hair and gaping mouth and swallowed a party of Agaria. Agyasur is another demon of fear: the Agaria were born from him, and must pay him all the reverence due to a parent. As we have seen, it is very dangerous to kick the fire or throw away a torch.

It may be that in such stories we have examples of that 'antecedent stage of religious awe which', as Otto says, 'is daemonic dread (compare the horror of Pan) with its queer perversion, a sort of abortive offshoot, the "dread of ghosts". It begins to stir in the feeling of "something uncanny", "eerie" or "weird". It is the feeling which, emerging in the mind of primeval man, forms the starting-point for the entire religious development in history. "Daemons" and "gods" alike spring from this root.'

It is here that, according to Otto's famous theory of the Numinous, we find the Ira Deorum in its earliest manifestations. This ὀργή or Wrath, as it is in the Old Testament, has 'no concern whatever with moral qualities'. 'There is something very baffling in the way in which it is "kindled" and manifested. It is like a hidden force of nature, like stored-up electricity, discharging itself upon anyone who comes too near.'[1] This would be an admirable description of the demons of the forge and pit. No wonder that the poor, defenceless Agaria stands smitten into 'immobility', in a state of *stupor* or *tremor* before the energy, urgency and explosiveness of the *mysterium tremendum*, the *numen praesens*[2] which clothes with dread his humblest and homeliest possessions.

The Agaria's expression of this feeling is crude enough: it is hard to see the dignity of the Greek δεῖμα πανικόν in a screaming child who demands a meal of beef from the midst of the furnace. But to the Agaria such a conception is charged with Numinous. There is little adoration yet; little that we can call worship in the higher sense. But that is not surprising. It is hard to bow in adoration before a Burning Bush if it is likely to singe your beard.

The sense of elementary Numinous may be again illustrated in the following story from the Motinala Range:—

> Kariya Kuar was marrying off his thirteen sons. He was taking them home along with their wives. Suddenly they all fell senseless to the ground. Kariya Kuar fussed about, running now here and now there, killing every sort of animal for every sort of god, but it was useless. At last he brought a naked sword and was about to cut off his own head. Then Dulha Deo[3] and his Devi appeared and said, 'We are your ancestors. In the old days everyone gave us food-sacrifices as they were taking the bride and bridegroom home. But you have not once taken our names.' But Kariya Kuar cried, 'Lies! Lies! What can you do? Gods have two heads, you've only got one'. But Dulha Deo said, 'I'll

[1] R. Otto, *The Idea of the Holy* (Oxford, 1926), p. 15. [2] ibid., p. 18.

[3] Dulha Deo is the godling of the hearth and the marriage bed. He is widely worshipped by Chokh and Mahali in Udaipur and Jashpur States.

show you that I am a god'. He made all the senseless well again. Then Kariya Kuar fell at his feet and said, 'Come home with us and we will honour you when a child is born and at every marriage, and you shall live in the hearth'.

Even more revealing is a story from Mawai.

Dulha Deo is the son of Thakur Deo. He quarrelled with his father as to who was greater. So Thakur Deo went from village to village troubling the people and sending sickness everywhere. Dulha Deo went from house to house, burning one, bringing death to another, blindness to a third. In this way, the Agaria soon learnt to worship Thakur Deo outside the village, and Dulha Deo inside the house.

The godlings, to put it plainly, are a great nuisance, and the more of a nuisance they are the more they are honoured. Towards Lohasur, there is a curiously ambivalent attitude; he is hated and feared, but he is also loved and trusted.[1] He may destroy the smithy, but he also protects it and provides the iron. In fact, while the Christian idea of the son's attitude to his Heavenly Father represents the ideal father-son relationship, the Agaria's notion of his relations with Lohasur seems to reflect much more exactly the real facts of family life.

The Agaria's fear of the godlings and anxiety about their proper treatment is a very genuine one. It appears in many dreams, of which I will give two examples.

I was making many sickles and axes and went down to Kalauti (the lowlands) to Pandatarai Bazaar to sell them. Then Lohasur cried, 'Worship me! Worship me!' Two tigers began to fight. I was terrified and crept into a hole to hide.

I went to dig iron out of a pit, but I found nothing but earth. Then I heard a cry, 'Your pit is ruined. You have not given food-offerings to Lohasur.' The earth fell on me and I was buried in the pit. I couldn't breathe and I screamed loudly.

The sexual symbolism in these two dreams—entering the hole and going down into the pit—is particularly interesting

[1] This may be one reason why the Agaria seem unable to decide whether Lohasur is male or female.

if Lohasur represents the father and all the ambivalent emotions that the father can excite.

The menace of the dead. Another type of supernatural interference in the life of the Agaria comes from the dead. On page 126 I have recorded a story about the young men who, when the implements in their smithy broke, thought it was due to the hatred of their dead father and went to dig up and break his bones. Another story comes from Mawai area.

> A man and his wife went together for iron from their pit. As the man went into the pit, a Baiga and his wife came by. The Baigin was in her period and her shadow fell on the pit. She said, 'Friend, this pit is very deep'. As she said this, the earth fell in on to this Agaria and he was buried, only his foot remained sticking out. The others saved him and took him home. Four years later he died and became a ghost and went to live in that pit. Whenever anyone came near, he troubled him. So at last we made a hammer, tongs and anvil in his name and put them in the pit, and there was no more trouble.

Many methods, of course, are adopted to quieten the uneasy spirits of the dead. Grave-furniture is often placed in the tomb. 'When a man dies,' said an Agaria of Bahapur, 'he comes as a ghost demanding gifts. When my own father died, he wanted all the tools of the smithy—bellows, tongs and hammer. When we put these in his grave, he gave us no more trouble.'

The Chokh Agaria make a ring of grass and put it on the toe of the corpse saying, 'Take this. If anyone comes here, do not trouble him. If a child comes, do not trouble him.' They break an earthen pot by the corpse and sprinkle *haldi*-oil upon it.

In Mawai, the Patharia Agaria generally burn very old men, though they bury the younger dead. 'For the ghosts of old men are very terrible; but if their bodies are burnt they lose some of their power.' On the tenth day, when they perform the Bara Nahawan rites, the men and women bathe separately. On the way back from bathing, the men walk in file. The leader picks up a stone and hands it to the man behind him, and so it passes down the line. The man at the end spits on it and throws it away. By this means the evil ghost of the dead is prevented from following the mourners home. In the house itself, the men break a chicken's leg [1] and allow the blood to fall on an earthen pot, so that as the blood mingles with the water, so the soul of the dead will mingle with the godlings and become a *deo*.

At the same time the women are bathing in the nearest stream, and when they have bathed they catch any living creature, fish or frog or crab, put it in a pot of water and bring it home. There they place it in the courtyard and burn incense before it. They catch a chicken and give it rice, saying 'Are you so and so?', naming the dead person. If the chicken does not eat the rice, it means that the dead person is angry and refuses to return home. After trying for an hour, they throw away the water with the living creature and let the chicken go. But if the chicken does eat, they believe that the dead person's soul is now in it and they take it into the house and kill and eat it.

The Asur Agaria of Uprora have a different method. On the tenth (Daskarma) day, after bathing they make a pattern with rice-flour on the floor of the house and put a wooden seat (*pidha*) on it. On the seat they put a pot of water and a leaf-cup of *khichri*. The women go down to the stream to catch a living creature. The men appoint the magician as the Joha, blindfold him and hide him in the house. When the women have caught some living creature, they let it go in the river saying 'Take thy soul, give to us, come now live in thy house'. Then they return home. Now the men, taking their hammers, go down to the stream. They hammer '*tin tin tin*' with the light hammer on the welding hammer and say, 'Come, please come, to thy house'. Then the soul of the dead comes with a gust of wind into the house. If the mother of the house has died they all cry, '*A be dai O!*' or they call

[1] The chicken is kept and when it is grown, the *samdhi* of the dead comes and eats it.

on the father or brother or whoever it is by name. 'Come into thy house. Do not stay out in the jungle. Come and live in thy house. Do not stay out in the jungle.' Now when the soul of the dead enters the house like the wind it eats the *khichri* and the blindfolded Joha watches. When it has finished eating, they all ask the Joha, 'Has it come or no?' He replies, 'It has come'. Then they all come in to see. There on the food they will find finger-marks and the pattern of rice-flour will be disturbed by feet. If there are no marks, they call the magician to discover why.

By these methods, the souls of the dead are appeased and brought to live happily in the home where they will remain until they find a body in which they desire to return to human existence. To prevent the evil ghost of a man finding his way back to trouble the living, the Agaria use the customary means of carrying the corpse by a zigzag route, taking it five times round the grave or pyre, breaking a leg of the cot on which the body has been carried, and throwing the pick with which the grave has been dug three times across it.

All these precautions witness to the dread and horror in which the Agaria hold the ghosts of the unquiet and unsatisfied dead, for these usually reveal their hostility by causing the iron-pit to collapse or by breaking the implements in the smithy.

The menace of the menstruous woman. Danger from the ghosts of the dead and even from the godlings can be largely averted by taking the proper precautions. But there is no protection against the irresponsible and unpredictable behaviour of the menstruous woman. The rules are perfectly simple and everyone knows them but herself. She must not go near the pit. She must not cook. She must not approach a new furnace or new smithy where the Virgin Iron will be prepared. She must not go near the heavy hammer or the anvil. She must not bring water for the work in the smithy. But she may enter the smithy, she may touch the iron and blow the bellows, she may touch the furnace and the forge and all the other implements. Only the new furnace and the heavy hammer and anvil at all times are taboo.

Agaria life is shadowed—it is no exaggeration to say so—by the fear that these rules will be broken. The fear is more intense because breach of the rules is punished so catastrophically. Twenty years ago in Markuta, for example, an Agaria called Dhami went to his pit; his wife was with him carrying the baskets. On the way she entered her period without realizing it. When Dhami went into the pit, the sides collapsed upon him and as he was struggling to escape a tiger came and seized the wife. Fortunately there were other people there and they drove the tiger away and rescued Dhami. Baghesur Pat fell on one of them and ordered them to give food-sacrifice and all was well.

In Mawai, an Agaria of Indri had great difficulties because his hammer was touched by a menstruous Gondin. The next day no iron came from the furnace; the flames leapt up and the mouth of the furnace was broken. The Chokh Agaria say that they are not afraid of witches; what they dread is the shadow of a menstruous woman anywhere in the smithy. In Motinala, a menstruous woman touched the hammer and when they next went to the pit they were attacked by a tiger. That cost them a black pig, turmeric and milk for sacrifice to Lohasur.

In Motinala Range also, a woman touched the stone anvil. When the Agaria next went to the pit, the earth fell in on him and he was killed. Another time, the heavy hammer was touched by a menstruous woman and the owner of it got aches in his arms and shoulders; he obtained very little iron from his furnace and that was poor and brittle. In Akaldharria (Kawardha State) a menstruous woman went to an iron-pit. The party was attacked by a tiger, and the iron they brought home was not extracted properly and the implements made with it broke. In Markuta, a menstruous woman touched the hammer and when her husband next used it, it broke.

These are serious matters, not only spiritually but economically. For in every case, the magician has to be called—and paid, and offerings have to be made—and paid for. Now it is a black pig, now a goat, now milk and coconuts. Sometimes a new furnace has to be built, or the family has to move to another village. For so poor a tribe, there is every cause for anxiety. And there is no way of checking the evil.

Sometimes the husband also is affected. Thus a God-dhuka Lohar of Patandadar (Raipur) said that he too must not go to the pit while his wife was in her period.

This sometimes appears as a conflict between husband and wife in dreams.

> I was blowing my bellows and extracting iron. But none came and the furnace broke. I was very angry and went to beat my wife. 'You are in your period,' I shouted, 'and you touched the bellows: that's why they are broken.' Then a *sadhu* hit me and I went round and round searching.

Curiously, however, it is *not* dangerous to touch the bellows.

The menace of witchcraft. The danger of witchcraft is very real to the Agaria and not a little of their timid and nervous attitude to the world around them is due to it. The witch can, in the first place, spoil the work in the smithy. Once in Lalpur (Mawai) a witch made a charm of *urad* pulse, a black chicken and *chirona* clay and plastered it on top of the furnace. Then all the ore turned into slag and no true iron could be extracted. In Rewa State, a witch took the bark of a tree struck by lightning, and made an image of it with her own excreta. She stripped herself naked and went round the image seven times, killed a black chicken and shook herself in ecstasy. She cried, 'Let not his iron fall rightly nor his tools turn rightly'. She picked up the bark and went to the smithy. Holding her breath she thrust it into the roof. 'Then everything went wrong.'

This happened in Mugdara Village. Matters were put right by the magician, but the witch tried again and this time they caught and beat her. In Dobgarh (Rewa State) some years ago a witch tried to ruin the work of the smithy (and in effect all the work of the village which depends on iron for its industries) by this same means. The magician fell into a trance and saw the bark in the roof. He threw it away and made an offering of a pig and a virgin goat, a red cock and three coconuts, and all was well.

I will now give two fragments of autobiography, dealing mainly with the period of childhood, which will vividly show the life of anxiety that a child has and the part that the witch plays in intensifying that anxiety. The first is from the life-story of Dewan (Patharia Agaria) of Basni village in the Motinala Range.

> When I was six years old I went with my parents to Kuman Village, because Lohasur gave my father a dream that in Kawardha (where I was born) we would not be able to get good iron. So my father lived in Kuman for a year, but the iron was not good and everything we made broke. Then my father fell very ill, but when we gave food-offerings he recovered.
>
> Then we went to another village. I was perhaps thirteen years old. I loved a Gond girl there. But she was a witch. I went one day to the Mawai bazaar with some iron tools to sell, and she asked me for money. I had none to give. She was angry and gave me some parched gram. On that gram was her magic. I was a boy and ignorant. I sneezed, but I didn't understand the warning, and ate up all the gram. At once I had a severe pain in the belly and began to vomit. I fell down senseless. My parents were frightened and gave offerings to Lohasur, and I recovered.
>
> Soon after that my father made a compact with Lohasur and said that if he failed to fulfil his side of it, then I would die or go mad. My father failed, and I became dumb. Lohasur carried me off in the middle of the night to the iron-pit and hid me there for three days. My parents were very frightened and searched everywhere for me. Then they made offerings to Lohasur and he gave them a dream. The next night he brought me back and put me in the bed beside them. My speech then returned to me.

Consider too how witchcraft threatens the life of Manbod, a Chokh Agaria of Thanakar village in the Uprora Zamindari.

> When I was a child, the Zamindar's chaprasis gave us so much trouble that we ran away. When I was about four years old a cobra coiled round my hand. My father caught the cobra in the tongs from the smithy and I was saved. When I was older we went to Surguja. There I made a sickle

and went to a Gond's house to sell it. I ate *pej* there and got fever. As I was sleeping that Gond's daughter-in-law put magic on my privates and they swelled up and I could hardly hobble home. Later I went to work for a Kawar; his daughter-in-law was a witch and I loved her. The Kawar discovered us and threatened to kill me, so I had no more to do with her. But she was angry and put magic in my pipe. When I smoked it I fell senseless.

I could fill a volume with witch-stories; they are the commonplaces of Indian village life. They fill the consciousness of every Agaria child and impress him deeply with the dangers of existence. Sometimes a man also practises 'black magic'. I have only once had this described to me by someone who would admit it. I ought not to give his name but he was an Agaria. 'I had a Gond enemy,' he said. 'He struck me with his magic, but I sent it back. Another Agaria took away my daughter-in-law and I went many times to him for the bride-price, but he wouldn't give it. So I put my magic on him and he died. I took a loan from a Lamana and we quarrelled. He took my wheat by force. So I sent a snake to bite him. He was nearly dead when they sent for me to save his life.'

A bad conscience is a fruitful source of fear, and those Agaria who have taken to plough-cultivation through economic necessity believe themselves to be living in a state of 'sin' and thus exposed to supernatural dangers. It is true that this feeling is not so strong as among the Baiga. The Baiga who deserts his *bewar* and tears the breast of his Mother the Earth with the plough forfeits his 'protected status': he is exposed to the attacks of godlings and witches, he is no longer privileged against wild animals, he is in a state of mortal sin. The Agaria have no particular objection to using the plough;[1] but they believe that they were put into the world to do iron work and that it is dangerous and futile for them to leave it.

[1] But in Lapha some Asur said 'The earth is our mother, and we were born from her, so we must not dig her breast. Our mother has said, "If you dig my body, you'll never get enough to eat".' But I doubt if this is typical. The name Birjhia, a sub-caste of Asur, is probably derived from *bewariya*, a worker in shifting cultivation.

Thus, a Patharia Agaria of Rewa State said that 'it is a sin for an Agaria to do ordinary cultivation. For the Agaria Raja started iron work. But nowadays, since Government taxes us so heavily and prevents us cutting *sarai*, we have taken to cultivation and we get every kind of disease and even so cannot fill our bellies. In the old days, we got few diseases, the godlings and ghosts did not attack us and we got all we wanted to eat That was because we were faithful to iron.' Another typical statement is this: 'It is sinful for the Agaria to do either plough-cultivation or *bewar*-cultivation. We got iron and charcoal from Bhagavan when he gave their work to all the tribes of the world. Our Raja Logundi worked in his smithy, not in a field. Now when many of us do field-work, our bullocks die and we get wretched food.'

The Chokh Agaria, however, say that it is not actually wicked to plough, but that they can never succeed at it. The same thought was put vividly by a Patharia of Gaonra (Mawai). Mother Earth,' he said, 'is the wife of the Gond, and she is faithful to them. When we try to seduce her, she gives us deformed children.' The Agaria's crops are always poor.

To the general economic depression, therefore, must be added this sense of hopelessness and belief that they have done the wrong thing, a thing that will expose them to many evils.

We have already seen how dangerous life is and how narrow the path of safety. A ritual error may well cost a man his life, the breaking of a taboo may lead to great disaster. Let us consider a few minor taboos, each of which adds its small contribution to the general sense of danger and alarm.

Thus, it is very dangerous to take an oath on iron.[1] Near

[1] To swear on iron is old as Herodotus who describes (i, 165) how the Phocaeans dropped a mass of iron into the sea, swearing never to return home till it appeared again on the surface. In the contemporary world, this oath is common. Among the Sema Naga 'a rare and serious form of oath is that taken by cutting iron, which if a man do falsely, members of his clan die off without apparent cause, such is the power of the metal when treated disrespectfully'.—Hutton, *The Sema Nagas*, p. 166. Dr Hutton also tells of a man coming into his court with a *dao* and a bit of umbrella wire prepared to take this oath, and quotes another who had to desert his house

Karanjia it is said that if a man swears on Virgin Iron, whether his oath be false or true, he will die. It is equally dangerous to swear on charcoal or on fire. Many instances are remembered in the villages. In Motinala, an Agaria of Koelari stole something and swore by iron, picking a bit up and holding it in his hand, that he was innocent. That night a great fire broke out on his threshold, he could not escape and he was burnt to death.

In Thakurkheta, a Chokh Agaria called Bharat swore on a bit of iron, and his son died at once. In Andhyarko (Rewa), an Agaria took an oath on iron. 'Lohasur ate him up and he died in fifteen days.' In Karangra (Rewa) an Agaria swore by fire, and Agyasur set fire to his house. As a result of this, an Agaria told us, 'we may lie or tell the truth but we leave iron and the fire alone'.

Salt is another holy and dangerous substance. If a man borrows some salt and fails to return it, there is danger that he may melt and dissolve like salt in water. The Agaria do not usually put salt in the water with which they temper their iron.

Colour taboos should also be carefully observed. The wearing of a red cloth may set fire to the smithy. If an Agaria wears black he may spoil the iron and the charcoal, for Lohasur and Koelasur are black, and are worshipped with black sacrifices. Yellow is also dangerous, for it is the colour of Dulha Deo, the godling of marriages when the yellow turmeric is used. At the time of a marriage, when yellow clothes are worn, the Agaria have to be very careful to appease Dulha Deo properly. Otherwise he may be jealous and send a snake to bite one of them.

and site and build a fresh house in another place because he had cut a bit of iron in a fit of temper. It is said too that although the people of Ballycroy in Erris on the coasts of Connacht but little regarded an oath on the Evangelists, the really binding oath was that taken on a human skull together with any iron object such as a bunch of keys.—*Folk-Lore*, Vol. XXXIV, p. 339. The Hausas of West Africa also swear on iron, usually a knife or bayonet.—*Folk-Lore*, Vol. XXI, p. 202. The Jur tribe of the Sudan regard oaths taken on the anvil of a dead smith as specially binding.—Crawhall, op. cit., p. 43. See also E. W. Hopkins. 'The Oath in Hindu Epic Literature', *J.A.O.S.*, Vol. LII (1932), pp. 316ff.

So far we have considered the dangers and disasters that come to the Agaria from within the tribe itself. But there is also menace from without, from the stranger, from the Government, and from poverty and hunger.

The Agaria are unusually afraid of strangers. Their alarm is not the alert, excited fright of the Baiga who run away into the jungle like a herd of startled deer; it is a hopeless miserable fear that makes them dull and stupid. Sometimes it is painful to meet them. In Singia village, the Asur Agaria were so frightened that they sweated and trembled as I talked to them. In Mawai and Motinala, of course, I am not a stranger and I do not know how they would regard one. But in Bilaspur and Raipur, their terror was very distressing. In a village in Udaipur State, I found a group of Chokh Agaria in the bazaar, and took a photograph. In a few moments, a wave of fear had passed over the bazaar; the Agaria were on their feet and running, soon everyone was running, streaming out of the village into the jungle.

The camera is naturally especially alarming to them. 'You have taken away all our strength and our *jiv* (soul) into that little box,' said Dhansai (God-dhuka Lohar) of Patandadar after I had photographed him. In Nunera, the idea was that the camera was a sort of X-ray and could look through the clothes and the skin to the liver, and thus attack it for purposes of magic. But later, after they had been shown a picture of an Agaria furnace which, after examining upside down and declaring to be a dog they at last recognized with shouts of delight, some of them even demanded to be photographed.[1]

This fear of the stranger is, of course, ultimately due to constant outside interference with the Agaria's life. In

[1] Fear of the camera is, however, fairly common among aboriginals. When Sir G. A. Grierson was taking photos for his *Bihar Peasant Life*, he once found no child allowed to face the camera. The Government was then building a bridge across the Gandak and the people thought children were going to be buried under the foundations. Another time it was thought he was collecting carts and boats for the Egyptian War or that he was counting the wells because he knew a famine was approaching.—Grierson, op. cit., p. 4.

Balaghat, the once-flourishing iron-smelting industry has been almost destroyed. In Mandla, heavy taxation reduced the number of furnaces from sixty-five to nineteen in thirty years. In some Raipur Zamindaris, where the God-dhuka Lohar are forbidden to use *sarai* trees for charcoal and any kind of charcoal-burning has been made difficult and expensive, most of the old furnaces have been abandoned. In Rewa State, a similar prohibition has reduced the Agaria to beggary. In the Bilaspur Zamindaris, although in the main taxation is low, the people are subjected to constant harassment by zamindari subordinates. All lower officials naturally expect their iron implements and those of their families to be repaired free of charge, and to be given free axes, sickles and knives. Government has made many attempts to check the evil of *begar* (forced unpaid labour) and *rasad* (free supplies), and in recent years there has been an undoubted improvement. But in remoter areas the evil lingers. *Begar* seems to be rooted, not in any particular system of Government, but in the less reputable tendencies of human nature.

No wonder then that the stranger in the village, especially a stranger who is making inquiries, should cause alarm. 'The tax is going to be raised again! They are going to forbid us to make charcoal! He probably wants a free hatchet.' Such thoughts pass rapidly through the Agaria's minds as they see a visitor approach.

This particular form of anxiety is reflected in many dreams, in fact the Agaria seem to have more nightmares about officials than about any other subject! The following dream, which has an obviously sexual latent meaning, refers to the constant (and I believe illegal) interference with the villagers in their gathering wild honey.

> I went with two men to the jungle. We found some honey in a hollow tree. I began to take it out with my hand. Someone hit me on the face, and my axe fell to the ground.

The real point of conflict with authority is charcoal-burning. This is reflected in a number of dreams.

I was coming from the jungle with a load of charcoal. The Jungly Sahib (Forest Officer) met me and abused me.

I went to make charcoal in the forest. The Forest Guard caught me. He shouted, 'Why have you cut such a big tree?' He tied my hands together with rope and beat me. But his clothes caught fire. He fell at my feet crying, 'Save me, save me'. A tiger came by chasing a sambhar and I cried '*dohoo*!'

Begar, the taking of free supplies and labour, is a continual annoyance.

I was sitting in the smithy and making an axe. A chaprasi came to the smithy and shouted at me that I should come and do his work immediately.

And then above all these other fears, running through them and giving them strength, is the constant dread of poverty and hunger, the failure of the capricious iron, misery and want leading to death itself. The Agaria are the poorest of the aboriginals, and among the shortest-lived. 'The earnings of the charcoal are never enough; as the Agaria eats he grows thin.' Consider this dream which represents a fundamental Agaria anxiety.

In the pit I dug out a lot of iron. But when I brought it home I found that it had turned into stones.

To dream of a broken limb means that the iron will be brittle.

I was working iron. My arm broke as I was beating my wife. She ran away. Then came a Gond and tied it up with string. He abused my wife saying, 'You have broken the arm of a Karigar (craftsman)'.

To dream of iron flowing like water is equally ominous.

I was reducing iron from the furnace. It went soft and flowed like water. My wife abused me.

The following dream means that on the morrow the fire will not burn properly.

Loharin Bai was blowing my bellows. The furnace went red hot. Then I went home. Loharin Bai said, 'But what do you want? Are not your eyes opened yet?'

How far have the fears and anxieties of the Agaria a sexual basis? I should say very little. There is plenty of reason for their anxiety, and if those reasons could be removed I have no doubt that they would live happier and more peaceful lives. The dread of impotence and castration, which is a prominent feature of Baiga psychology, is far less in evidence among the Agaria. Indeed, in the only *Vagina Dentata* story which seems to have originated among them, the Agaria hero triumphantly overcomes his peril and emphatically is not castrated. But the theme does occur sometimes in dreams, though usually in a form different from the Baiga in that the danger of sexual intercourse is not due to teeth in the vagina but rather to long pubic hairs which make a noose and amputate the penis.

> In my dream I went to a woman. There was a great deal of hair in her vagina. It caught my penis and cut it off. The woman abused me. 'Away with you, you eunuch. You don't know how to do it.' She pushed me away.

> I was asleep. Two women came and tied a string round my penis and began to pull at it. But I got up and stripped them both naked. One of the women had her pubic hairs woven in a plait. Then they both seized me and with their pubic hairs tied me up.

> A woman came and slept with me in my dream. She caught my penis and pulled it. Her pubic hairs were like needles and they pricked my penis and testicles and a lot of blood flowed. I washed away the blood and woke.

It will be said that these fears are not peculiar to the Agaria: the dread of angry and erratic demons, the contagion of menstruous women, the threat of witchcraft menaces the whole of village India. Nor, unhappily, is the dread of poverty and death confined to the blacksmith. But the fears which assail any neurotic are the common anxieties of mankind, but exaggerated and perhaps imagined.

The same is true of the Agaria. Their spirit has been broken by long decades of slow material decline and they have lost their power of resistance against the common dangers of animist life. Every furnace abandoned means one less temple to Lohasur; wherever charcoal-burning is forbidden, there is less honour done to Koelasur. No longer is the Virgin Fire kindled, no more is the Virgin Iron extracted in villages where the smelters have been driven from their ancestral occupation to agriculture.

Seeing this, the Agaria is afraid, for he sees the end of his people. He already sees the day when no one of his race will again drive into the lintel of the house the all-protecting nail or fasten about the feet of children the thunder-scaring anklet.

This will be so. Unless the protective tariff (in the shape of greatly reduced taxation) already imposed by Government in certain areas, is extended and maintained, unless some effort is made to educate the tribe in an improved technique, unless an enlightened public opinion lifts from them the stigma of social inferiority, the Agaria are doomed to extinction within a few decades.

This should not, and need not, be so. The Agaria could be saved, their industry revitalized, their religion and culture preserved, easily and at a ridiculously small cost. Immediate improvement would be gained by the appointment of a couple of touring propagandists who would study the primitive furnace, devise means for its improvement, and then educate the Agaria in better methods; by the reduction of the tax on the furnace to a purely nominal one as in Bastar so that it would act as a sort of protective tariff against the competition of 'bazaar' iron—which itself is protected; by the strictest watch on *begar*, on any form of forced unpaid repairs or free supplies of iron taken by subordinate officials or landlords.

The preservation of the Agaria depends almost entirely upon the Government of the Central Provinces, especially when that passes into Indian hands. I would commend to them some words from that extraordinary document composed by Asoka after his conquest of the Kalinga Kingdom—

> Even upon the forest tribes in his Dominions, His Majesty has compassion, though advised to destroy them in detail, and though the power to harry them is in His Majesty's hands. For His Majesty desires for all animate beings security, control over the passions, peace of mind, and joyousness.

APPENDIXES

APPENDIX I

DISTRIBUTION OF THE AGARIA ACCORDING TO THE CENSUS OF INDIA

	1891	1911	1921
Balaghat	..	30	..
Bilaspur	2,013	2,619	1,921
Chang Bhaker	..	482	..
Chanda	27	..	..
Damoh	148	18	..
Drug	..	3	..
Jashpur	..	53	..
Jubbulpore	1,850	273	..
Kanker	..	64	..
Kawardha	458	129	..
Korea	..	956	..
Mandla	564	793	..
Narsinghpur	78	9	..
Raigarh	198	870	..
Raipur	306	..	..
Saugor	189	..	..
Seoni	..	..	..
Surguja	..	2,592	1,740
Udaipur	..	608	..

TOTAL OF AGARIA IN THE CENTRAL PROVINCES AND STATES—

1891	5,832
1901	1,604
1911	9,500
1921	3,661

Appendix II

DETAILS OF THE IRON-SMELTING FURNACES IN THE CENTRAL PROVINCES

'The only part of India in which the old indigenous methods of smelting ore are still carried on to any appreciative extent is the C.P., which produced nearly 4,500 tons of ore and supported nearly 300 native furnaces' in 1916 (*R.G.S.I.*, Vol. XLVIII, Pt. II, p. 46).

The following figures are based on the annual and quinquennial surveys of the mineral production of India in the *Records of the Geological Survey of India*, Vols. XLVIII to LXXIV.

Year	Saugor	Jubbulpore	Mandla	Chanda	Balaghat	Raipur	Drug	Bilaspur	Total
1909 ..	13	26	65	9	4	230	56	103	510
1910 ..	18	24	63	5	4	238	49	91	494
1911 ..	19	27	63	13	4	..	39	84	249
1912 ..	19	30	52	9	4	228	36	73	451
1913 ..	19	29	49	20	..	181	40	99	437
1915 ..	..	..	..	..	..	..	..	..	307
1916 ..	..	..	..	..	..	..	..	..	309
1917 ..	..	..	..	..	..	157	52	103	312
1918 ..	..	..	..	..	..	..	..	..	232
1919 ..	..	..	..	..	..	..	34	125	159
1920 ..	..	..	..	..	..	..	92	133	225
1921 ..	..	..	..	..	..	..	26	129	155
1922 ..	..	..	..	..	..	..	19	129	148
1923 ..	..	..	..	..	..	..	19	100	119
1924 ..	..	..	..	..	..	..	..	..	229
1925 ..	4	1	35	..	..	68	..	103	211
1926 ..	4	1	36	..	..	68	..	102	211
1927 ..	3	1	47	..	..	48	11	95	205
1928 ..	3	..	54	..	..	14	16	102	190
1929 ..	3	..	53	..	..	12	11	95	174
1930 ..	1	..	57	..	..	13	..	53	124
1931 ..	1	..	49	..	..	3	..	53	106
1932 ..	1	..	51	..	..	3	4	59	118
1933 ..	1	..	54	..	..	2	4	52	114
1934 ..	..	..	56	6	..	3	5	50	120
1935 ..	..	..	52	2	..	22	5	46	127
1936 ..	..	..	43	4	..	2	5	38	92
1937 ..	..	..	38	4	..	3	6	59	110
1938 ..	..	..	21	..	..	50	6	59	136

APPENDIX III

CHEMICAL ANALYSIS OF AGARIA ORE

The Chief Chemist of the Tata Iron and Steel Company at Jamshedpur was good enough to analyse a number of specimens of iron ore, metal and slag from the Dindori Tahsil. The following specimens were sent:—

1. *Chāwariya* ore dug from pits in the Motinala Range. Considered the best of all.

2. *Chāwariya*, dug from pits in the Karanjia Range. Also considered very good.

3. *Bhāwariya*, dug from pits in the Motinala Range. Good.

4. *Pondo*, gathered from the surface of the ground in Motinala. Considered by the Agaria to be a pure heavy ore.

5. *Katarra*, collected from the banks of streams in Motinala. Of poor quality.

6. *Charki*, dug from pits in Motinala. Tools made from this are said to break readily.

7. *Jak-makka*, dug from pits in Motinala.

8. *Pondo* iron in the state called by the Agaria *dhidha*; it has been extracted from the furnace after an hour and a half's smelting. From Motinala.

9. *Pajar* iron extracted from *chāwariya* ore from Motinala. It has had an hour-and-a-half in the furnace and been further refined for two hours in the forge.

10. *Mail*, or slag, from a furnace in the Motinala Range.

CHEMICAL ANALYSIS

A. *Iron Ore*

	1	2	3	4	5	6	7
SiO_2 ..	13·10	3·78	9·90	6·00	2·92	10·24	4·60
Al_2O_3 ..	2·68	2·94	2·94	5·52	4·69	9·74	8·20
TiO_2 ..	0·10	0·10	trace	0·70	0·50	1·60	0·70
FeO ..	trace	trace	trace	0·26	1·94	0·38	1·29
Fe_2O_3 ..	69·20	80·36	70·21	79·22	77·93	70·36	73·22
MnO ..	0·70	1·33	1·90	0·49	0·15	0·27	0·06
P_2O_5 ..	0·120	0·460	0·220	0·192	0·925	0·215	0·765
CaO ..	trace	trace	trace	0·30	0·40	0·20	0·20
MgO ..	1·15	0·72	1·44	0·22	0·52	0·23	0·28
H_2O ..	13·00	9·80	12·60	7·32	10·20	7·12	11·00

B. *Metal*

	8	9[1]
C	0·78	0·42
Mn	0·10	0·15
S	trace	trace
P	0·140	0·043
Si	0·075	0·48

C. *Slag*

	10	10A
SiO_2	18·00	16·72
Al_2O_3	9·02	9·70
TiO_2	0·30	0·70
FeO	53·40	53·79
Fe_2O_3	10·01	9·29
Met. iron ..	1·60	0·80
MnO	4·75	6·71
P_2O_5	0·450	0·435
CaO	0·40	1·40
MgO	2·16	0·94
Carbon	0·28	..

[1] This sample is mixed with about 5 per cent slag of composition, see analysis of 10A.

APPENDIX IV

BIBLIOGRAPHY

Abbott, J. .. .. *The Keys of Power* (London, 1932)

Archer, W. G. .. *The Blue Grove* (London, 1940)

Balfour, E. .. .. 'The Migratory Tribes of Natives in Central India', *J.A.S.B.*, Vol. XIII

Ball, V. .. .. 'Geology of the Aurunga and Hutar Coal Fields', *M.G.S.I.*, Vol. XV. (Gives an account of the Agaria.)

Jungle Life in India (London, 1880)

Banerji-Sastri, A. .. 'The Asuras in Indo-Iranian Literature', *J.B.O.R.S.*, Vol. XII

'Asura Expansion by Sea', *J.B.O.R.S.*, Vol. XII

Begbie, L. F. .. *The Iron and Steel Industry in the Central Provinces*

Berriedale-Keith, A. .. *Indian Mythology* (Boston, 1917)

Birdwood, G. .. *Industrial Arts of India* (1880)

Bose, P. N. .. .. 'The Iron Industry of the Western Portion of the District of Raipur', *R.G.S.I.*, Vol. XX

Cammiade, L. A. .. 'Iron-smelting by Kois', *Man*, 1931.

Coghlan, H. H. .. 'Prehistoric Iron Prior to the Dispersion of the Hittite Empire', *Man*, Vol. XLI

Cracroft, W. .. 'Smelting of Iron in the Khasya Hills', *J.A.S.B*, Vol. I

Crawhall, T. C. .. 'Iron Working in the Sudan', *Man*, Vol. XXXIII

Crooke, W. .. .. *The Popular Religion and Folklore of Northern India* (London, 1896)

Tribes and Castes of the North-West Provinces and Oudh (Calcutta, 1896)

Dalton, E. T. .. *Descriptive Ethnology of Bengal* (Calcutta, 1872)

Day, John .. .. *The Prehistoric Use of Iron and Steel* (London, 1877)

De Brett, E. A. .. *Chhattisgarh Feudatory States Gazetteer* (Bombay, 1909)

Dikshit, K. N. .. *Scope of Pre-History and Anthropological Work in India*

Dowson, J. .. .. *A Classical Dictionary of Hindu Mythology* (London, 1879)

Drake-Brockman, D. L. *Mirzapur, A Gazetteer* (Allahabad, 1911)

Dutt, U. C. .. .. *Materia Medica of the Hindus* (1877)

Elwin, Verrier .. *The Baiga* (London, 1939)

Fausböll, V. .. *Indian Mythology according to the Mahabharata* (London, 1903)

Fermor, Sir L. L. .. 'The Mineral Resources of the C.P. and Berar.' This was first written by Sir L. L. Fermor in 1918 in *R.G.S.I.*, Vol. L. It was revised by him in 1927 and by Dr M. S. Krishnan in 1939 in *R.G.S.I.*, Vol. LXXIV

Forsyth, J. .. .. *The Highlands of Central India* (London, 1871)

Friend, J. N. .. *Iron in Antiquity* (London, 1926)

Garland, H. .. *Ancient Egyptian Metallurgy* (London, 1927)

Grant, Sir C. .. *Gazetteer of the Central Provinces* (Nagpur, 1870)

Grierson, Sir G. .. *Bihar Peasant Life* (Patna, 1926)

Grigson, W. V. .. *The Maria Gonds of Bastar* (London, 1938)

Hadfield, R. .. 'Sinhalese Iron and Steel of Ancient Origin', *Journal of the Iron and Steel Institute*, Vol. LXXXV (1912)

Hallett, M. G. .. *Ranchi District Gazetteer* (Patna, 1917)

Held, G. J. .. .. *The Mahabharata* (London, 1935)

Hole, R. S. .. .. 'The Iron Industry in the Central Provinces', *Agricultural Ledger*, Vol. V, No. 17, pp. 1–27 and Vol. VII, No. 14, pp. 146–60

Hughes, T. W. H. .. 'Note on the Iron Deposits of Chanda', *R.G.S.I.*, Vol. VI

Ibbetson, Sir D. C. J. .. *Outlines of Panjab Ethnology* (Calcutta, 1883)

Iyer, A. K. .. .. *The Cochin Tribes and Castes* (Madras, 1909)

Iyer, A. K. .. *The Mysore Tribes and Castes* (Mysore, 1935)

Kitts, E. V. .. .. *Compendium of the Castes and Tribes found in India* (Bombay, 1885)

La Touche, T. H. D. .. *A Bibliography of Indian Geology*, G.S.I., 1917

Lawrence, A. J. .. *Report of the Land Revenue Settlement of the Bhundara District* (Bombay, 1867)

Lester, I. E. .. *Indian Iron* (Stourbridge, 1912)

Lovat Frazer .. *Iron and Steel in India* (Bombay, 1919)

Low, Sir C. E. .. *Balaghat District Gazetteer* (Allahabad, 1907)

Luard, C. E. .. *Rewa State Gazetteer* (Lucknow, 1907)

Marten, J. T. .. *Census of India, 1911*, Vol. X, Part I

M.G.S.I. .. .. *Memoirs of the Geological Survey of India*

Mellor, J. W. .. *Treatise on Inorganic and Theoretical Chemistry*, Vol. XII, pp. 482–520

Nelson, Sir A. E. .. *Bilaspur District Gazetteer* (Allahabad, 1910)
Drug District Gazetteer (Calcutta, 1910)
Jubbulpore District Gazetteer (Bombay, 1909)

Oldham, R. D. .. 'Report on the Geology of Parts of Manipur and the Naga Hills', *M.G.S.I.*, Vol. XIX

O'Malley, L. S. S. .. *Palamau District Gazetteer* (Calcutta, 1907). Revised edition by P. C. Tallents (Patna, 1926)

Partington, J. R. .. *Origins and Development of Applied Chemistry* (London, 1935)

R.G.S.I. .. .. *Records of the Geological Survey of India*
Quinquennial Reviews of Mineral Production in India in *R.G.S.I.*, Vols. LVII, LXIV and LXX

Report of the Central Provinces Provincial Banking Enquiry Committee (Nagpur, 1930)

Reuben, W. .. .. *Eisenschmiede und Dämonen in Indien* (Leiden, 1939)

Rickard, T. A. .. 'The Knowledge and Use of Iron among the South Sea Islanders', *J.R.A.I.*, Vol. LXII

'Primitive Smelting of Iron', *American Journal of Archaeology*, Vol. XLIV

Risley, Sir H. H. .. *Tribes and Castes of Bengal* (Calcutta, 1891)

The People of India (London, 1915)

Robertson, Sir B. .. *Census of India, 1891*, Vol. XI, Part I

Roughton, N. J. .. *Census of India, 1921*, Vol. XI, Part I

Rowney, H. B. .. *The Wild Tribes of India* (London, 1882)

Roy, Sarat Chandra .. 'A Note on Some Remains of the Ancient Asurs in the Ranchi District', *J.B.O.R.S.*, Vol. I

'Distribution and Nature of Asur Sites in Chota Nagpur', *J.B.O.R.S.*, Vol. VI (1920)

'A Note on Totemism among the Asurs', *J.B.O.R.S.*, Vol. III (1917)

'The Asurs—Ancient and Modern', *J.B.O.R.S.*, Vol. XII (1926)

Rudman, F. R. R. .. *Mandla District Gazetteer* (Bombay, 1912)

Russell, R. V. .. *Census of India, 1901*, Vol. XIII, Part I

Saugor District Gazetteer (Allahabad, 1906)

Russell, R. V. and Hiralal, R. B. .. *The Tribes and Castes of the Central Provinces of India* (London, 1916)

Sarkar, B. K. .. *The Positive Background of Hindu Sociology*

Sayce, R. U. .. *Primitive Arts and Crafts* (Cambridge, 1933)

Schoff, W. H. .. 'The Eastern Iron Trade of the Roman Empire', *J.A.O.S.*, Vol. XXXV (1915)

Schrader, O. .. *Prehistoric Antiquities of the Aryan Peoples* (London, 1890)

Shoobert, W. H. .. *Census of India, 1931*, Vol. XII

Tawney, C. H. .. *The Ocean of Story*, Revised by Penzer (London, 1924–8)

Temple, Sir R. .. *Report on the Administration of the Central Provinces up to 1862* (Nagpur, 1923)

Reports on the Zamindaris and other Petty Chieftaincies in the C.P. in 1863 (Nagpur, 1923)

Thomson, W. B. .. *Report of the Land Revenue Settlement of the Seonee District* (Bombay, 1867)

Thurston, E. .. *Castes and Tribes of Southern India* (Madras, 1909)

Vans Agnew, P. .. *A Report on the Subah or Province of Chhattisgarh written in 1820* (Nagpur, 1922)

Verchere, A. M. .. *J.A.S.B.*, Vol. XXXVI, Part II

Ward, H. C. E. .. *Report on the Land Revenue Settlement of the Mundlah District* (Bombay, 1870)

Warth, H. .. .. *Report on the Iron District of Chota Baghal in Kangra* (*Panjab Gazette*, May, 1873)

Watts, Sir G. .. *Dictionary of the Economic Products of India* (London, 1890), Vol. IV

Wynne, F. H. .. 'Native Methods of Smelting and Manufacturing Iron in Jabalpur', *Trans. Inst. Min. Eng.*, Vol. XXVI, pp. 231–45

IDENTIFICATIONS

anjun .. *Hardwickia binata*, Roxb.
bar .. *Ficus bengalensis*, Linn.
dhanbahar *Cassia fistula*, Linn.
dhāmin .. *Grewia vestita*, Wall.
dhauhara *Zizyphus rugosa*, Lam.
dub .. A grass, *Cynodon dactylon*, Pres.
gaur .. *Gavaeus gaurus*
gohariyār A tree
haldi .. Turmeric
karra .. *Holarrhena antidysenterica*, Wall.
katai .. *Flacourtia ramontchi*, L'Hérit.
kerketa .. A bird
khair .. *Acacia catechu*, Willd.
kodon .. *Paspalum scrobiculatum*
kosam .. *Schleichera trijuga*, Willd.
kumjun .. *Hardwickia binata*, Roxb.
kussera .. A bird
kutki .. *Panicum psilipodium*
mahua .. *Bassia latifolia*, Roxb.
mohlain .. *Bauhinia vahlii*, W. and A.
munjni .. *Hardwickia binata*, Roxb.
parsa .. *Ficus retusa*, Linn.
sāmbhar .. *Cervus unicolor*, or *equinus*.
sāj .. *Terminalia tomentosa*, W. and A.
sarai .. *Boswellia serrata*, Roxb.
sukla .. The grass *Heteropogon contortus*
tilai .. A tree, perhaps *Wendlandia exserta*, D.C.
tuma .. A gourd
urad .. *Phaseolus radiatus*

INDEX